LOW-SO
GOOD

LOW-SO
GOOD

A Guide to Real Food, Big Flavor,
and Less Sodium
with 70 AMAZING RECIPES

JESSICA GOLDMAN FOUNG

Photographs by JOHN LEE

CHRONICLE BOOKS
SAN FRANCISCO

"An apple a day keeps the doctor away."

An apple-five-spice pie keeps guests coming back for seconds.

Text copyright © 2016 by Jessica Goldman Foung.
Photographs copyright © 2016 by John Lee.

Library of Congress Cataloging-in-Publication
Data available.

ISBN 978-1-4521-3508-3

Manufactured in China

Designed by Emily Dubin
Food styling by Lillian Kang
Typesetting by Hillary Caudle

10 9 8 7 6 5 4 3 2 1

Chronicle Books LLC
680 Second Street
San Francisco, California 94107
www.chroniclebooks.com

MIX
Paper from
responsible sources
FSC™ C008047
FSC
www.fsc.org

ACKNOWLEDGMENTS

It seems strange to say, but I am truly thankful that lupus and kidney failure entered my life. They led me to discover far cooler things about myself and the world around me, and, above all, they allowed me to grow closer to an amazing group of humans I get to call family and friends. These people rally behind me at every step and push me to believe in even the most far-out miracles. They believed in my strength to survive, they believed in my mission to heal with food, they even believed I could write a book (or two). Because of them, kidney failure means having more, not less. So I'd like to take a moment to say thanks.

To Nomi, my most discerning taste-tester and favorite mayhem-maker. May you always wear two different-colored shoes. Let your joy and imagination run wild. And forever draw outside the lines. Also, eat your peas.

To Alejandro, the best half-Chinese, quarter-Mexican, eighth-Irish, eighth-German husband; cheerleader; and patient partner in crime I could ever dream of.

To my mom (Smoosh) and my dad (Johnny), for giving me life, not once but many times over. For encouragement, continually. And for soft shoulders to land on. As well as a kitchen to cook in when our oven breaks.

To the team, Uncle Rondo, Sarah, Aba, Tia, Tim, Mo Mo, Yeh Yeh, Ya Ya, Andrea, Cara, Samara, and Ale, for helping keep the house clean, the baby entertained, and the date nights on the calendar.

To the food folks, Stephanie Hua, Catherine McCord, Phoebe Lapine, Andrew Wilder, Stephanie Weaver, Max Falkowitz, Irvin Lin, Tracy Benjamin, Cheryl Sternman Rule, Jess Thomson, Food52 Crew, Denise Woodward, Gaby Dalkin, Visra Vichit-Vadakan, Mei Li, Firefly Restaurant, Haley Sausner, Bruce Cole, Nojo Restaurant, and Greg Dunmore, for being generous with your wisdom and for welcoming low-sodium so warmly into the greater culinary world.

To the pros, Jenni Ferrari-Adler, Adelaide Mueller, Rebekah Peppler, Jenais Zarlin, Sarah Billingsley, Emily Dubin, Hillary Caudle, Doug Ogan, Ellen Wheat, Vanessa Dina, John Lee, Lillian Kang, Emma Star Jensen, Veronica Sjoen, Stephan Lam, Barb Stuckey, Dr. Rachel K. Johnson, Erin McCormick, Nikki Gepner, Katy Wilkens, Beth Shanaman, Karsha Chang, and Heather Bandura, for believing in my words, my recipes, and my mission.

To my friends, all of you; you and you and you, too—who accepted my low-sodium food and lifestyle from the very beginning. Who tested recipes. Ate recipes. Created recipes. And continually inspire new recipes.

To the caffeine providers, the crews at Bernie's, Philz on 24th, and La Boulange, for letting me work for endless hours in your establishment while sipping very small cups of coffee.

To my two kidneys, Frank and Stein, who taught me everything about perseverance and conquering the impossible. Without you two, none of this would be possible.

CONTENTS

INTRODUCTION

Congratulations, my friends. You are about to experience food and flavor like never before.

Bland and boring. Low-sodium diets have a pretty bad reputation. I get it. You lose the salt, you lose flavor. You lose your favorite foods. You lose out on the social fun of sharing a pizza. But after twelve years of low-sodium cooking, dining, and living, I can say with confidence that none of these rumors hold true.

After being diagnosed with lupus-related kidney failure in 2004, I started on a low-sodium diet with determination, willing to do anything to stay healthy and strong. As someone who likes to eat great food (and feed others), I was equally resolute to make this new regimen more than a prescription, and more than just palatable. It had to be as good as anything I ate before losing the salt, or better.

Which brings me to years of eating ridiculously well— like, five-star-level deliciousness—at home, abroad, and with some of the most amazing chefs at the helm. I've spent years conquering all the seemingly impossible high-sodium challenges. So if you really believe that keeping a low-sodium diet means being doomed to meals of steamed chicken breast, eaten alone while watching *Golden Girls* reruns, think again. Those low-sodium misperceptions are just plain wrong.

In the following pages, you'll discover that a low-sodium diet can be anything but plain. With the right attitude, the right tools, and your righteous imagination, anything is possible on a low-sodium diet, including big flavor and meals shared with friends. And, yes, even bacon.

This guide will help you discover, step by step, the low-sodium potential that lies before you. From the tip of your tongue to the tines of your fork. In your home and in your office. When eating by yourself or with others. We will start by exploring the basics of sodium and salt, and the many ways to eat and live with less of it. Then, we'll cover the basics of the kitchen and the grocery store, so you become as confident as possible with your cooking adventures. Because, often, the concept of making meals from scratch feels scarier than lowering the sodium. After that, we leave the house and explore solutions to sodium-challenges that occur at work, with friends, and when traveling (to name just a few). And we'll complete the guide with delicious low-sodium recipes to keep you satisfied any time of the day. These have been woven throughout the guide so you can put all the lessons and tips (and cooking equipment!) to immediate use. By the end, I promise, you will find that once you lose some of that sodium, you will gain more than you could have imagined.

While most of the words in this book come directly from my life and real experiences, you'll also hear from a few experts: registered dietitians, salt-eating food writers and bloggers, a former boyfriend (now husband), and even a food developer. They participated in the writing of this book in order to share their wisdom about everything—from decoding labels to dating to storing spices. But they are also here as friends, a small sample of the diverse community that helps me eat better and live better and who often joins me at my table. Beyond being wise, these friends serve as proof that you will not go low-so alone.

Which brings me to another important point: I wrote this book with you in mind, but it is not just for you. It is for everyone. Because in its most basic form, a low-sodium diet is a diet free of processed food and full of whole, fresh ingredients, or, as I like to say, "low-so" food is just "slow food" with the letters mixed around. Whether you know people who are on a plant-based diet, doing "the Whole 30" challenge, or simply "eating clean," the core principle remains the same: Ditch the junk for real ingredients. And the tips, recipes, and advice in this book are truly applicable to anyone—from those on a special eating plan to those looking for fresh ideas on how to eat more fresh food. So don't hog this book for yourself—share it. There's literally something for everyone in here.

But, now, back to you. If you're completely new to this whole low-sodium thing, use this book as your starting line and let it help you ease into a new routine. If you consider yourself a low-so pro, use this book as a reference guide; flipping to pages as needed, adding more tricks to your already well-stocked arsenal. And if you ever find yourself in a sodium-related challenge or a recipe rut, use this book like a set of jumper cables to get a boost of creativity.

No matter where you find yourself, use this book as a companion, to not only all the other cookbooks and guides out there but also the professional advice and assistance you receive from your health-care providers and dietitians. Use it to create food you crave and a life you enjoy. Use it to make you a more confident cook. Use it to change food obsessions from fake cheesy puffs to cayenne dusted polenta fries. And in the end, use it to transform the way you feel about low-sodium diets and see it for what it really is; real, good food that will make you feel really good.

I am not a doctor, or a nutritionist, or a dietitian. Nor a rock star, or a karate expert, or a culinary school–certified chef, for that matter. What I am is a motivational eater. And with a dozen years of experience cooking, dining, and adventuring under my non–black belt, I know a thing or two about finding and making satisfying low-sodium food wherever I go. I have devoured cookbooks, and taught myself how to make everything from salt-free bread to no-sodium Bloody Marys. I have asked tons of questions of professionals—both the cooking and the medical kind. And over time, I've replaced the long list of "no you cannots" with enthusiastic "oh hell, yes you cans!" You might even say that I've kicked major high-sodium challenges in the butt, karate-style. The advice in this book is meant to help you do the same, by filling you with enthusiasm and inspiring you with creativity when it comes to your new diet, as well as directing you to valuable resources for further information. But remember, when it comes to your health and the specifics of your diet, always consult your medical professionals about what's right for you.

···1···
TRANSFORM

Let's Go Low-So

Imagine a world where you could improve your health just by eating. Not with thick protein shakes or chalky meal replacements, but with bold, bright food. Food that makes your mouth water, that entices your friends to come over for dinner, that deserves to be on the cover of a cookbook. Wouldn't that be amazing?

Well, this world exists. For most people, just by filling their plates with less processed foods and more fresh ingredients, they can reduce their risk of heart disease, diabetes, and other health issues.

So what is this tasty solution called and where has it been all your life?

I'm simply talking about a low-sodium diet. You've most likely heard your doctor, dietitian, or TV news anchor mention it before. That was when any mouthwatering excitement began to fade.

Visions of tasteless chicken, soggy vegetables, and hours spent prepping in the kitchen have long kept people away from giving a low-sodium diet a fair chance. Fear of changing routines and losing favorite comfort foods drive people away from the diet instead of toward it. And while people have the opportunity to improve their health with less sodium, which seems like a no-brainer, no one is taking the bait.

That's because the bait still isn't very appetizing. Low-sodium diets continue to be depicted not as food, but as a prescription, one that requires deprivation and ditching convenience and routine (a.k.a. the familiar). And after receiving a sobering diagnosis that replaced your clean bill of health, it's understandable why people might refuse to give up anything else, like culinary comforts.

To inspire people, we need to change the way we talk about low-sodium food—in look, feel, and taste. Even in name (we'll get to that). This approach to healthful eating must shift from something medical to something culinary. It must allow people to not only stay well, but live well. It must transform from something enforced to something we enjoy. Which isn't a difficult task, because in the end, we are simply talking about replacing the muddled taste of packaged meals with real food and real flavor.

So get ready to ditch the "diet" concept and dive into a total low-sodium transformation—or what I like to call the "low-so" life—which you'll discover is full of fresh ingredients, strong spices, and beautiful meals to share with others.

UNDERSTANDING SALT AND SODIUM

Before cutting down on salt and sodium, it's important to understand the what, the where, the why, and the how. What is the difference between table salt and sodium? Where do salt and sodium exist in your food and your routine? Why does salt make food taste so good? How much do you need—or need to minimize—for good health? And how can you cook successfully without it?

By learning the answers to these questions, you'll be better prepared to avoid high-sodium traps, mimic salt in cooking, and maintain a balanced and healthful diet, which will make the whole low-so switch a lot easier and a whole lot tastier.

TABLE SALT AND SOURCES OF SODIUM

You may have heard someone make the following statement: "I don't eat a lot of sodium. I never salt my food."

The truth is, the saltshaker is not the only source of sodium. Actually, the salt you use (or don't use) while cooking and before you dig into dinner contributes only about 10 percent of the sodium you consume, according to the American Heart Association.

Although people tend to use the two terms *salt* and *sodium* interchangeably, sodium is a component of the table salt you use for cooking and sprinkling. Table salt is 40 percent sodium and 60 percent chloride. Sodium also exists in most foods naturally, like carrots (42 mg per large carrot), eggs (70 mg per egg), chicken thighs (80 mg per 3-oz [85-g] boneless, skinless thigh), and lobster (150 mg per 3-oz [85-g] lobster).

Sodium also hides in unexpected places, like milk (about 100 mg per 1 cup [240 ml]), soy sauce (more than 100 mg per 1 Tbsp), your favorite salad dressings (about 135 mg per 1 Tbsp ranch dressing, depending on brand), baking powder (more than 400 mg per 1 tsp) and baking soda (1,249 mg per 1 tsp), as well as medications (like antacids). So even if you don't "salt" your food, sodium is found in other ingredients you use when cooking and eating, from processed foods to the produce aisle. And these all contribute to your daily total.

NOTE: All sodium counts given in this book are based on averages provided by the USDA National Nutrient Database for Standard Reference Release 26 (ndb.nal.usda.gov/ndb/search).

WHY WE NEED SODIUM AND WHY SOME OF US NEED LESS

Sodium is an essential electrolyte for our basic, everyday bodily functions, such as balancing fluids, transporting nutrients, transmitting nerve impulses, and contracting muscles. As Rachel K. Johnson, PhD, RD, and American Heart Association spokesperson, notes, "Sodium is also needed to replace losses from sweat in people who engage in heavy physical activity." The bottom line is: We need sodium to stay healthy and to survive.

Depending on your health needs and sodium sensitivities, however, too much sodium can "hold excess fluid in the body," Dr. Johnson says, putting stress on your body, increasing blood pressure and risk of disease. For these populations, she adds, "eating less sodium will help minimize the rise in blood pressure as well as reduce the risk of developing other conditions associated with too much sodium, such as stroke, heart failure, osteoporosis, stomach cancer, and kidney disease."

So how much sodium should you be consuming? The number will be different for each person, depending on age, race, health, and predisposition for certain diseases. It's essential to consult a doctor or registered dietitian to find the right sodium-intake plan for your individual needs. But currently, the USDA's 2010 Dietary Guidelines for Americans (cnpp.usda.gov/dietaryguidelines) recommends an upper limit of 2,300 mg of sodium a day. And for more than 50 percent of the population—those who are older than fifty-one; African American; or have high blood pressure, diabetes, or chronic heart or kidney disease—the guidelines recommend less than 1,500 mg of sodium a day.

To put this in perspective, 2,300 mg of sodium is equal to 1 tsp of table salt, and 1,500 mg is about ¾ tsp of table salt or a little more than 1 Tbsp of soy sauce. And let's just say, most people—nine out of ten Americans, according to the American Heart Association—take in more than double the lower limit, around 3,400 mg of sodium. Factor in high-sodium, fast-food meal choices and sometimes people hit those numbers by lunch. Gulp.

That's because more than 75 percent of the sodium people consume comes from packaged goods, processed foods, and restaurant meals. But you don't need to hide out in your kitchen only eating raw vegetables. We all just need to learn how to make smart food choices.

So, "low-so" food really *is* just "slow" food with the letters mixed around. Lowering sodium in its simplest form means using fresh ingredients, ditching processed products, enjoying the process of making real food, and getting creative in the kitchen to revise favorite recipes.

TOP SOURCES OF SECRET SODIUM

The Centers for Disease Control and Prevention and the American Heart Association recently put the spotlight on six surprising foods that are top contributors to the sodium in our diets, all commonly found on pantry shelves, restaurant menus, and people's cravings lists. They call them "The Salty Six." You can keep the Six from sneaking too much sodium into your daily diet by having them on your radar and knowing how to replace them with lower-sodium choices.

BREAD

Sodium Facts: You might not think of two pieces of bread as an unhealthful choice. But if you're watching your sodium intake, each slice can equal more than 200 mg of sodium, depending on the product.

Lower-Sodium Solution: Depending on your sodium needs, reduce those numbers by using one slice of bread instead of two. Buy low-sodium or no-salt-added bread. Use sturdy greens, corn tortillas, or sodium-free sushi nori to make a wrap. Try using sodium-free matzo crackers for an open-face sandwich. Or fire up the oven and make your own loaf!

COLD CUTS

Sodium Facts: According to the American Heart Association, a 2-oz [55-g] serving (or about six thin slices) of deli meat can equal more than half the day's recommended 1,500 mg sodium intake.

Lower-Sodium Solution: Look for low-sodium or salt-free meat products (they exist), or make big batches of roasted chicken or meat on the weekend to fill salads and those low-sodium sandwiches all week long.

PIZZA

Sodium Facts: With the dough, sauce, cheese, pepperoni, and other salty toppings like olives, even one slice of pizza can easily deliver half your daily 1,500 mg sodium allotment.

Lower-Sodium Solution: Depending on your sodium needs, you can simply choose toppings wisely, sticking to low-sodium options (like vegetables versus sausage). You can make your own dough and sauce from scratch. Or even use chickpea flour to make a ready-to-eat pizza crust (see page 94) in less time than it takes to order and wait for delivery.

POULTRY

Sodium Facts: When it comes to chicken (and even beef, pork, fish, and shellfish), some manufacturers plump the protein with salty solutions before it hits the store, increasing weight and price, not to mention upping sodium content in chicken as much as 500 percent.

Lower-Sodium Solution: Avoid items with "added broth," "percent solution," "enhanced," "brined," and even "natural flavoring" listed on the label in small print. Look for "air-chilled" and "no water added" to identify products that are plumping-free. And when in doubt, read the nutritional information: Natural chicken should have 70 to 90 mg of sodium per 4 oz [115 g].

SANDWICHES

Sodium Facts: I think you know what's coming by now. Between the bread, the spread, the deli meat, and the cheese, a sandwich ends up being a high-sodium choice.

Lower-Sodium Solution: Get creative and ask your local sandwich shop to wrap your sandwich in lettuce instead of bread. Use any of the bread and meat swaps suggested on page 120 to make your own low-so subs at home. Or use your favorite sandwich fillings as inspiration for a salad instead.

SOUP

Sodium Facts: A single 1-cup [240-ml] serving of canned soup can range from 100 to 1,000 mg of sodium. If you have double that amount of high-sodium soup, you've already exceeded the 1,500 mg sodium per day limit.

Lower-Sodium Solution: Let's just agree that freshly made soup will always taste better than canned soup. Of course, low-sodium soups and even salt-free stock options exist, which are great to have on hand for convenience. Just make sure to consult your physician to make sure these products fit within your dietary needs, because some may use potassium-chloride salt substitutes for flavor.

Above all, remember to inspect the label of any product and search for high-sodium key words and clues (more about that on page 74). With a keen eye and a quick flip of a can or package, you'll quickly become a skilled sodium sleuth and an expert in eliminating high-sodium products before they hit your plate.

And don't forget about medications. Sometimes sodium sneaks its way into pills and vitamins, too. So check labels and, when in doubt, talk to your doctor and pharmacist.

SALT SUBSTITUTES

While salt replacements exist, not every substitute is meant for every body. "Low-sodium salts" and "no-sodium salts" use potassium chloride to replace a percentage or all of the sodium chloride. For most people, potassium chloride is well tolerated in moderate amounts. But some people on kidney-friendly diets or certain medications—like diuretics or heart or blood-pressure medications—may need to avoid these products because of potential risks of elevated blood-potassium levels.

For those who must avoid potassium chloride, the good news is that several companies make sodium- and potassium-free spice and herb blends, or use nutritional yeast and kelp to offer salt-like taste. When selecting one of these, be sure to buy those products labeled "MSG free." Do not use these products if you have a yeast intolerance or allergy. Be aware that seaweed contains iodine and, in some cases, may interfere with thyroid functions, so it's best to use on an occasional basis. Alternatively, if you *can* handle a little more sodium, try using small amounts of salty ingredients in place of the shaker, like a sprinkle of shredded Parmesan (90 mg per 1 Tbsp) or goat cheese (around 100 mg per 1 oz [28 g]); chopped olives (50 mg per olive, depending on brand) or low-sodium sweet pickles (30 mg per 1 cup [140 g], chopped, depending on brand); or panko bread crumbs (40 mg per ½ cup [30 g]), crumbled low-sodium crackers, or flavored seaweed snacks. No matter what salt substitute you choose, remember to always consult your doctor or dietitian to pick a salt substitute that's safe for you.

TABLE SALT VERSUS SEA SALT

Sea salt can boast that it has bigger and flakier crystals than table salt, and also a more natural taste. But one thing table salt and sea salt still have in common is sodium content. The dietary guidelines for daily sodium limits still apply, even if the salt is from the Himalayas or is mixed with truffle bits.

EXPLORING THE FIVE TASTES

Now that we're better acquainted with salt and sodium, let's get to know our tongues a little bit better, too. Because this licking and lapping device does a lot more than rescue drips of sauce from the corner of your mouth.

The tongue actually plays a very important role in helping us know what tastes good (mint chip ice cream, hooray!) and what tastes bad (moldy cantaloupe, boo). Of course, the nose is also involved, but we'll talk about that in a second. By giving your tongue what it's looking for, you'll end up with a satisfying low-sodium meal.

Covered in taste buds, our tongues can detect five distinct tastes: sweet, sour, bitter, umami (or savory), and salty. It's a combination of these elements that move dishes from boring to pleasant to memorable to "let's make this again immediately." An understanding of the tastes and how to combine them will help you quickly fine-tune a dish or make something up, on the fly.

Here's the mind-blowing part of the lesson: Each of these five tastes can be found in whole foods, naturally. No bottles, no sauces, no seasoning, no salt or sodium necessary. That's right. Mother Nature made her own spice rack with fruits, vegetables, and meat. So let's explore the five tastes with this simple plate of raw ingredients.

SWEET

Let's start with the taste we probably *think* we know best: Sweet. When we think of sweet, we typically think of fruit—cobblers, strawberry-topped waffles, and banana smoothies. But it's time to start thinking of sweet ingredients as a friend of savory food, too.

The next time you see rosy raspberries or plump nectarines, transform them into a sauce for grilled meat or mix them into a vegetable-heavy salad. And don't forget that nonfruit items—like peas, corn, and basil—are sweet, too. A dash of natural sweetness will balance and enhance other flavors in a dish.

Try This: Take a bite of in-season berries. Then explore some nonfruit sweetness with fresh-from-the-cob corn kernels or Roasted Red Pepper and Butternut Squash Soup (page 243). Then go to the next level and try Roasted Fig and Tomato Slow Jam (page 162), on its own or atop a juicy pork chop or steak, and enjoy the dance of naturally occurring sweet, savory, and umami tastes.

SOUR

Adding something sour to a dish, like citrus or vinegar, is akin to splashing your face with cold water. It's a quick way to wake up your food. If you want to resurrect leftovers, a squeeze of lemon will do the trick. When that salad needs a little extra oomph, try a dash of vinegar. And if that soup hits only one note, add another with a tangy dollop of Greek yogurt.

Try This: Don't tell your dentist, but take a bite of a lemon wedge. Then sample Lemon Chicken Orzo (page 172) or Macaroon Custard Tarts (page 225) to see how well a sour ingredient plays with sweet and savory ingredients.

BITTER

Some people wince at the thought of adding bitter ingredients to their dishes. But just the right amount of bite offers a pleasant surprise to the palate, especially in typically mild or somewhat sweet dishes like mashed potatoes, shrimp, or roasted salmon. Here's the thing about bitter ingredients, whether you're talking onions or wasabi: By adding a little heat and something sweet, bitter ingredients mellow out so they become pleasant instead of piercing.

Try This: To experience a mild bitter flavor, try raw radish on its own or in Radish-and-Onion Yogurt Spread (page 179). Or go for broke with a bite of raw radicchio or a slice of horseradish. Then try one of the Kale Salads for Different Seasons (page 182) to experience how a little sweetness from avocado and the sour of citrus balances out the bitterness in the greens.

UMAMI

When people think of umami, they think of high-sodium products like soy sauce, teriyaki sauce, and kimchi. But umami (or savory) flavor actually exists naturally in mushrooms, tomatoes, beef, and even green tea. And umami flavor actually gets stronger when ingredients are aged, dried, cooked, cured, or simply paired with other umami-rich foods. So if you need to increase the savory taste of a dish, go for more umami.

Try This: Add shiitake mushrooms to your next vegetable stir-fry and enjoy the savory boost. Then try Genmaicha Microwave Soup (page 122) or Cauliflower Steaks with Curry Mushroom Gravy (page 203) for a multiplied umami experience.

SALTY

You're probably thinking, how can you create a salty taste without salt? Well, remember that most foods have sodium in them naturally. We can use that fact to our cooking advantage. Using ingredients like beets, meat, and shellfish that are naturally higher in sodium, you can infuse favorite typically salty dishes with natural salty tastes. No saltshaker needed.

Try This: Start by chewing on a piece of celery. Wow, kind of salty tasting, right? Then make Carrot–Sweet Onion Dressing (page 169) to add balance to sweet and smoky Grilled Lettuce Salad (page 171) or try Toasted Rice Patties (page 180) with their salty tasting seaweed sprinkle.

MIMICKING SALT: ANYTHING SALT CAN DO, YOU CAN DO BETTER

Now that we know how to replicate each of the five tastes with whole ingredients, let's focus a little bit more on salt and how it enhances our taste experience. To do that, let's turn to my friend Barb Stuckey, who is an actual food developer (which is a real job, people!).

Barb wrote a book called *Taste What You're Missing*, which is all about getting more flavor from your food. As the executive vice president of marketing and sales at Mattson (a food and beverage development company), she is an expert at improving the taste of food. She understands the actual "science-y" side of why a bowl of creamy mushroom soup makes us drool. And she knows exactly what happens when we sprinkle a little salt on top.

According to Barb, salt plays five main roles in enhancing the taste of our meals:

+ It magnifies the taste of an ingredient.

+ It wakes up the flavor.

+ It releases volatiles, or the aromas found in food ingredients (oh hey, nostrils!).

+ It balances the other tastes.

+ It makes things taste salty.

But here's what's really cool. Just like we can mimic the five tastes with whole ingredients, you can easily replicate each of these salt-enhancing traits without touching the saltshaker.

Salt magnifies the taste of an ingredient. Sprinkling a little salt on a tomato will magically increase the essence of tomato, which is a great trick for making bitter or out-of-season tomatoes more palatable. But there's another way to achieve the same level of flavor enhancement; simply apply time and heat. By giving tomatoes a slow roast, you can intensify the tomato flavor. The same goes for a stew braised for hours in the oven or all day in a slow cooker. The longer dishes cook, the more the flavor gets coaxed out of the ingredients.

Salt wakes up the flavor. When a dish tastes flat or leftovers taste old, a little salt gives food a second chance. But a splash of something sour will achieve the same results. And while citrus juice offers an awesome effect, don't forget the peel. By adding the zest of that lemon or orange, you will also release the smell of the citrus, which will activate that nose of yours. Smelling food is actually 90 percent of tasting it.

Salt releases volatiles. Volatiles are the essences emitted from a food that help us smell it and taste it. Salt helps release these volatiles. But heat also releases volatiles. This is why you toast spices before using them, and why the aroma of sautéed garlic and onions make your mouth water.

Salt balances the other tastes. If you want to test this, try making a chocolate chip cookie without salt. It tastes flat. But that doesn't mean you can't make really good low-sodium chocolate chip cookies (or any dish) without salt. You just need to replace the salt with something else to enhance the other tastes. Whether you use a sprinkle of chili powder or ground cardamom, an extra taste element (spice, color, smell) goes a long way in rebalancing chocolate chip cookies. Or any recipe you decide to make salt-free.

Salt makes things taste salty. Ten minutes ago, you would have said this was an impossible challenge to resolve. But now you know that you can find salty tastes in whole ingredients. By using beets, celery seed, or even shrimp shells (when making a broth), you can add a salty kick to favorite recipes.

Barb adds that increasing umami in a dish will help curb the natural craving for salt. And by playing up the other senses—touch, smell, and sight—you can help distract the palate and enhance the food in other ways, like using interesting textures, pleasant odors, and pretty colors.

FINDING FLAVOR

Now that you know what salt does to your food, let's replace it—with a new approach to food as well as a new attitude. Because to successfully remove the salt from favorite dishes, you must not only fill the gap—with spice, texture, or color—but also flip your perspective. And that's why we are about to Rediscover, Rebel, Relate, and Refocus.

REDISCOVER: ALTERNATIVE FLAVOR BOOSTERS

When it comes to flavor-enhancing alternatives, the options are endless. You can increase the taste and appeal of your food by simply exploring new cuisines; adding unexpected texture; using a grill or slow cooker to add smokiness and depth; or serving your finished dish on those gorgeous inherited china plates you have yet to use. Use the following ingredients, tools, and cooking tricks to replicate all of salt's flavor-boosting powers without using a single grain of it.

SPICES, HERBS, VINEGARS, OILS, CITRUS

From paprika to cinnamon, the world of spices will enhance even the simplest of meals (like roasted chicken or sautéed vegetables). And don't forget about flavored vinegars, flavored oils, fresh and dried herbs, and citrus. But remember, check labels. Even spices, oils, and vinegars may contain salt or seasoning. Buy only items marked "no salt added" or containing 0 mg of salt. If something doesn't exist, or you feel bold, make your own flavored oils, vinegars, and spice blends, like Maharaja-Style Curry Powder (page 195).

UNCOMMON PAIRINGS

The more you surprise yourself and your palate, the less you'll miss salt. Take creative liberties with recipes and add uncommon ingredients to the mix. Make a pasta sauce with puréed pumpkin. Use jams instead of steak sauce. Toss salads with juicy berries instead of dressing. You'll be swept away by the surprising, low-sodium combinations.

COLOR AND FEEL

As the adage goes, you eat as much with your eyes as with your mouth. The look of your plate proves just as important as what you put on it. So don't shy away from brightly colored dishes and foods. Mix up textures as well, putting creamy and crunchy ingredients together. The more there is to see and feel, the less you'll search for the salt.

OVENS, GRILLS, AND SLOW COOKERS

Not all flavor comes in a bottle. You can create a tasty meal with just an oven, a slow cooker, or a grill. When you roast ingredients or stew them, the heat and longer cooking times magnify the natural sweetness and savory tastes in your ingredients. A grill will add a smoky essence to your dishes. Throw smoking chips on the coals to further infuse your ingredients, from peaches to fish, with smells of hickory, mesquite, cherry, and apple, to name a few options.

CATHERINE McCORD
PLAYS WITH HER FOOD

....

Let me introduce you to Catherine McCord, the founder of Weelicious.com, author of One Family. One Meal. and Weelicious Lunches, and a whiz when it comes to making healthful food for her entire family. But before you ask what a kid's meal has to do with low-sodium diets, let me remind you that enjoying salt-free food comes down to attitude. Who says adults aren't just as picky and green-aphobic as toddlers? No matter who you need to feed, a little fun goes a long way, especially when trying something new. Whether it's the addition of color (purple cauliflower!), a twist on an old recipe (baked potato tacos!), or turning dinner into a family event, use Catherine's advice to make healthful meals into happy meals.

We know that whole foods are better for our bodies. The question is how to make them the star of the meal and have fun doing it at the same time. I've spent years doing research—my lab being my kitchen, my mice being my family—to find cool ways to incorporate as much nutrition into our meals while adding tons of color and flavor too. Here are five tips—kid approved and adult applicable—for getting anyone onboard.

+ We eat with our eyes, so the more vibrant the plate, the more visually exciting the meal becomes. Instead of boiling broccoli, gently steam it to keep the nutrients and emerald green color intact. Make sure every meal includes colorful fruits and vegetables to brighten up the plate.

+ When foods have visual appeal, they're instantly more exciting. Cutting foods into fun shapes can transform them. For easy appetizers, try using a melon baller for watermelon and put on skewers, or cutting cucumbers into sticks or coins.

+ For kids (and adults!) who resist vegetables, offer toasted sesame seeds in a shaker or a sauce to spoon on top. That way they can doll up their food themselves—making it more fun and interactive—while adding vitamins at the same time.

+ Instead of getting stuck in a food rut, switching things up day to day can keep your diet, and your menus, nutritionally balanced and exciting at the same time. Try having fish on Monday, chicken or meat on Wednesday, and a few vegetarian meals in between. Variety really is the spice of life.

+ Get everyone involved in making every meal. By involving family and friends in the cooking process, picky eaters of all ages will get more excited about the foods they've made and are about to eat.

REBEL: LESSONS FROM JAMES DEAN AND LADY GAGA

Remember those yearbook polls where people got voted "best looking," "most likely to rule the world," or "most likely to be famous"? Well, I was voted "teacher's pet." No big surprise, for a total nerd/perfectionist.

But my high-school classmates got it all wrong. Over the years, I developed a total bad streak. I'm now a real mischief-maker. And when it comes to cooking, you won't find me following anyone's directions.

Most of the old low-sodium rules told you what *not* to do. Which is why people don't want to give it a try. So you need to pull a James Dean or get all Gaga and break the rules. Low-sodium cooking requires coloring outside the lines, pushing against the conventional, and yes, rewriting those recipes. So take charge. When you act a little bad, your food will start to taste really good.

RELATE: TOP CHEFS AND OTHER SPECIAL DIETS

Most people believe that taking on a low-sodium diet means removing themselves from the greater culinary community and the big foodie table. Why? Because low-sodium food often gets painted as not gourmet, not chef caliber, and not worth serving to others.

But this is all sorts of wrong. And I'll prove it.

First let's look at shows like *Top Chef* and *Iron Chef* and pretty much any cooking competition on the Food Network. To win, the talented contestants must think out of the box to meet crazy food challenges (you can only use anchovies and chocolate!) or invent new versions of old favorites (shrimp pot pie!). Their level of creativity and inventiveness is thrilling to watch, and that is exactly what you're about to do as a low-sodium cook.

In making dishes without prepared foods, from scratch, and with less-salty ingredients, you'll be forced to use more innovation, more imagination, and more personal flair. Just like the pros. This kind of creativity sets the good cooks apart from the great cooks. And means exciting, impressive meals. So, in fact, low-sodium cooking doesn't make you a noncook; it makes you a culinary force to be reckoned with. Tom Colicchio, bring it on.

As for being part of a culinary community, let's look to some other special diets, like raw food, vegan, gluten-free, and Paleo. Today, celebrities, food publications, and even the restaurant industry warmly welcome these restricted eating plans. People don't see them as diets, but as a valuable part of the food world. Like low-sodium, they use creativity to overcome limitations. And they've added a whole new vocabulary of ingredient swaps to the culinary playbook. We wouldn't have cauliflower pizza crust or zucchini noodles without them.

So why doesn't low-sodium food get the same love? One difference, enthusiasm. People on gluten-free, vegan, vegetarian, and Paleo plans are proud, not apologetic. They put their creations front and center versus hiding them—at parties, at potlucks, and on the pages of magazines.

Which is all to say that if you see low-sodium as a great thing, others will too. Be proud of your low-sodium creations. And remember to share your discoveries with others on special diets, because just like you:

+ Vegans love cheese substitutes and meatless hot dog swaps

+ Paleo fans can always use another grain-free bread idea

+ Plant-based eaters love vegetable-heavy entrees and noodle dishes

+ Whole 30 followers benefit from travel advice, dining tips, and 1-hour homemade bacon

+ Anyone who works in an office will appreciate tips on better desk lunches

+ Everyone wants an excuse to eat more avocado

If it helps, go ahead and give your program a new name—like "eating real" or "unprocessed" or, of course, "low-so"—if that makes you feel more empowered. Remind yourself that your low-sodium ways are no different from the other healthful eating missions your peers take on. Own it. And when there's a salty ingredient you need to replace, look to other special diets for confidence and ingredient-swapping inspiration. Then, channel your inner James Dean or Lady Gaga, give it a try, and create the next "kale chip."

PHOEBE LAPINE
TALKS SPECIAL-DIET TIPS

....

Everyone with any special diet shares the same challenge of eliminating ingredients while staying satisfied. Those who eat gluten-free, dairy-free, or anything-free can share strategies and tips. I tapped cookbook author, private chef, vegetarian, and gluten-free eater, Phoebe Lapine, to let you in on some secrets to eating well with special food needs.

SEE GAINS, NOT LOSS:
Let your food limitations be your biggest motivator to fall back in love with your kitchen. Allow the restriction to unlock your sense of creativity and adventure. And think of it as an opportunity to try new things instead of an ongoing struggle to forgo old favorites. If you're open to it, you'll discover many more new things that you love.

EAT OUT, SPEAK UP:
When you eat out, don't feel ashamed of being vocal. Communicate with hosts if you're their dinner guest. Let them know in advance that you have an allergy or dietary restriction. Trust me, they'll be more upset by the fact that you can't eat their lasagna, than by the opportunity to make something that fits your needs.

LOVE WHAT YOU EAT:
You eat with your eyes first, so take an extra five minutes to plate your food beautifully and garnish with fresh herbs. Turn meals into an activity. Make it fun. It sounds so silly, but even eating things with your fingers is a simple pleasure. So put dinner on a stick or in a taco. And reconnect with your food.

ANDREW WILDER
TALKS GOING UNPROCESSED

....

Cleanses, detoxes, and clean eating—people love the idea of pressing the restart button on their health. We all know friends and coworkers who proudly share their plans to cut the junk for days or weeks at a time. So how is that any different from going on a low-sodium diet? It isn't. For further proof and inspiration, I asked my friend Andrew Wilder, founder of EatingRules.com and creator of October Unprocessed, to share his story of eating clean, eating well, and actually (although unintentionally) eating less sodium, all while building a supportive community.

In October 2009, I had my "aha!" moment. I was walking in a parking lot on perfectly level ground, and felt like I was walking through molasses. My legs ached and my body simply didn't want to move. I was thirty-two years old, and it struck me that I really shouldn't feel like that. I started thinking about how what I ate affected my body. And I was struck by a simple idea: What would happen if I went for an entire month without eating any processed foods?

This question would have been laughable just a few decades ago. But nowadays, it seems that almost every food comes with an ingredient list laden with extra sugar, fat, and salt. And preservatives. And flavorings. And artificial colors. After realizing just how much of that junk I was putting into my body, I decided it had to stop.

So I tried it, along with my friends Dana and Lindsey. A month of no processed foods. It was revelatory. My expectations and my sense of taste were recalibrated. I started to identify individual ingredients in the foods I ate. I didn't crave those salty snacks. I found myself often in the kitchen, excited to see what I could cook next. Above all, I simply felt better.

A few months later, I started my blog to help others find the same joy in real, unprocessed food. And when October came around again, I decided to see how many people might want to try a similar challenge. I set up a "pledge" page on my site, where people could sign their names and see the list of everyone else who had committed. I also invited other bloggers and experts to share guest posts throughout the month. By the end of the first official "October Unprocessed," 415 brave people had signed the pledge on my site.

That was back in 2010. I've led the challenge each year since then, and it's grown every time. In 2013, more than 15,500 people took part!

Nowadays, I eat unprocessed almost all of the time, but it still helps to take a month each year (especially before the gluttonous holiday season!) to hit the reset button and take a fresh look at what I'm eating. I hope you'll consider joining me this coming October—or year-round!—and take control of your health and happiness by experiencing the joy of eating real, unprocessed food.

REFOCUS: GAINS VERSUS LOSSES

For the visual learners, or for those who need a little more convincing, here's a list of gains versus losses when taking on a low-sodium diet. Of course, there are the obvious points to make about overall health and wellness as well as time and cost. But here are some other perhaps less obvious takeaways.

GAINS

+ You will get more acquainted with your palate.

+ You will become more confident cooking, even when using leftovers.

+ You will become more knowledgeable about vegetables and proteins.

+ You will explore new spices and herbs.

+ You will form more meaningful relationships with the people who feed you.

+ You will become more adventurous and interesting.

+ You will throw better dinner parties.

+ You will inspire loved ones to spend more time in the kitchen.

LOSSES

+ You may have to spend less money on processed and prepared foods.

+ You may have to eat fewer chemicals, ingredients you cannot pronounce, and junk.

+ You may talk less to your pizza guy and more to your butcher.

+ You may see less of your doctor.

+ You may spend less time eating in front of the TV and more time at a beautifully set table.

+ You may use fewer recipes and more of your own creativity.

+ You will eat fewer processed foods and enjoy more of the process of making food.

7-DAY TASTE BUD REBOOT

Let's get your tongue back on track and recalibrate it so that instead of needing the over-saltiness of processed ingredients, it starts detecting the nuanced flavors in real foods again. To do that, you will need to eat incredibly tasty, fresh food for seven days. I'm talking breakfast, lunch, dinner, and even snacks. I know, rough. But you can do it! And the meal plan on pages 31–32 will set you and your taste buds on the right course.

You will be making all your meals from scratch, which will feel overwhelming. But think of this as a food boot camp—there are big rewards for big effort. It's only one week, and it's more about switching up your routine than confining you to your stove forever. Pick a relatively calm seven days with a relatively clear calendar. And trust me, I've streamlined the recipes, the ingredients, and the heavy equipment so most of the hard work happens at the beginning. I've included a shopping list and prep guide to make every step efficient.

The reboot officially starts on Sunday afternoon with a roasted chicken and a few hours of heavy meal prep (all while that bird cooks). I chose Sunday because it is usually the emptiest day of my week and you'll have to be home while that chicken cooks, but do what works for your schedule. Dinner always feeds two people; all breakfasts, lunches, and snacks are just for you. Add bulk or go rogue following the Additional Ways to Taste More with Your Taste Buds suggestions. Freeze any extras (see page 68) for some real, fast food later on. And remember this is not a dietary or medical meal plan, but a processed-food detox. So always consult your medical professionals to make sure you're eating what's right for you and your health.

SHOPPING LIST

PROTEIN

+ 1 dozen large eggs

+ One 3- to 4-lb [1.3- to 1.8-kg] fryer chicken

+ 8 to 10 oz [225 to 285 g] salmon fillets

+ 8 to 10 oz [225 to 285 g] tilapia fillets

VEGETABLES

+ 3 avocados

+ 3 red bell peppers

+ 1 large bunch of broccoli (with stem)

+ 1 head butter lettuce

+ 1 large butternut squash, pre-cut into cubes, or two 10-oz [285-g] bags diced frozen butternut squash

+ 4 carrots

+ 1 large bunch of cauliflower (with leaves)

+ 1 bunch cilantro

+ 1 bag frozen corn, no salt added

+ 1 large English cucumber

+ Garlic, pre-peeled

+ 1 jalapeño chile

- + 1 large bunch Lacinato kale (about 24 leaves)
- + 1 bag spinach, pre-washed
- + 2 sweet potatoes
- + 1 yam
- + 1 zucchini

FRUIT

- + 2 apples
- + 2 bananas, ripe or overripe
- + 2 limes
- + 2 lemons
- + 1 large mango or pineapple, or 1 lb [455 g] cubed fresh mango or pineapple
- + 2 nectarines

DAIRY

- + Coconut milk beverage, unsweetened
- + Two 6-oz [180-ml] containers soy or coconut yogurt
- + One 6-oz [180-ml] container Greek yogurt

MISCELLANEOUS SUNDRIES

- + All-purpose flour
- + Black or pinto beans, no salt added
- + Chipotle chiles, dried
- + Coconut flakes, unsweetened
- + Corn tortillas
- + Pepitas or pumpkin seeds, unsalted
- + Popcorn (microwave or kernels), unsalted
- + Quinoa or brown rice

- + Raisins
- + Rice crackers, sodium-free
- + Rice noodles or spaghetti, sodium-free
- + Spices for "everything spice" and jerk rub: caraway seeds, sesame seeds, celery seeds, mustard seeds, garlic powder, onion powder, black pepper, paprika, cayenne pepper, cumin, cloves, and cinnamon.
- + White chia seeds
- + Nori sheets, sodium-free

ADDITIONAL WAYS TO TASTE MORE WITH YOUR TASTE BUDS

This meal plan is based on what I would typically make and eat in a week. Once you've completed your seven days, you'll most likely cook in a less pre-planned manner. For those nights, try the following ideas to give fresh food a boost of flavor.

For added bulk, add more vegetables by:

- + Roasting broccoli or cauliflower and tossing with harissa sauce
- + Grilling zucchini or asparagus and dressing with lemon juice, lemon zest, and fresh dill
- + Sautéing leafy greens in a little coconut milk and grated ginger
- + Steaming green beans and drizzling with olive oil and crushed nuts

Go beyond white rice and noodles with:

- + Flavorful grains like farro, quinoa, or brown rice
- + Riced cauliflower or broccoli
- + Baked yams, sweet potatoes, or roasted eggplant topped with pasta sauce or pizza toppings

Swap out high-sodium sauces for:

+ Grilled fruit salsa

+ Roasted tomatoes

+ A blend of olive oil and herbs

At the table, sprinkle on:

+ Dukka spice or crushed nuts

+ Dried dill and salt-free garlic powder

+ Red chili pepper flakes

+ Freshly chopped parsley or chives

SUNDAY PREP
ORDER OF OPERATIONS

To get ready for this week's reboot, today you'll be prepping the ingredients for Sunday Chicken with Roasted Roots and Fruits (page 223), Harissa Hot Sauce (page 164), Avocado Green Goddess Dressing (page 168), Cauliflower Rice, Pea, and Edamame Salad (page 197), Cauliflower-Nut "Ricotta" (page 196), Toasted Pepita Mix (page 176), and Banana Chai–Chia Pudding (page 112). By following this list, you will make the most of your oven, your kitchen tools, and your time.

1. Steep the dried chipotle chile in hot water for 30 minutes for the Harissa Hot Sauce.

2. Broil the bell peppers for 15 to 20 minutes for the Harissa Hot Sauce.

3. Prepare the Sunday Chicken with Roasted Roots and Fruits and put it in the oven.

4. Using a food processor, rice the cauliflower for the Cauliflower Rice, Pea, and Edamame Salad.

Transfer 1½ cups [630 g] to an airtight container for Monday's lunch.

5. With 2 cups [840 g] of the riced cauliflower, make the Cauliflower-Nut "Ricotta," skipping the steaming and using whatever citrus juice you have on hand.

6. Take a clean-up break.

7. Using the food processor, rice the broccoli florets; then using the grater attachment for the food processor, shred the broccoli stem for the Cauliflower Rice, Pea, and Edamame Salad.

8. Using the grater attachment for the food processor, shred three of the carrots.

9. Rinse out the food processor.

10. Use the food processor to make the Harissa Hot Sauce.

11. Rinse out the food processor.

12. Use the food processor to make the Avocado Green Goddess Dressing.

13. Cut the kale leaves into ribbons, chop the kale stems, and transfer to separate airtight containers or bags for storage.

14. Make the Banana Chai–Chia Pudding.

15. Make the Toasted Pepita Mix.

16. Toast the coconut flakes.

17. Take a breath and a bow, and eat your chicken dinner.

THE 7-DAY TASTE BUD REBOOT MEAL PLAN

SUNDAY

DINNER

Legs from the Sunday Chicken (shred the remaining chicken) over two-thirds of the Roasted Roots and Fruits (save other one-third for Monday's lunch) mixed with a large handful of massaged or sautéed kale ribbons

MONDAY

BREAKFAST

Soy or coconut yogurt with diced mango and toasted coconut

SNACK

Toasted Pepita Mix with a small handful of popcorn

LUNCH

Cauliflower rice with half of the leftover shredded chicken, leftover roots and fruits, Avocado Green Goddess Dressing, squeeze of lime or lemon

DINNER

Oven-broiled salmon (cook it all and save one portion for Tuesday's lunch) glazed with Harissa Hot Sauce, served over a large handful of massaged or sautéed kale and a handful of spinach

MAKE AHEAD

Prep a cucumber baguette (see page 120) with half of the cucumber for Tuesday's lunch
Cut remaining cucumber into snacking sticks
Mix up caraway seeds, sesame seeds, celery seeds, mustard seeds, garlic powder, onion powder, and black pepper for "everything spice"

TUESDAY

BREAKFAST

Banana Chai–Chia Pudding

SNACK

Rice crackers with avocado and "everything spice"

LUNCH

Cucumber baguette filled with Cauliflower-Nut "Ricotta," topped with leftover harissa salmon

DINNER

Roasted Pepper and Butternut Squash Soup (page 243) with the remaining shredded chicken (save one portion for Thursday's dinner)

MAKE AHEAD

Make Mini Hash Brown Quiches (page 208) for Thursday's breakfast; cut two quiches into "croutons" for Wednesday's lunch
Roast the sweet potato for Friday's lunch

WEDNESDAY

BREAKFAST

Soy or coconut yogurt with raisins, cinnamon, and toasted coconut

SNACK

Cauliflower-Nut "Ricotta" with DIY tortilla chips and cucumber sticks

LUNCH

Green salad with a handful of spinach, a large handful of kale, Avocado Green Goddess Dressing, and quiche "croutons"

DINNER

Spicy shrimp (see page 199) over rice noodles or spaghetti with two handfuls of shredded carrots and a large handful of spinach, sautéed

MAKE AHEAD

Cut 1 apple into 1-in- [2.5-cm-] thick rounds for "toast" for Thursday's snack

Make Banana Chai–Chia Pudding (page 112) for Friday's breakfast

THURSDAY

BREAKFAST

Two Mini Hash Brown Quiches, halved, with Greek yogurt and "everything spice"

SNACK

Sliced apple "toast" with Cauliflower-Nut "Ricotta"

LUNCH

Shrimp "taco" wrapped in butter lettuce with Avocado Green Goddess Dressing, shredded carrots, shredded broccoli stems, diced mango, and corn

DINNER

Eggs poached in leftover Roasted Pepper and Butternut Squash Soup, served over quinoa or brown rice (save half of the cooked grain for Saturday's dinner)

MAKE AHEAD

Cut 1 apple into matchsticks; make nori roll filled with Cauliflower-Nut "Ricotta," apple matchsticks, and shredded broccoli stems for Friday's snack

FRIDAY

BREAKFAST

Banana Chai–Chia Pudding

SNACK

"Ricotta," apple, and broccoli nori roll

LUNCH

Sweet potato half loaded with sauteed spinach, black beans, diced avocado and jalapeño, and Greek yogurt

DINNER

Corn-Broccoli Burgers (page 201; halve recipe and save two burgers for Saturday's breakfast), wrapped in butter lettuce with shredded carrot, Greek yogurt, and Harissa Hot Sauce

MAKE AHEAD

Make a spread with the other half of the sweet potato and a dollop of Harissa Hot Sauce for Saturday's lunch

SATURDAY

BREAKFAST

Leftover Corn-Broccoli Burgers with sautéed spinach and a fried egg on top

SNACK

Toasted Pepita Mix with a small handful of popcorn

LUNCH

Open-face tortilla tostada with sweet potato spread, black beans, corn, and Greek yogurt

DINNER

Grilled tilapia with jerk rub (see page 256) with grilled mango and zucchini skewers, over leftover quinoa or brown rice, topped with cilantro and lemon

TAKE THE LEAP: ONE MONTH TO LOW-SO SUCCESS

Because this is a guide, let me take your hand and lead you into the world of low-sodium living. With this workbook—full of weekly journaling, eating plans, and cooking-related activities—we'll kick-start your new diet. Together. Step by step. Until your "low-so" life is oh so good.

Every week, you'll use the suggested exercises to make small changes in your meals and habits. Nothing too scary or drastic, just tiny shifts to help you keep the foods and activities you love in your life versus cutting them out. Ultimately, you're designing a low-sodium routine that works for you. By the end, your taste buds may still crave salt or a slice of pizza, but you will see big changes in your pantry, your confidence, and your enthusiasm—you will have created the foundation for many good low-so things to come. Feel free to begin these exercises as you read this book or once you've finished it. Remember you can always flip to a new section if you hit a high-sodium stumbling block. And don't be afraid to recruit a friend (or a whole gang of pals!) to refresh eating habits along with you—a surplus of support, accountability, and creative thinking never hurt. So when you are ready, let's jump in and do this.

A WORD FROM STEPHANIE WEAVER, RECENT LOW-SO CONVERT AND FOUNDER OF RECIPERENOVATOR.COM

Research and my experience have shown that our taste buds adapt to low-sodium diets in two to three months, depending on the level of sodium that was eaten at the start. If you have been on a high-sodium diet full of processed foods, it may take you longer to adjust to this new way of eating. I tried to do it overnight, which I don't recommend. And taking it step by step as Jessica suggests will make it far easier.

But don't get discouraged if food doesn't taste quite as great for a few weeks. There will be a moment down the road when you bite into an organic cherry tomato and suddenly, *pow!* It tastes like the most incredible candy. That's when you'll know that your taste buds have healed and that low-sodium foods will start to taste better to you than in the past.

WEEK 1

This week is about prep work and gathering everything you need to make your low-sodium switch as easy and flavorful as possible.

MENTAL GAME

Before you start eliminating sodium, you must understand where it already exists in your diet. Spend at least three days recording everything you eat, including drinks and the amount of table salt you use (measure it!). Then calculate the sodium content in the ingredients, recipes, and prepared meals you consumed by using the USDA National Nutrient Database (ndb.nal.usda.gov), the USDA SuperTracker (supertracker.usda.gov), and sites like MyFitnessPal .com (myfitnesspal.com/recipe/calculator) and apps like Sodium Tracker. Make note of the ingredients or meals that surprised you most in terms of their sodium content, like:

+ Did you eat more sodium for breakfast than expected?

+ Was there an ingredient you eat daily that was higher in sodium than you thought?

+ Or, on the flip side, were there products and meals that were surprisingly low in sodium?

ROUTINE SWITCH

Now let's focus on the social side of eating, because when we eat out and with others, we tend to choose higher-sodium options and give in to high-sodium food traps. But don't worry, you don't need to cut out these outings. Just be aware of how often they occur on your social calendar and how they add to your weekly sodium intake. Then you'll be prepared to make smart sodium choices. Spend one weekend observing your social eating habits and make note of:

+ How often did you eat out?

+ What was the sodium content of your meals outside of the house (including drinks)?

+ Were there any lower-sodium options available?

TAKE NOTE

Finally, let's face your low-sodium "fears" head-on. Take a moment to think about what scares you most about a low-sodium diet and what you believe will be your biggest challenges, like:

+ How to eat low-sodium while at work?

+ How to order at your favorite restaurant?

+ How to make low-sodium dinners during a busy week?

Then list proposed solutions, because the best way to overcome an obstacle is with a plan.

EXTRA-CREDIT ACTIVITIES

Give yourself a leg up on this low-sodium journey by carrying out the following tasks:

+ Clear the shelves and refrigerator of high-sodium items and packaged goods—get rid of temptation.

+ Head to the grocery store for a research trip to familiarize yourself with what's available. Take your time and read every label.

+ Curl up with your computer, some favorite cookbooks, and food magazines and get inspired. Pick five recipes that excite you, even if they contain high-sodium ingredients. File them away—we'll get to those later.

WEEK 2

This week, we'll ease you into your low-sodium diet with a few changes at a time. But when it comes to introducing your palate to new flavors, we're going to dive right in. Get ready to go on a taste adventure, and to use your new discoveries to help replace high-sodium favorites in your daily routine.

MENTAL GAME

Start transforming those taste buds with a test-drive. This week, make one meal each day featuring a vegetable or spice you've never used before. Explore uncharted food territory, and then write down:

+ Which new flavors and textures did you enjoy?

+ What meal or meals did you like best and why?

+ Were there dishes where you still craved salt? If you answer yes, note what you would try next time to boost the taste of the dish (other than salt).

ROUTINE SWITCH

This week, overcome a big sodium challenge—work-day lunch. Whether you go out for lunch and order something lower in sodium or bring meals with you to the office, make a point to avoid high-sodium choices. Make note of the following:

+ Your favorite low-sodium lunch creations.

+ The meals that felt the most difficult to make or were the most unsatisfying.

+ How you will avoid unsuccessful lunches next time.

+ Your ideas for making work lunches easier, tastier, and less time-consuming.

TAKE NOTE

At least one day this week, write down everything you eat. Tally up the sodium amounts. See where you made the greatest changes and where high-sodium food still poses a challenge. Write down the answers to the following questions:

+ How do you plan to avoid high sodium next week?

+ What are you enjoying about your low-sodium diet?

+ What do you miss most about your old diet?

+ What are your own ideas to help fill those lifestyle and food gaps?

EXTRA-CREDIT ACTIVITIES

Do some prep work. Spend Sunday filling your fridge with vegetables, proteins, grains, and leafy greens to use for lunches and dinners all week long. Does this make your low-sodium meals easier and tastier?

Explore more. Take one simple recipe (tacos, rice bowls, pasta, or a frittata) and make it every night that week, using different ingredients and spices to transform the dish. Focus on discovering new flavor combinations and cuisines.

Redo a recipe. Do you crave Grandma's famous casserole or a recipe from one of your favorite cook-books? Whatever the dish, try giving it a low-sodium makeover of your own by substituting low-sodium ingredients and spices.

WEEK 3

Have you noticed that the challenges are becoming less daunting and you're starting to feel like a low-so pro? This week, we'll refine all those low-sodium skills you're mastering and continue to practice overcoming high-sodium obstacles with our newfound tools: Creativity and confidence.

MENTAL GAME

If you miss snacking and midday salty treats, don't just reach for the bag of potato chips. Make a list of low-sodium snacking swaps. Use resources like Pinterest, kid-focused cookbooks and blogs (school lunches are full of great ideas!), and other special-diet sites for inspiration. Prepare some new low-sodium snacks for your week ahead. Maybe even take a few pictures of your favorite bites and share them on Pinterest. Now who's the expert?!

ROUTINE SWITCH

If eating outside your home seems scary, practice makes perfect. Plan a dinner out with friends. Use your low-sodium dining tools (see page 100) to prepare for a smooth meal. Then write down your thoughts about the experience:

+ What surprised you most—the food, the service, your friends' reactions?

+ What would you do differently next time?

+ What restaurant do you want to try next?

TAKE NOTE

One day this week, write down everything you ate and, once again, tally up those sodium amounts. See where you made the greatest changes and which high-sodium foods still pose a challenge.

EXTRA-CREDIT ACTIVITIES

Did you discover a great low-sodium product on the Internet and wish it was in your local market? This week, meet with a store manager and ask if they can carry the product for you. Do you miss going to your favorite local spot, like a pizza joint or sandwich shop? Make a date with the restaurant manager and ask what kind of deal you might be able to work out so you can continue to be a loyal customer *and* eat low-sodium. You never know what's possible if you don't ask. And you might end up with a personalized pizza or sub on the menu.

WEEK 4

Do you realize you've reached the last week of your low-sodium switch? All the hard work of the past three weeks will truly make the low-sodium days, weeks, months, and years ahead easier, tastier, and better than you could have ever imagined. Let's celebrate.

MENTAL GAME

Even though your taste buds may still be adjusting, hopefully you have realized that your life need not be any less flavorful or fabulous than before. You've become an expert of sorts, not only on sodium but on cooking real, good food, too. So pat yourself on the back and brag a little bit about your accomplishments this month:

+ What was the most difficult cooking skill you attempted (and mastered)?

+ What was the most terrifying ingredient you bravely used (and ate)?

+ What was the best low-sodium dish you ate or cooked (and devoured)?

ROUTINE SWITCH

Low-sodium food need not be consumed alone. Remember, we're talking fresh, flavor-forward food that anyone would enjoy. So it's time to invite friends, coworkers, and loved ones to taste your delicious low-sodium food creations. And this week, whether it is a work lunch or a small dinner party, take the leap and host your first low-so get-together. You cook, they eat, everyone wins.

When you share your low-sodium meals with your friends, pay attention to their reactions. Sure, they may miss the salt. But they may also notice the interesting textures, the beautiful colors, and unfamiliar spices you used. Write down their feedback and use it to boost flavor the next time around as well as to boost your confidence.

EXTRA-CREDIT ACTIVITIES

One of the easiest ways to eat well away from your home is by teaching your friends and loved ones how to cook low-sodium, too. And you can kick-start their low-sodium adventures with a fun, themed potluck, like an Iron Chef No-Salt Battle or an off-season Thanksgiving dinner. Or by using any of the recipes in this book. Assign guests to different parts of the meal and then give them confidence by educating them and encouraging their creativity. Help them understand what to avoid and, most important, which low-sodium substitutes and ingredients they can use. Be sure to provide favorite low-sodium websites, resources, and your own tips. Then let everyone gather around your table and dig in. Not only will you find joy in making good food for those you love, but your crew of family and friends will now have all the information, skills, and recipes they need to provide low-sodium food for you, too.

··· 2 ···

LEARN

Becoming an Expert

Learning to ride a bike didn't happen overnight. First, you had to scoot around on a little three-wheeler and propel yourself forward with your feet. Eventually, you got the hang of the pedals. And finally, you found enough confidence to lose a wheel and your parents' helping hands, and take off on your own. You found your balance, charted your own course, and learned new tricks like popping wheelies and climbing steep hills.

Learning to cook (and cook low-sodium) is just like riding a bike. It doesn't happen overnight and you'll need support and guidance in the beginning. But very quickly, you find your confidence, your balance, and your sense of adventure. And just like biking, there are always new things to learn and new tricks to add to your repertoire.

So remember, when that roasted chicken falls on the floor, pick yourself, and that chicken, up and try again. Or, if you are like my grandmother, wipe it off and serve it anyway. Just like biking, the more you cook—and eat out and eat with others—the better and more comfortable you will get at it. Living low-sodium is a skill that only improves with practice and time. So give yourself plenty of both.

WHERE TO START: FEARS AND FUNDAMENTALS

For many people, the biggest challenge of low-sodium cooking is not the sodium, but the cooking itself. To new cooks, the kitchen feels like a pretty scary place with a lot of potential for disaster, from overdone meat to messes. So before we launch into cooking lessons, let's face those kitchen fears and kitchen basics to discover just how forgiving food preparation can be.

BIG FEARS

Today, not much scares me when it comes to cooking. I have overcome my fear of frying. I am tackling my anxieties about baking, one pie crust at a time. And I'm always looking for a challenge to convert culinary panic to pluck. Sometimes, I forget what it feels like when cooking is brand new or unfamiliar. Thanks to Facebook, though, I asked one question—"What scares you?"—and received more than forty answers; all solvable with simple solutions. So let's tackle the most common intimidating issues right now, and officially break that barrier between you and your stove.

CLEANUP

Minimize kitchen cleanup by doing the dishes while you cook. When waiting for something to roast or water to boil, use that time to wipe and wash. Use nonchemical cleaners so you do not contaminate your food. And if you're really "cleanup phobic," start with one-pot recipes. That way you can ease into your cook-and-clean routine.

SMELLY INGREDIENTS

If the lingering smell of fish bothers you, simply open a window or turn on the stove-top fan while cooking to diffuse the scent. Or arm yourself with a spray bottle of citrus or lavender water to spritz while you cook and when the meal is done.

UNDERCOOKING AND OVERCOOKING INGREDIENTS

First of all, use the right-size pot or pan. Too small and you'll crowd your ingredients, meaning some of that pasta or broccoli or chicken will end up underdone or limp. Second, use cooking thermometers so you can get correct finishing temperatures (like medium-rare, medium, well-done) for different proteins. And third, check the texture and temperatures of ingredients near the end of the allotted cooking time. That way, you can stop or add time according to the doneness you desire.

TIMING MULTIPLE DISHES

If you decide to tackle a meal that includes side dishes, come up with a game plan before you cook. That may mean chopping and measuring ingredients a day before, or cooking part of the dish ahead of time. Then, when it is go time, set several timers and label each with the name of the dish it is timing. That way, you can make the salad while you roast the lamb, all without forgetting about (and burning) the quinoa.

RANDOM INGREDIENTS

If a recipe calls for a special trip to a special store or includes something you've never heard of, use the Internet to figure out where to buy that item and how to use it. But if this still feels like too much effort, skip that recipe altogether, or turn it into a weekend adventure and tackle it with friends, or come up with your own substitutes for the hard-to-find ingredients.

MISSING INGREDIENTS

You go shopping. You get home. You forgot the onion. Sound familiar? Do not let this stop you from cooking a recipe. When you do not have something in an ingredient list, don't panic. Your meal will be okay without it. Ask yourself: What else do I have on hand that would work as a substitute? What's hiding in the freezer that might save the day? Remember: This is not a moment for a breakdown, but a moment to get creative.

BASIC SAFETY AND EFFICIENCY RULES

Now that you no longer fear the kitchen, let's take a moment to go over some basic pointers for keeping cooking safe and efficient.

Always wash your hands before you start cooking and anytime you've touched raw meat, eggs, or fish. That way you'll keep your food germ- and bacteria-free. Also wash cutting boards and other tools, bowls, and surfaces, too, after use, so there's no cross-contamination. And, if you clean as you go, be sure to use nonchemical products. I know of no recipe that calls for bleach in the ingredient list.

Before you begin a recipe, take the time to read it all the way through, start to finish. That way you'll know to keep the dry and wet ingredients separated, to put the basil in at the end, and to soak those beans a day ahead. If you have time to prep some ingredients before you start, even better. Good prep means quicker cooking and more successful meals.

Never toss dirty knives or other sharp objects in the sink. Even if you think you'll remember that you put them there, you're risking a nasty cut. To avoid accidents, set aside a tall cup or bowl where you can safely put your dirty knives, blade down, while you finish making the meal. Then clean them when you're done and at full attention.

Always have a pen on hand. Because of your special diet or even your palate, you'll adjust many recipes, adding a spice here or a seasonal ingredient there. Successful alterations can be easily forgotten, so make sure to note your additions or changes right on the recipe pages.

Always take your time; don't rush. Cooking a meal from scratch can be a really relaxing and rewarding experience. Even on the busiest nights, this time in the kitchen can generally be an opportunity to unwind. So enjoy yourself. If you need help getting Zen, squeeze a little lemon juice into a glass of water (the aroma will calm you), turn on some music, and go to your culinary happy place.

Messes happen. Even with the best intentions, disasters strike. It's important to have a broom and dust pan, mini vacuum, nontoxic cleaners, and a fire extinguisher handy, just in case. If you're prepared for the worst—dramatic quinoa spills, dropped Thanksgiving turkeys, and the "great pine nut fire of 2010"—cleanup won't seem that bad.

AVOIDING COMMON MISTAKES

Because messes, spills, and maybe a few flames are unavoidable when you experiment in the kitchen, we should spend a minute to chat about common cooking mistakes and ways to prevent them, beyond the five-second rule but before calling the fire department. So here's my list of common kitchen disasters (that I may or may not have committed) and how to avoid them.

BLENDERS, FOOD PROCESSORS, AND MISSING TOPS

Whether you've had too little coffee or you've got too many misplaced parts, remember that a topless blender or food processor means a coating of "natural paint" on the walls, floor, ceiling, and you. So take the time to put on the top and hold it down. If you're in a pinch, use a tight-fitting kitchen towel to keep all the ingredients inside. If you're blending something hot, like a soup, make sure to let it cool a bit before putting it in the blender. If not, you'll have a literal hot mess.

COOKIES, CAKES, AND UNFOLLOWED DIRECTIONS

If you're like me, you don't always have all the right ingredients on hand, which can be a big problem when it comes to baking. So for those times when you throw caution to the wind and use orange juice in place of eggs, don't be surprised that your cookies and chocolate cakes don't rise or look like they are supposed to. But don't worry either. When baking fails strike, simply rename the recipe (cookies are now cookie crumbs) and turn those deconstructed baked goods into an ice-cream topping, a pie crust, a parfait, or a sweet mix-in for an afternoon yogurt snack.

DISHES AND OVENS; FOIL AND MICROWAVES

Not all dishes are ovenproof, and not all containers can be safely used in the microwave. It's important to check that your chosen vessel can be used in your chosen cooking appliance. Know which items should never go in a microwave, such as metal (twist ties, stainless steel, aluminum foil), plastic, Styrofoam, and takeout containers.

FISH EN PAPILLOTE AND UNPLEASANT TASTES

I learned this lesson the hard way: Aluminum foil + acid = inedible. So when making fish en papillote, use parchment paper (but don't broil it). Or, if using foil, be sure to omit acidic ingredients like vinegar, white wine, tomatoes, and citrus.

PARCHMENT PAPER AND OVEN TEMPERATURE

Only *you* can prevent oven fires. The easiest way to do that is to make sure to keep flammable items and ingredients far away from the broiler heat coil, especially parchment paper (which can be used only at oven temperatures below 425°F [220°C]). If you do decide to roast nuts in the oven, watch them closely; or go the safest route and toast them in a dry, hot pan on the stove top.

POTATOES AND DISH DISPOSAL

There are a few items you should never put down your disposal: Glass, oil or grease, expandable foods (like rice and pasta), and, yes, potatoes. Whether shredded, peeled, or mashed, potatoes will turn into glue, and the disposal blades will stop working. Meaning you will need to call a repairman on Thanksgiving Day. Toss potatoes or peels on the compost pile instead.

BUILDING YOUR LIBRARY

What's wonderful about cooking is that you don't need to go to culinary school to learn how to do it. Today, with the many available cookbooks (and now television and the Internet and magazines), you can learn everything you need to know, from the basics to fancy desserts, on your own time, in your own kitchen.

But where do you start? It probably makes sense to start with the basics, such as knife skills, steaming rice, and sautéing vegetables. But make sure you also throw in specialty subjects that excite you. Do you love Vietnamese food? Pick up a few cookbooks on Vietnamese cuisine. Are you interested in sauces? Start with a primer on everything from hollandaise to beurre blanc. Do you have a favorite restaurant you've visited or always wanted to visit? Many of them have their own cookbooks now, which means you can re-create famous dishes at home.

Whatever the dish, the cuisine, or the specialty, you'll learn skills with every recipe you try—the most important one being confidence. And you'll quickly collect recipes for favorite dishes, weekly standards, and even your own recipe makeovers that get passed on to family and friends.

To get you started on your low-so education, here are some suggestions for books, magazines, TV shows, and Internet-based cooking resources that provide the instruction you need to do everything from boiling eggs to making elegant pastries.

ON THE SHELF

Cookbooks have taken over prime real estate in my home. I read cookbooks in bed as a way to unwind. I've been known to take them on vacation, even if I have no plans to cook. If you came over, you'd find that the cookbooks on my shelves range from classics to low-sodium-specific to specialty cuisines. Which is all to say that, just because you need to limit the salt in your meals, doesn't mean you have to limit the inspiration on your shelves (and counter and bedside table). Every cookbook will teach you something, even if you have to adjust recipes. So arm yourself with texts that teach you the basics as well as those that make your mouth water.

CLASSICS AND COOKING SKILLS

It's useful to have a few books on hand that act as reference guides. With the books by Mark Bittman and *Cook's Illustrated* magazine, I learned how to poach eggs, chiffonade basil, and bake fish en papillote. When you're ready to start making up recipes of your own, these more instructional books help you do just that. Once you understand the basic idea behind a dish, you can go from there.

LOW-SODIUM GUIDES

Some books help you to become an expert in losing the salt in recipes and replacing it with lots of flavor. From baking to making soy sauce substitutes, these texts show you how to surpass any sodium challenge and make really tantalizing meals. Look for books by the low-sodium forefathers, Donald A. Gazzaniga and Dick Logue; Bobbie Mostyn's *Pocket Guide to Low Sodium Foods*; anything by the American Heart Association; and, of course, *Sodium Girl's Limitless Low-Sodium Cookbook*.

SPECIAL-DIET INSPIRATION

Remember, low-sodium diets have a lot in common with other special diets. Vegetarian, vegan, Paleo, raw, and gluten-free guides will give you lots of ideas for exciting ingredient substitutions.

WORLD CUISINES AND OTHER SPECIALTY SUBJECTS

Get your cooking passport ready and maybe grab a butcher's knife. Whether you want to make dim sum dumplings, use a sous vide, or cut up a whole hog, books are available that will teach you how to do that and much more.

ON TV

I have to take a moment to thank television, because that's where I truly began my culinary career. Watching cooking shows and cooking competitions taught me that it was okay to play with food and ingredients. By seeing professional, celebrity chefs put their own twists on traditional dishes, I knew I could have the same sense of fun and creativity in my kitchen.

COOKING COMPETITIONS

Want to learn more about flavor combinations and unfamiliar ingredients? Then check out shows like *Chopped, Iron Chef, Top Chef*, and pretty much any of the cooking competitions on television these days. By watching chef-testants getting judged on skills, knowledge, and creativity, you'll pick up a lot of tips on flavors, plating, and how to avoid major cooking mistakes.

COOKING SHOWS

For visual learners who want step-by-step instructions, cooking shows are a perfect fit. Even if hosts use ingredients that you must avoid, it is all about inspiration and actually seeing someone brown meat in a pan or whisk eggs. By watching other people put foods together with ease, you'll feel more confident when it's just you, the written instructions, and your kitchen.

ON THE WEB

These days, the Internet offers boundless information and learning opportunities, from recipes to video tutorials to actual online cooking schools. Whether you need to Google a term or ingredient or just watch someone make crêpes, you can find it online. Like with the cookbooks on your shelf, don't limit the kinds of recipe sites and blogs you visit. Even salty resources are good for learning purposes, and you can then adjust the information as necessary.

BUILDING YOUR SKILLS

Some people think that because you eat a low-sodium diet, you can't take cooking classes. Well that's just plain silly. Even if you can't eat the final product, you can learn a lot from going through the paces. And, food experiences don't have to be limited to dinners out or taking classes. Even by spending time at the farmers' market or going fishing, you'll become more knowledgeable and passionate about the food you eat, which is a secret weapon when it comes to cooking. Meals made with love always taste better. Plus, you can often pick up the best cooking tips from the farmers and fishermen themselves. So take part in cooking classes, farm tours, and other food adventures, and build some skills beyond the stove.

CHEAT SHEET: HOW TO CUT STRANGE FRUITS AND VEGETABLES

To sharpen your skills, let's get you started with some odd-shaped fruit and vegetable prep. Some fresh items can seem really daunting at first sight—like butternut squash, corn on the cob, jicama, watermelon—especially when a recipe simply calls for cubes or kernels without explaining how to get them. Once you've tackled these unwieldy-looking foods, no shape, size, or husks will scare you again.

BUTTERNUT SQUASH

Start by cutting off both ends of the squash with a large, heavy, sharp knife. Then use the knife to cut it in half, separating the neck from the body. Use a sharp peeler to take off the skin, working around the curves. Slice the neck (with no seeds) into disks. If there's a spongy core in parts, just scoop it out with a spoon. Then cut into cubes. For the seedy body, cut it in half and then scoop out the seeds with a spoon. Cut the halves into half-moon shapes and then cube. If you're using only part of the squash, store leftovers in airtight bags in the freezer for the next time you need recipe-ready squash.

CORN KERNELS

Remove the husk (the green leaves) and the silk (the silky threads). Place the corncob on its side on a cutting board. While holding the stem, use a sharp knife (directed away from you) to slice the kernels off one side, getting as close to the core as possible. Rotate the cob a small turn and cut kernels off another side. Continue cutting and rotating until you've sliced off all the kernels. And don't forget to use the remaining cob. You can rub it on a grater to capture the corn milk or save it to toss in your next soup or stew for a sweet, milky flavor. If you don't have time to do that today, put the cob in an airtight bag in the freezer and do it later.

JICAMA

Rinse the jicama bulb, then peel. You then want to use the peeler for a second spin around the bulb to totally remove the fibrous top layer. Next, use a sharp or serrated knife to cut off both knobby ends. Set the jicama on one of the flat sides. Slice it in half, top to bottom, and set aside one half. Lay the other half on its wide side and cut it into half-ovals ½ to 1 in [12 mm to 2.5 cm] thick. Then stack a few of those ovals on top of each other and cut the jicama into fries or matchsticks or cubes, depending on how you plan to use it. Repeat with the other jicama half.

WATERMELON

Wash the outside of the melon. Set the watermelon on a cutting board that will catch the juice, if you have one. Otherwise, have some paper towels ready to soak up the excess juice. Use a large, sharp knife to cut both ends off the melon and then, while on its side, cut the melon in half. Lay one half aside. Lay the other half on its center-cut side and use the knife to trim off the rind, leaving only the red flesh. Cut the fruit into any shape you like, cubes or wedges. Transfer the melon to an airtight container. Repeat with the other watermelon half. Store in the refrigerator for up to 1 week.

OTHER ODDLY SHAPED PRODUCE

Anytime you want or need to learn how to cut a particular ingredient, be it fennel bulbs or whole ducks, hit the Internet. Whether you learn best via the written word, instructional videos, or adorable infographics, there's a variety of demos that will teach you how to do almost anything. And when you need a refresher, you can reread or rewatch anytime.

STEPHANIE HUA
TALKS SMART COOKING

....

Although I never went to cooking school, as I found myself diving deeper into the world of food, I started making friends with people who did put in time at real culinary institutions. So I tapped my friend Stephanie Hua, founder of LickMySpoon.com and graduate of the San Francisco Cooking School, to give us a quick lesson in smart cooking.

I've picked up some great tips from watching great cooks work, voraciously consuming food media, and training at the San Francisco Cooking School. Here are a few tips on how to cook smarter and faster.

BATCH MOTIONS
In cooking school, one of the first things we learned was the importance of working efficiently. You'll work faster if you batch together similar motions. For example, if you need to cut up several onions, don't peel and slice each onion one at a time. Instead, peel all the onions at once, and then cut them all at once, without having to put down your knife. The work will go twice as fast.

TASTE AS YOU COOK
Learn to taste and season throughout different stages of preparing a dish rather than just at the end. This allows you to build layers of flavor as the different ingredients in the dish come together, resulting in a more complex and cohesive end product. Also, if you're constantly tasting, you can troubleshoot a problem before it's too late.

KEEP YOUR KNIVES SHARP
A sharp knife will make prepping so much easier, and safer! A dull knife will not only make you exert unnecessary energy, it will actually bruise vegetables or delicate herbs because you are crushing cell walls rather than slicing through them. Test your blade on a tomato. You should be able to slice through cleanly with minimal effort and pressure. If you are smashing it, it's time to sharpen that knife.

PEEL IN BOTH DIRECTIONS
Most vegetable peelers have a double edge on the blade, which means it can actually peel forward and backward! Try it! You just peeled that carrot twice as fast. You're welcome.

THE MAILLARD REACTION
Let's get nerdy. The Maillard reaction is chef-speak for the chemical reaction that occurs when you brown food—think seared steak or that golden crust on baked bread. As you expose the food to heat, the amino acids react with the sugars, and you end up with a golden brown deliciousness. So, the lesson here? Roast, caramelize, and sear away! It's amazing the flavors you can coax out by roasting some veggies. Apply this principle to nuts and seeds, too. Toasting them will bring out aromas and flavors that would otherwise remain dormant.

REDUCTIONS PACK A PUNCH
When you reduce a liquid down, you essentially evaporate off the water and concentrate the flavor. Try adding reduced stocks, vegetable juices, or fruit juices to bring big flavor to your dish.

THE RD AND ME—
BUILDING A GOOD RELATIONSHIP WITH YOUR DIETITIAN

....

You've set a time to meet with a registered dietitian (RD) to discuss your low-sodium plan. To make sure that time is well spent, four wonderful dietitians from Northwest Kidney Centers—Erin McCormick, Nikki Gepner, Katy Wilkens, and Beth Shanaman— have generously shared their tips on getting the most from your appointment.

Be Fearless: The best relationships, including the one with your RD, are built on honesty. But Shanaman says many people will withhold information for fear of being judged for bad habits. Just remember, your RD wants to help you, not scold you. So release the fear and tell the truth.

Take Note: Both McCormick and Gepner say that keeping a food journal prior to your visit will greatly increase the RD's ability to tailor advice to your specific needs, tastes, budget, and routines. Before your first visit, Gepner suggests keeping a food journal for at least three days, including a workweek day and a weekend, and don't forget beverages (hidden sodium traps!). Jot down any questions you have—the more information you bring in, the more you will learn.

Include Your Team: McCormick says that if someone helps you cook or do the food prep and shopping, be sure to bring them along to your appointment. That way, everyone will be informed. The more support you have, the easier making adjustments will be.

Good Ear: Gepner says that a good RD should be an excellent listener. By asking questions and meeting often, you will find that your RD offers more personalized suggestions that fit into your life, not get in the way of it. A successful low-sodium plan will be one that gels with your priorities and your goals.

Small Steps, Big Changes: When facing all the adjustments required of a low-sodium life, some people feel overwhelmed instead of enthusiastic. So McCormick says to "set small achievable goals and celebrate every success."

Turn the Table: Shanaman says to constantly ask people what they eat, "in the waiting room, at the gym, at the grocery store." That includes your RD, too! You never know what tips you'll pick up or what new foods you'll discover.

You're the Boss: Wilkens says that an RD's job is to "set the table with healthful choices." Then it's up to you (the patient) to choose which ideas fit best for your life and put them into practice. Above all, if you ever feel like your RD does not understand you or your needs, Wilkens says it's worth it to look for another RD. Because you're the boss, and you're in charge of picking a team to work for and with you.

BUILDING A LOW-SODIUM PLAN

Now that you're learning how to cook, it's important to learn how to eat. That means creating your own personalized low-sodium plan. Working with your doctor and dietitian, first figure out how much sodium (and other essential nutrients) you should eat every day for your body and health needs. Then spend a few days tracking your sodium intake to discover where sodium sneaks into your meals, or use your notes from the One Month to Low-So Success exercises on page 33. Remember, most sodium doesn't come from just that saltshaker.

Once you identify the foods you should eat less of or avoid, focus on the foods you can enjoy. Curb feelings of loss by making a game plan. Fill your refrigerator, cupboards, and work cubicle with products, spices, and snacks you can and want to eat. And for every favorite item you have to ditch (morning bagel), come up with a satisfying, low-sodium alternative (toasted tortilla with homemade guacamole).

With these steps and the help of your health-care team, you'll figure out the right guidelines for your body, your needs, and your lifestyle. And going low-sodium will start to feel like second nature, transforming "burden" to "no big thing."

CONTINUED EDUCATION

Talk, share, and read constantly, because the learning never ends. You'll master Moroccan cuisine, only to then begin a journey into homemade nut butters, pickles, and bread. You'll think you have found your ultimate BFF spice, only to find another that steals your heart. Even after twelve years of passionate, self-led cooking adventures, there are plenty of skills and subjects I have yet to master. So get ready for a lifelong journey of education.

For your low-sodium diet specifically, this continued education is essential. Everybody and every body is different, and so it's important to constantly consult with your health-care providers to make sure your diet continues to fit your needs through the many years ahead of you. Nutritional labels, dietary guidelines, and your own medical condition may change over time, and therefore your diet needs may change and shift, too.

··· 3 ···

PREP

Setting Up Your Kitchen and Pantry

It's totally normal to be afraid of the kitchen. There are hot stoves, too many different types of pots and pans, and shelves full of canned ingredients that you will no longer use. The unfamiliarity of this space may cause you panic. It may keep you from trying a recipe. And worst of all, it may drive you to another night of take-out.

But good food starts in the kitchen. So before we even talk about recipes or heating up that stove, let's outfit your space with everything you need to feel comfortable and confident, and to actually cook great tasting low-so food. First you need to stock the pantry, the fridge, your spice rack, and your counter with all the tools (edible and mechanical) that make cooking a pleasant experience. With the huge array of options, though, this may feel like a daunting task. So we'll cover the basics of what's available and give you the information you need to make the right choices for you and your space.

Once you've gathered your tools, the next step is using them to their full potential. Because what's the point of buying a food processor or a jar of cloves if you hardly ever take them off the shelf? That means storing food properly, stretching spices and equipment beyond their most basic tasks, and stocking the kitchen with items you need to get you through any emergency—whether a dry chicken or an earthquake. In the end, you'll replace your fears with everything you need for a fully functioning kitchen. And you'll be prepped and ready to tackle the low-so adventures ahead.

Above all, whether you live in a tiny studio apartment with a countertop hot plate or in a luxurious suburban farmhouse with an eight-burner stove, it's important to make your cooking space an efficient and inspiring workspace. This might mean coming up with creative storage solutions or buying space-saving appliances, so you have room for all your new stuff. It also means giving your walls a pop of color and some personal flair, so you design a room you love.

To transform your space, simply start here: What about your kitchen bothers you the most? What doesn't work? What serves as the biggest roadblock when cooking, or drives you to eat cereal for dinner?

Once you have your answer, fix it. Check out online resources like Pinterest.com and interior-decorating blogs or design magazines for budget-friendly kitchen solutions. Go feng shui or go to Ikea. Just spend time and a little money buying what you need—from a stockpot to a fresh coat of paint—that will make your low-so cooking easy and enjoyable.

KITCHEN ESSENTIALS

There are some scenarios in life where having the best and most-updated equipment is extremely important, like skydiving and rock climbing. But when it comes to your kitchen, don't let a barren setup or a tight budget stop you from cooking. You only really need a few basic items to start cooking, like a knife, a pot and a pan, and a source of heat. Everything else is about ease, efficiency, and exact measurements.

As your kitchen adventures expand, so will the range of your cooking tools. And this chapter will acquaint you with an overview of what's available. Decide which items you want to buy now (measuring spoons); and which to keep for future purchases (a slow cooker).

Just remember, the only real essentials are those that fit within your current space and budget. So before we go shopping, let's chat about a few ways to help limit clutter and over-spending.

Pick Multitaskers Over One-Trick Ponies: When purchasing big items, choose the ones with a range of talents and impressive résumés, like food processors that can chop vegetables, make dressings, and even mix bread dough. These items will earn their place on your counter.

Size Matters: When buying your essential items, go for versions that are lighter and smaller, like an immersion blender versus a stand-up blender. You will save precious cupboard space, and if they're easy to store and lift, you'll use them more often.

Try to DIY: Certain items, like biscuit cutters, can be replicated just by using metal measuring cups or empty metal cans. When considering buying an item, also consider if you can craft it yourself.

Bargain Shop: You don't need to buy everything new. Keep an eye out for discounts and sales. Scout second-hand stores, flea markets, and garage sales. Shop on sites like eBay and Craigslist. And create gift registries on houseware websites to get the pricier items you covet for holidays and birthday presents.

Purge Regularly: If you find yourself swimming in serving spoons or trays or mismatched measuring cups, take the time to spring clean throughout the year. You can even host a utensil or serving ware "swap party" with friends to get rid of your unused goods and maybe pick up something you've been wanting.

Splurge Consciously: Make room for special items, like colorful enamel pots or holiday place settings. There's always space for beautiful things that make cooking fun.

TRACY BENJAMIN
TALKS SUMAC

....

For a lady who loves black-and-white stripes, Tracy Benjamin (founder of Shutterbean .com and co-host of the Joy the Baker podcast) sure knows a lot about creating colorful food—in look and flavor. Just one peek at the rainbow of Popsicle creations on her blog and you'll see what I'm talking about. I asked Tracy which spice she likes to use when something needs a little pop. And no surprise, it's electric!

Sumac is a tart, citrus-like spice that comes from the Middle East. It can be used in place of fresh lemon juice since it adds a nice fruity, salty tang to recipes. It's perfect on fish or chicken, mixed in vinaigrettes, or sprinkled on top of rice dishes. I happen to love it in a fattoush (a salad traditionally made of fresh vegetables and toasted pita bread), Greek salads, and even meatballs because it brightens up the flavors and adds nice oomph.

UTENSIL ESSENTIALS

Part necessity and part preference, the following items are ones I have acquired over the years. These are the "absolutes," or tools I take out weekly or daily. I have also included a list of the fun items, which you do not need in order to conquer a recipe but may make your time in the kitchen more colorful and thrilling. When picking items for yourself, think about what you like to cook; how much space you have; and how many people you generally feed. Make sure items are easy to lift and clean, so you will use them often. Versatility trumps good looks and nifty gadgetry, and new doesn't mean better. Make sure your kitchen tools fit your home and lifestyle.

THE ABSOLUTES

BAKING PANS AND COOKIE SHEETS

Baking pans have rolled edges, while cookie sheets do not (although some have one edge for gripping purposes). You use a baking pan for anything where you want an edge (like for focaccia or flatbread) as well as recipes that release juices (like when roasting vegetables). And leave the cookie sheet for, basically, cookies, biscuits, or other pastries. If you can buy only one, start with the rimmed kind because they're the most versatile. Choose thicker or heavy-gauge materials, like aluminum or a steel-aluminum combination, to prevent warping and uneven cooking. Nonstick will work too, but your metal utensils will scratch those. Make sure to buy pans according to your budget and the size of your oven.

BLENDERS

While it will take up some kitchen space, a counter-top blender will smooth out those smoothies, sauces, and soups. Look for a model with long metal blades, a powerful motor, and angled sides, which will keep the food moving so that it doesn't clump at the bottom. Also, an immersion blender is very handy. Just stick it in the liquid mixture, press a button, and blend. It even whips cream. Super-easy to clean, immersion blenders are lightweight and space efficient. Look for one with a strong motor, easy-to-press buttons, and a blending cup, which will keep ingredients closer to the blade when blending smaller volumes of liquid.

BOX GRATER AND MICROPLANE

I constantly use a Microplane grater for zesting citrus and grating spices like nutmeg and cinnamon. A tradi-tional box grater is not just for shredding cheese; use it to grate raw zucchini, squash, and carrots for raw additions to salads, yogurt dips, and healthful fillers for meatballs and pasta.

CANNING JARS

Canning jars have been around for ages and are the Swiss army knives of the container family. Use them to transport salads or soups, whip up heavy cream in minutes, emulsify dressings with a quick shake, or mix up cocktails. They come in different sizes and glass colors. They make nice food-gift containers, and are perfect for keeping fresh herbs in a bit of water (see page 78).

COOLING RACKS

Beyond holding baked goods or other pans while they cool, wire cooling racks can sit on top of large baking sheets to make fish sticks, Salt-Free Bacon (page 93), and other dishes when you want to keep small pieces of meat crispy and clear of juicy drippings.

CUTTING BOARDS

You'll want several of these, because you should prepare your meat and vegetables on separate cutting boards to avoid cross contamination. Some people get different colors to keep track of which is which. Choices of material range from plastic to wood to bamboo—I prefer plastic because it does not warp like wood and I can put the boards in the dishwasher. Pick ones that will stay put on your counter while you chop, either with a grip or because it is made of heavier material so they won't slide.

COFFEE/SPICE GRINDER

Nothing wakes your palate up like the aroma of freshly ground spices—just wait until you make your own Maharaja-Style Curry Powder (page 195). Although using a mortar and pestle will get the job done, it takes quite a lot of effort. This double-duty appliance, however, will turn those salt-free seeds and spices (or coffee grounds) into a fine powder in minutes.

DUTCH OVEN

I have a major crush on my enameled cast-iron Dutch oven. While some girls dream of wedding dresses, I dreamed of a bridal registry filled with enameled Dutch ovens in every color. You can use them on the stove and in the oven. They're great heat conductors and tall enough for deep-frying. They work for long-cooking braises, stews, and soups, and even for baking a round loaf of bread. Start with a 5-qt [4.7-L] one, fall in love, and add other sizes as you can.

FIRE EXTINGUISHER

Just in case. You may never need it, but you'll be glad it's there if you do. Read the instructions so you'll be prepared. And be sure to follow the tips on how to avoid ever needing to use it (see page 44).

FOOD PROCESSORS—LARGE AND SMALL

If you have a small food processor, you can finely dice garlic or onions without tears, blend a sauce in minutes, chop nuts quickly, and grind whole spices. But don't forget the larger version. Beyond chopping, grating, or ricing vegetables (à la Cauliflower Rice, Pea, and Edamame Salad [page 197]), a standard food processor will purée soups and make dough, quickly and easily, whether bread or broccoli gnocchi (see page 235). Just be sure to keep all the blades it comes with, because each has special superpowers.

KNIVES

A sharp knife means safe slicing. And while you may eventually collect a whole set of knives (serrated bread knife, steak knives, etc.), a medium chef's knife with a 6- or 7-in [15- or 17-cm] blade is the easiest to hold and will get the job done. It's handy to have a second, cheaper large knife for backup when chopping and cutting tougher ingredients, like nuts and butternut squash, that may dull the blade. A medium-size serrated knife works best for foods with hard exteriors (like lemons and crusty bread) and ingredients that squash with pressure (like tomatoes). The teeth of the blade break through the skin or crust, making way for a clean slice.

LOAF PAN

You don't need a bread maker for Super-Simple Sandwich Bread (page 149); you only need a loaf pan. But you can also use this multitasking pan for roasting small portions of vegetables and making meatloaf. I prefer nonstick material, since it browns the bread more than aluminum and makes for easy cleanup.

MEASURING CUPS—LIQUID AND DRY

There are different measuring devices calibrated for liquid ingredients (usually see-through glass or plastic, with a pouring spout) and for dry ingredients. Make sure the cups you buy are in standard sizes with clear markings and sturdy handles. Dry measuring cups do not reflect true volume measurements, and as such do not correspond to liquid measures. A standard set of dry measuring cups should include ¼-cup [60-ml], ⅓-cup [80-ml], ½-cup [125-ml], and 1-cup [250-ml] scoops.

MEASURING SPOONS

At some point, you'll become confident enough to just sprinkle and pour spices and oils as you cook. But when trying a recipe for the first time (or when baking), get those measurements right with measuring spoons. Just like for measuring cups, favor clear markings and functionality over cute design.

MUFFIN TINS

Muffin tins most commonly come in jumbo (usually 6 large wells), standard (12 medium wells), and mini sizes (24 small wells). I prefer nonstick material and a wide edge for easy holding and cleaning. While these tins are most commonly used for muffins and cupcakes, they can also be used in any recipe that calls for ramekins, or to make smaller portions of savory meals, like Mini Hash Brown Quiches (page 208), meatloaf, and lasagna. You can also use the muffin wells to hold your chopped and diced ingredients, or to freeze individual portions of pesto or tomato sauce.

NONCHEMICAL CLEANERS AND SMALL VACUUM

If cleaning up keeps you from cooking, then get over it and get yourself the supplies that make messes and spills no big deal. If your cleaning products are nonchemical and easy to get to, then you can clean as you cook and avoid a "stacked dish" disaster zone after the meal is over.

NONREACTIVE BOWLS

Ceramic, glass, stainless steel, and enamel-coated metal all fall in the nonreactive category. To start, buy a three-piece set of heavy bowls (for example, ceramic) that will stay put while mixing and whisking. Then get a second three-piece set of heatproof bowls (for example, stainless steel) to use as a double boiler.

OVEN MITTS

Safety first. Don't try using towels.

OVENPROOF BAKING DISHES

Square, rectangle, and oval. Glass, ceramic, and cast iron. You'll find a wide range of ovenproof baking dishes in various sizes and shapes and materials. For ultimate versatility, choose those that are broiler-safe, like ceramic. And start with a square dish (8 by 8 in [20 by 20 cm]) and a rectangular dish (9 by 13 in [23 by 33 cm]), which will work for most desserts, casseroles, and recipes in this book. As a plus, if you buy glass, ceramic, or enamel, they can also be used at the table for serving dishes, because they're really pretty.

PARCHMENT PAPER AND ALUMINUM FOIL

Having these on hand will make cleaning easier. I line my baking sheets and pans with parchment or foil to limit residue and mess. Remember: Use parchment when cooking acidic ingredients to avoid tinny tastes, and use foil when you plan to cook at temperatures hotter than 425°F [220°C] to avoid a fire.

PASTRY BRUSHES

Having a few of these on hand will let you grease pans and dishes, frost cookies, and paint your meats with marinades before they go into the oven or on the grill. Natural bristles work best.

RAMEKINS

These small ceramic dishes are perfect for so many uses, such as individual pot pies, baked eggs, and tiny versions of big dishes. They also serve double-duty as food prep bowls to hold your chopped onions and spice rubs, and triple-duty as serving dishes for dips and spreads.

REUSABLE STORAGE CONTAINERS

Going low-sodium often means packing food for work, travel, and any occasion where you eat away from home. That's why it's important to buy spill-proof storage containers with tight, well-sealed lids. I prefer glass over plastic containers, which are usually microwave safe. If you choose plastic containers, make sure they are BPA-free.

RICE COOKER AND SLOW COOKER

Meet your two favorite low-sodium sous chefs. When you have limited time and energy, these appliances do most of the work for you. No overcooked or burnt food, guaranteed(ish). While pricier models boast more features and presets, I find that basic, less-expensive versions, with usually only one or two heat settings, get the job done.

ROASTING PAN WITH RACK

A roasting pan should be deep enough to hold roasting juices and wide enough to fit the largest item you ever plan to cook in it. While you do not need a rack, it will keep fatty meats from soaking in their juices, leaving the skin nice and crispy. Avoid nonstick pans and choose one made from heavy material, like clad stainless steel, to prevent burning and uneven cooking. But you need to be able to lift the darn thing, so buy one with sturdy handles that you can easily maneuver. If this item would be a splurge, and you never plan to roast a huge turkey, use any ovenproof dish, tall enough to hold drippings, instead.

ROLLING PIN

If you're in a real pinch, you can always use a clean, label-free wine bottle to roll out your dough. I've done it plenty of times. But a wooden rolling pin will allow you to get those perfectly thin pie crusts, pizza doughs, and pasta sheets. I prefer a straight French rolling pin without tapered ends or handles since I find they require less work (and strength) on my part. Be sure to choose a length that fits your drawer or storage space.

SALAD SPINNER

Beyond drying your washed lettuce and vegetables, you can also use a salad spinner to help evenly distribute salad dressing right before serving.

SALT AND PEPPER GRINDERS

If you find yourself with a pair of S and P grinders, don't throw the salt one away. S can also mean "spice," so fill it with other whole spices or a mix of seeds, like coriander, cumin, and caraway. Then grind and sprinkle your spice and pepper at the dinner table. How's that for a salt-free makeover?

SAUCEPAN

This pan, which looks like a pot, has high sides and a lid. It is a kitchen workhorse and you'll use it for rice, soups, sauces, steamed vegetables, and even hard-boiled eggs. Look for products made of nonreactive and high heat–conducting materials, so you get even cooking without burning. And choose saucepans with long handles for easier lifting.

SKILLET

If you can only get one kind of pan to start, go for a 10- to 12-in [25- to 30-cm] stainless-steel skillet (also known as a frying pan) with an aluminum core, preferably with a lid and an ovenproof surface and handle so you can use it for roasted vegetables, frittatas, and Chickpea-Flour Pizza crust (see page 94). Make sure the pan is large enough for the amount of servings you usually cook. You don't want to crowd items in a pan.

SPATULAS

When it comes to spatulas, you want one that flips and one that scrapes. A flat, thin-edged metal spatula will easily slide under your Coconut "Panko" Pork Tonkatsu (page 218) and turn it to crisp on the other side. If you use nonstick pans, buy a heatproof silicone spatula, to avoid scratching your cookware. For scraping, a small rubber or silicone spatula will stir and scoop all that whipped cream from the bowl onto your cake. But unlike metal or silicone, a rubber spatula may melt, so be careful when using it near the stove.

STEAMER BASKET

Here's a surprising multitasker. Your steamer basket will not only steam vegetables when placed in a pot with a bit of water; it will also help you make Hickory-Smoked Fish Spread (page 228), and can double as a small colander.

STOCKPOT

As the name suggests, a stockpot is mainly used for making stock. But it also works well for making a large batch of soup, chili, or pasta, and for blanching vegetables (see page 69). Sizes range from small (6 qt [5.7 L]) to large (20 qt [18.9 L]), and shapes vary from tall to wide. So pick what makes sense for your kitchen and cupboard space. For even cooking, choose products made from heavy, heat-conducting materials—like stainless steel with an aluminum core. Be sure to test-drive the handles. You want them to be sturdy so you can lift a full pot safely.

THERMOMETERS

Test, don't guess! Use digital thermometers to test the doneness of meat (meat thermometer), the temperature of oil (candy/deep-fry thermometer), and the true temperatures of your oven and fridge. Just be sure to buy the right kind for each task. If you can find it, perhaps purchase a multipurpose product.

TIMER

Whether it is the one on your phone or a cute ceramic rooster, you will need a timer that works. You may want to get several for those evenings when you are cooking many dishes at the same time.

TONGS

Tongs will turn roasting veggies, flip searing meat, and pluck a lobster from boiling water. And, of course, help you avoid scorched fingertips. Start with 8- or 10-in [20- or 25-cm-] tongs for best maneuverability and safety. Make sure they open and close with ease and have heat-safe handles. I prefer those that lock for easier storage.

VEGETABLE PEELER

You have two basic choices for peelers—the straight swivel and the Y-shaped. I prefer the straight swivel, because you do not have to rotate your wrist to use it. But buy the one that feels right for you. A vegetable peeler will clean carrots, make vegetable ribbons, and create a pile of chocolate curls.

WOODEN SPOONS

A few of these will stir your soups, mix your cookie dough, and even tell you when your oil is hot (see page 146). Plus, they stand up to heat, whereas plastic spoons may not, and they do not scratch delicate cooking surfaces. Their woody material will absorb smells and colors, however, so if you can, buy two spoons—one for sweet items and one for savory.

FOR LOOKS, FOR EASE, FOR FUN

APRON

No one will make you wear an apron in the kitchen. But sometimes, by just tying one on, you suddenly feel more capable, and perhaps freer to make a mess. Like a superhero's cape or a pop singer's stage name (ahem, Sasha Fierce), your apron gives you the confidence to tackle new recipes, ingredients, and techniques. (Capes are just a little too dangerous when you're working with open flame.)

CHERRY PITTER

Yes, a cherry pitter is a single-skilled tool, but it will get you through a mound of cherries faster than using a straw and more safely than using a paring knife. You'll enjoy using it when you make Pickled Cherries (page 249).

FOOD SCALE

Even if you do not portion or weigh your food, a digital scale proves essential when trying a new baking adventure or substituting whole grains or gluten-free mixes for the regular flour in a recipe. You may even find that it makes measuring ingredients easier than filling a cup or spoon, as you can just pour them directly into one bowl.

GRILL PAN

With this pan in your kitchen, you won't need a barbecue or even the sun to get the charred lines and roasted flavor of a grill.

HAND MIXER

Less expensive than a stand mixer, an electric hand mixer works well for small mixing tasks, like whipping cream and blending cake batter. Plus, the metal whisks detach so they can be washed in the dishwasher for easy clean up, or licked by eager onlookers.

JULIENNE PEELER OR SPIRAL SLICER

This device can turn your vegetables into spaghetti-like noodles, making meatless Mondays more fun, lunch prep super-quick, and hot nights full of cool options.

MANDOLINE

A mandoline will slice vegetables into even, thin, pretty discs if you want to leave them raw for salads, sides, salt-free pickles, or sandwich toppings. Be sure to buy one with a safety guard. You can always chop veggies by hand, but the mandoline will make elegant slices quickly.

PASTA MAKER

You can always use a rolling pin to flatten your pasta dough, but a pasta maker with attachments will do the hard work for you. And it's so easy to use, you may be inspired to make homemade pasta more often.

RADIO OR PORTABLE SPEAKERS

To make cooking truly enjoyable, you might want to have some background music or listen to a favorite radio program. Having a little company will keep you grooving (or learning) instead of anxiously waiting for the pot to boil.

SMOKING CHIPS

I never thought wood chips would have a place in my home. But after learning how to smoke my own fish on the stove, I now like to have a stash of hickory, mesquite, cedar, and other fruitwood chips on hand. They lend a smoky flavor to everything from vegetables to meat and even fruit. And, of course, your sweater.

WAFFLE MAKER, SPRINGFORM CAKE PAN, AND ICE-CREAM MAKER

You may want to get these items. We will use them for recipes in this book and I think they're lots of fun.

PANTRY ESSENTIALS

Now it's time to open your pantry and fill those shelves with shelf-stable dry goods that will be lifesavers when you need a basic ingredient to make a dish, a few ingredients to throw together for dinner when you're in a pinch, or some low-sodium prepared items that allow you to cut corners. Here's what to keep in stock:

+ Baking powder, sodium-free

+ Baking soda, sodium-free

+ Beans, canned and dried

+ Coconut milk, canned

+ Flours; all-purpose, bread, chickpea, whole-wheat

+ Fruit, dried, unsulfured

+ Garlic, unpeeled

+ Ginger

+ Grains; quinoa, couscous, rice

+ Honey

+ Marinades and sauces, low-sodium

+ Molasses, unsulfured

+ Mushrooms, dried

+ Nori sheets, sodium-free

+ Nut and seed butters (including tahini), no salt added

+ Nuts and seeds, whole, unsalted

+ Oils; olive, coconut, vegetable, nonstick spray

+ Onions; red, white, yellow

+ Pasta, no salt added

+ Pizza dough mix, packaged and sodium-free

+ Popcorn, microwave, salt-free

+ Shallots

+ Sugars; brown, granulated, powdered

+ Sweet additions; puffed rice, marshmallows, dried cherries, dark chocolate chips, candied ginger, and anything that sounds good for yogurt or a sweet snack mix

+ Tomato products, canned, no salt added; diced, sauce, and paste

+ Tomatoes, dried, no salt added

+ Vegetable purée, canned, no salt added; butternut squash and pumpkin

+ Vinegars; unseasoned rice, balsamic, apple cider

FROM THE CREW AT FOOD52.COM— MAKING THE MOST OF YOUR PANTRY

Your pantry is always hiding tricks up its sleeves. It holds spices and staples and dinners that can come together in 20 minutes, even after weeks without grocery shopping. It is your greatest asset.

But there are still more ways to get the most out of your pantry—to deepen the flavors sitting in there, to stretch a can of no-salt-added tomato paste, to use the package of couscous sitting in the corner. Here are a few tricks you can use to maximize your pantry's potential.

Check the expiration dates on your oils. It's easy to forget about them, but they will go rancid within a certain amount of time. Keep an eye on that label, and consider storing more delicate oils—especially those made from nuts and seeds—in the fridge.

Same goes for spices! Don't keep them for more than a year. After that, they'll lose a lot of flavor, and won't do the heavy lifting you need them to do.

To get more flavor from your spices, toast them, which will turn their notes deeper, fuller, more spicy. Just heat a clean, dry pan over low heat, then toast whole spices until they turn fragrant. Coriander, cumin, and fennel seeds do especially well with this treatment. Then, grind them in a grinder—you'll be amazed at the enhanced flavor.

Toast your grains, too. Just think about risotto. Cooking rice in fat adds flavor to every grain. In the same way, toasting quinoa, farro, and millet—whether dry, or in oil—will add a nuttiness to an otherwise simple dish.

Label everything! The best way to ensure that your chickpea flour won't go bad is to remember that it exists. Label things clearly, and transfer staples like flours, sweeteners, dried beans, and lentils into clear, sturdy, reusable containers, like jars or food-safe plastic. This saves you money, too, since you're less likely to accidentally buy an ingredient that you already have.

When you have leftovers—like 2 or 3 Tbsp of homemade and salt-free tomato or curry paste, or extra coconut milk—freeze them. You can extend the shelf life of basically anything that will freeze. We're fond of ice-cube molds, which allow you to use only what you need.

Don't let nuts go rancid. The fat in walnuts, almonds, and pecans causes them to have a short shelf life, unless you store them in the fridge or freezer, where they will keep much longer. So give them a good chill.

SPICE ESSENTIALS

Clear out some cupboard shelf space or a few kitchen drawers, because we are about to go spice shopping. If you are like me, you'll end up with a minimum of twenty-five spices and blends to choose from at all times.

To get started, it is best to pick a few spices at a time or buy from bulk bins in smaller portions when trying something new. Then, take the time to get to know each spice. Smell it. Taste-test it with a blank canvas, like roasted chicken or potatoes, white beans, or steamed rice. Make note of the warmth, the sweetness, the spiciness, or the tingle it provides. Then, forget about being right or wrong when it comes to using it. Make up your own mind and your own rules about where it shines.

To help you, let me recommend my Six Salt-Free Starter Spices. These are your gateway spices. You can use them in pretty much any cuisine, from any region, with any ingredients, in an immeasurable number of combinations. Start with these six spices and experience big flavor beyond salt to build your spice confidence. And remember, sometimes salt is used as a filler for spices and blends. So look for products that clearly state "no salt added," "salt-free," or 0 mg of sodium on the nutritional label.

Cayenne pepper/red pepper flakes: A little heat (and a little citrus) will majorly wake up a dish. Cayenne refers to the ground form of the pepper, while red pepper flakes are the dried and crushed form of the pepper. They are both hot spices, but do not try to replace the same amount of one with the other—½ tsp of cayenne will pack more punch than ½ tsp of red pepper flakes. For those who like more mild heat, I suggest using flakes as I find them easier to gently adjust to your desired spiciness without going overboard.

Cumin (seeds and ground): Cumin adds a subtle heat to dishes without being too hot. The husky warmth of cumin pairs beautifully with everything from lamb to beans to butternut squash—and even grilled watermelon.

Dried dill: Tasty with vegetables, proteins, pasta, or just a simple serving of yogurt, this sweet and versatile herb adds a springtime brightness to your dishes.

Peppercorns: Freshly ground black peppercorns are more intense than prepared ground black pepper. So I encourage you to grind your own right before using. And why stop at black? You'd be surprised how many types of peppercorns there are. Try the range of varieties (white, green, pink, and Tellicherry) for different levels of spiciness.

Salt-free garlic powder: Simply put, this is the "salt" of salt-free cooking. You'll use it on everything to add a pleasant savory flavor and to bring out other natural flavors.

Smoked paprika: Smoky and sweet and colorful, this spice will become a favorite of yours. You may start using it in and on everything.

Here's where things start to get really wild and fun. There are countless other spices to try from all over the world, sold as whole seeds or ground powders. There are salt-free versions of blends you've probably heard of before, such as taco seasoning and curry powder, as well as many blends you may have yet to try, such as dukka and jerk seasoning. Don't forget about dried herbs. Unlike fresh herbs, they stand up to long cooking times and retain flavor without getting bitter. They also easily replace fresh herbs in a recipe—just use one-third as much. The point is, there are many flavors to try beyond the Six Salt-Free Starter Spices, so let's explore other favorites that are nice to have on hand.

TOP SIX WHOLE SPICES

+ Caraway seeds

+ Cardamom pods

+ Celery seed (not celery salt)

+ Coriander seeds

+ Fennel seeds

+ Mustard seeds

TOP SIX FRESH HERBS

+ Basil

+ Chives

+ Dill

+ Mint

+ Rosemary

+ Tarragon

OTHER SPICES TO HAVE ON HAND

+ Chili powder, salt-free

+ Cinnamon

+ Dried onion (voilà, onion dip!)

+ Extracts; vanilla, lemon, almond

+ Ground cloves

+ Ground ginger

+ Ground mustard

+ Ground nutmeg or mace

+ Sesame seeds

+ Star anise

+ Tea (Hint: Use to add subtle flavor to poached fish, cookies, and puddings—see Banana Chai–Chia Pudding, page 112.)

STRETCHING YOUR SPICES

Sometimes you buy a spice for a particular recipe only to let it sit in a drawer until you make that dish again. Which could be months from now. But just because a spice seems destined for a specific food doesn't mean that any spice can't reach far beyond its most common cuisines and uses.

For example, you may think cumin is best for BBQ rubs. But it is also a mainstay in Indian curries, Moroccan stews, and Mexican beans. It's also excellent on simple roasted carrots and adds a surprising smokiness to savory scones.

Use this cheat sheet to think beyond the obvious and stretch your imagination. And gain the confidence to tackle other spices in your rack on your own.

ALLSPICE (GROUND)
Spice starter: Gingerbread
Spice stretch: Meatballs, chutney, oven-fried chicken

CARAWAY SEEDS
Spice starter: Bread
Spice stretch: Scrambled eggs, potato salad, burger patties

CELERY SEEDS
Spice starter: Pickling liquid
Spice stretch: Matzo ball soup, egg salad, root vegetable gratin

CHILI POWDER
Spice starter: BBQ chicken
Spice stretch: Roasted cauliflower, creamy soup, lentils

CINNAMON (GROUND)
Spice starter: Pumpkin pie
Spice stretch: Chicken pot pie, glazed carrots, brown butter fish

CLOVES
Spice starter: Poached pear (whole cloves)
Spice stretch: Chili, pork tenderloin, mango sorbet (ground cloves)

COCOA POWDER
Spice starter: Brownies
Spice stretch: Rib rub, baked beans, enchilada sauce

COFFEE GROUNDS
Spice starter: Steak rub
Spice stretch: Ice cream, chocolate cookies, meringues

CURRY POWDER
Spice starter: Tofu
Spice stretch: Savory granola, hummus, currant scones

SHICHIMI (JAPANESE SEVEN-SPICE)
Spice Starter: Rice
Spice Stretch: Grilled peaches or watermelon, grilled corn, avocado salad

STAR ANISE (GROUND)
Spice starter: Braised beef
Spice stretch: Savory cranberry relish, berry crumbles, pancakes

ZA'ATAR
Spice starter: Lamb
Spice stretch: Meatballs, coleslaw, yogurt

CHERYL STERNMAN RULE
TALKS CARDAMOM

....

Cheryl is the kind of woman who agrees to meet a stranger for coffee on a busy summer day and answer endless question about writing, cooking, and life in general. That's how I first fell in love with Cheryl. The unknown doesn't scare her. She's generous with her time and knowledge. She's a natural-born teacher. And for many years now, she's kindly helped me navigate uncharted territory and, thankfully, turned into a dear friend as well.

Since that coffee date, I've not only become majorly obsessed with her as a human being, but as a vivid storyteller and recipe creator, too—examples of which can be found on her blog, 5 Second Rule, and her books, Ripe and Yogurt Culture. She's an expert at blending the familiar with the eye-opening—both in words and in food. That's why I asked her to talk to you about cardamom, to demystify this strange spice and show you how a little sprinkle will make the commonplace memorable.

I blame my nose, since before I ever tasted cardamom, I smelled it, and afterward I was pretty much done for. One whiff of the mysteriously floral spice and suddenly I spooned it everywhere—pancakes and cookies, curries and soups, cakes and muffins. But cardamom, which comes in green, black, and even white pods (I'm partial to green), as well as ground, is a spice that demands a certain restraint. It's fairly brash, and when overused it can bully subtler flavors and ingredients, forcing them into the background whether they belong there or not.

Chai drinkers have known about whole cardamom for ages, of course, because the pods are an essential ingredient in this popular milky tea. After bruising the pods to release their essential oils and let their flavor run free, they're steeped with their cousins (cinnamon, clove, ginger, and black pepper) to add intoxicating flavor and aroma to the classic Indian brew. I also add

bruised pods to saffron rice, to poaching fruit, to korma, to crème anglaise. (Lift out the spent shells before serving.)

Ground, cardamom is excellent in pretty much anything you'd use cinnamon in; oatmeal (try a drizzle of coconut milk with your cardamom), waffles, or applesauce. Scandinavians are especially fond of it in baking, especially in coffee cakes and pastry braids. Just go easy. Cardamom's a passionate spice, and a gentle nudge is more than sufficient to warm up your batter and set your heart aflutter.

JESS THOMSON
TALKS ABOUT THE ZING OF ZEST

....

Meet my soul sister, Jess. Besides talking like me, sharing a life with lupus, and, oh yeah, that whole first-name thing, we also both love all things food (and you can read more about her creations at Hogwash.com as well as in the many books she's authored). Beyond our similarities, what I adore and respect most about Jess is her ability to brighten up a room, a gloomy situation, and, yes, boring meals. So the next time your soup or salad has you down, just think, What would Jess do? She'd give it zest. And now she'll show you how.

You know what they say about how when life gives you lemons, you should make lemonade? Nothing against lemonade, but I think that's awfully shortsighted. Lemon zest, the sunny outermost layer every lemon wears with pride, is a delicious (and easy) way to add brightness and flavor to dishes year-round. Use it the way you use fresh herbs—liberally, in cold or hot foods, when you think something you're making needs a little more punch.

A quick note: Although lemon *zest* and lemon *peel* are often used interchangeably, the zest is technically the outermost yellow layer, while the peel includes the bitter white pith underneath. Both parts are edible, but the citric, floral flavor you're looking for comes from the natural oils found only in the yellow part. And there are three great ways to get the zest off a lemon, besides a kitchen knife.

First, you can use a Microplane grater to shave the zest off in soft piles. When it's grated finely like this, whisk lemon zest into any dry ingredient that goes into a baked good—think flour or sugar—for added flavor. I also love adding finely grated zest to vinaigrettes.

Second, you can use a so-called zester—a kind of medieval-looking instrument that looks like a handle with the world's most miniature set of brass knuckles at one end—to strip that yellow gold off in thin ribbons. I use these longer strips of zest when I want a more pronounced lemony punch. Try adding the ribbons from about one-quarter of a medium-size fruit to sautéed vegetables, chicken salad, any dish made with cooked grains, or to pickles of any sort.

Third, you can use a vegetable peeler to cut the zest off in strips 1 in [2.5 cm] wide. Use big strips of zest (which some call "peel") at "wine-thirty" (a.k.a. Happy Hour), or drop them into braises to add flavor to chicken or lamb.

The power of the peel (or zest) isn't limited to lemons. Use orange, lime, or grapefruit zest the same way. Save the rest of your citrus in the refrigerator to use later.

REFRIGERATOR ESSENTIALS

By now, you've assembled a useful selection of utensils, dry goods, and spices to support you in your food adventures to come. So let's talk about the leader of the operation: the fridge.

Your refrigerator is the compass that will set the course of your meals, and what's inside will mean the difference between merely edible food and unbelievable deliciousness. What you have in your fridge determines what you are able to make for breakfast, lunch, and dinner. Yes, you can happily get by with dried rice and beans. And I have. But a thoughtfully stocked refrigerator means flavorful flexibility and the ability to create impressive food whenever you want.

+ Eggs, large

+ Fresh fruit (like citrus and avocados)

+ Fresh herbs

+ Jams

+ Juice

+ Meat

+ Mustard, low- or no-sodium

+ Starch; potatoes, sweet potato, squash, corn

+ Vegetables; broccoli, leafy greens, carrots, zucchini

+ Yogurt

FREEZER ESSENTIALS

Take note of what you find in the store's freezer section and then re-create the convenience at home.

FROZEN DOUGHS AND CRUSTS

Whether you make your dough ahead of time or save the extra scraps, don't let your hand-kneaded work go to waste. For pizza and bread dough, oil it before placing in a plastic bag. Squeeze out all the air (or suck out the air with a straw), and then freeze. To use frozen yeast-based pizza dough or bread dough, let it thaw in the refrigerator for 4 hours and then rest at room temperature for about 10 minutes before baking.

To freeze uncooked pasta dough, sprinkle a baking pan with flour. Lay out the noodles on the pan, toss them in the flour, and then place the whole pan in the freezer. When hard, put the pasta in airtight plastic bags or containers, in individual portions. To use, skip the thawing process and plop frozen pasta right into your boiling water when ready to cook. Cook for 3 to 5 minutes for small, thin noodles, and 5 to 7 minutes for larger, thicker pastas.

For cookie dough, use a spoon or ice-cream scoop to portion out individual cookies, freeze, and then put into an airtight plastic container. Or shape cookie dough into a log, wrap in wax paper or plastic wrap, and freeze. Then, slice and bake from frozen as your sweet tooth demands. Add a couple of extra minutes to the bake time when starting with frozen dough.

For pie dough, press the extra dough into a metal or ceramic pie dish, wrap in plastic wrap (tightly!), and freeze. Then bake without thawing—like cookies, add a few more minutes of cooking due to the cold start. And don't forget to freeze the pie fillings, too, in pie-sized portions, to make things truly easy as pie.

FROZEN MEAT

You'll be happy you stocked up on steak, chops, chicken, and shrimp for those nights when you crave protein but didn't have time to go to the store. Consult the FDA Refrigerator and Freezer Storage Chart (www.fda.gov/downloads/Food/FoodborneIllness Contaminants/UCM109315.pdf) for optimal storage time to ensure safety and quality. Be sure to label your frozen meats with type and the date you froze it. Leave time for proper thawing in the fridge (not on the counter) overnight or longer. When cooking steaks or chops, though, it's actually best to skip the thaw and cook frozen. Just add some extra minutes to the cooking time depending on the size of the cut.

BLANCHING VEGETABLES

All low-sodium eaters and cooks must understand blanching, or quickly boiling, vegetables. Why? This technique (also referred to as "parboiling") will partially cook vegetables while retaining (if not enhancing) their bright hue—a great party trick for crudité platters and salads, as well as a time-saver when grilling or pan-frying tougher ingredients, like Brussels sprouts. It is also an essential step in freezing vegetables properly and safely.

Understanding blanching will also keep your meals low-sodium-safe, as many home cooks and chefs add salt to the blanching water. So when dining out, ask for vegetables to be kept raw, steamed, or blanched without salted water.

The technique for blanching is pretty much the same whether you've got corn or cauliflower. Fill a medium bowl with water and ice and stick it in the freezer to keep cold. Then fill a medium pot with water and bring it to a boil. If your vegetables need trimming, peeling, or cutting (like green beans or carrots), do the prep right before you blanch. Take the ice bath out of the freezer when the water is boiling and add the vegetables to the pot, in batches, if needed. When the vegetables are slightly tender, after 1 to 2 minutes (or 2 to 3 minutes for larger items like broccoli florets), use a slotted spoon to transfer them to the ice bath. When cool to the touch, transfer the vegetables to a paper towel–lined plate or give them a whirl in a salad spinner to dry off. Use the vibrant vegetables immediately, store in an airtight container in the refrigerator for up to 1 week, or freeze (see page 71) for up to 1 year.

IRVIN LIN
TALKS GOING ROGUE WITH GRAINS AND FLOUR

....

As the genius behind the blog Eat The Love and author of the upcoming Marbled, Swirled, Layered, *Irvin Lin knows what he's doing when it comes to baking. You should see the sweet holiday spread he cranks out every year. It's a cookie explosion.*

But what's really special about Irvin (and his baked goods) is that, while baking involves exact measurements and a bit of science, he's not afraid to experiment, especially when it comes to using grains and flours beyond the all-purpose kind. Kamut, amaranth, and spelt each have their own flavor profiles; which means, instead of hovering in the background, they can be the star of the recipe. Or like Irvin says, cookies no longer just have to be about the chocolate chips.

So enjoy these tips from Irvin to harness the power of grains and flours, and use them just like a spice to add something special to those cakes, breads, crumbles, and even salads.

GET TO KNOW YOUR GRAINS AND FLOURS

Buckwheat tastes "malty," amaranth is "grassy," Kamut is "buttery," and semolina is "crunchy." Once you understand the tastes and textures provided by each grain and flour, you can use them as you would spices to change the profile of your favorite recipes. So give it a taste. Then start switching things up.

MAKE YOUR OWN

While you can always ransack the bulk bins, you can also make your own flours at home. Use a food processor to grind nuts, oats, grains, and even coconut into a fine powder [like for the Lemon Zinger Bars on page 175]. Then experiment with small batches or even combine them to make your own mixes. Coconut and pistachio flour, anyone?

GIVE IT A TRY

When you have the confidence to start subbing grains and flours in your favorite recipes, use a scale and swap by weight. Usually you can successfully substitute 25 percent of the original all-purpose flour for any other grain. But if you're a little nervous, start with something simple, like a crumble, where the butter and sugar act as a safety net—failure is not an option when they're around. Another idea for something toasty; instead of using flour, try adding rolled oats, millet for a mildly nutty flavor, or almond flour for something buttery and a bit savory. Be warned, though, this will be your gateway substitution. There's no stopping you after that.

FROZEN VEGETABLES AND FRUIT

You can cook with corn and peaches all year long if you have them in your freezer. This is nice, especially during the winter root season when a little extra sweetness or color is greatly welcome. Just make sure you buy products with 0 mg of sodium or "no salt added." Or buy extra produce, wash ripe fruit and blanch vegetables, then freeze on trays. When hard, place into airtight containers or bags. And remember, you can freeze portions of pestos and vegetable purées in muffin tins or ice-cube trays (before placing in a plastic bag) to save freezer space and time.

LEFTOVERS

Don't be afraid to make big portions or double recipes. If you properly store leftovers, you can take the night off from the stove once in a while and still eat low-sodium. Just remember to cool food before storing, keep serving-size portions in airtight plastic bags or in plastic wrap to reduce moisture loss and freezer burn, and label with the dish name and date of preparation. Most cooked food keeps well frozen for 2 to 3 months. Beware: Pasta can become mushy when reheated. So if you know extra noodles are bound for the freezer, slightly undercook them.

SAUCES, STOCK, COCONUT MILK

Freeze these liquids in ice-cube trays. Once they've hardened, transfer the cubes to airtight containers. You can pull a few cubes out as needed. The coconut milk will separate when thawed, so simply remix it. These will keep for 3 months.

EMERGENCY ESSENTIALS

With your cupboards and refrigerator full, there's one last place people forget to stock with low-sodium goods: Emergency kits.

It took me years to realize that my bag of SOS items needed a major low-sodium makeover. The last thing you'd want during an earthquake or a Godzilla attack is not having the sustenance you need to stay healthy (and able to fight really large creatures). So beyond warm clothes, medical supplies, and water, make sure you pack a can opener and some of these nonperishables:

+ Low-sodium or no-salt-added soups

+ No-salt-added beans and vegetables

+ Low-sodium canned fish

+ No-salt-added granola bars

+ Baby food (Most baby food is packed full of good nutrition with little to no sodium)

··· 4 ···

SHOP

Getting More from
Shopping at the Market

My favorite place in the world is the grocery store. For many people, the market represents tedious errands, frozen dinners, or cleanups on aisle four. And for those of us on special diets, it can serve as a reminder of all the food we cannot eat anymore.

To me, the grocery store means endless possibilities. It is a warehouse of flavor and the starting line for many memorable meals to come. Going to my local market gives me inspiration. I go so often, everyone knows my name, which could seem a little embarrassing but is ultimately essential for cooking delicious low-sodium meals. When you have a relationship with your store, you also have a direct line to the people who can put your favorite products on the shelves.

But my excitement and confidence in wandering the aisles grew over time. This transformation required both instruction and a new set of shopping skills, which they don't teach in school. With a little extra know-how and practice, you, too, will not only begin to enjoy (and love) your trips to the store, but you'll get more from those aisles and shelves than ever before.

LESSON ONE: READ THE LABELS

Welcome to shopping school. Let's begin by talking about the contents of the market. There's the fresh stuff—produce, meats, and fish—and then there's the packaged stuff—dairy, deli, and anything in a bag, box, or can.

When it comes to figuring out the nutritional content of fresh foods, use resources like the USDA National Nutrient Database for Standard Reference for sodium averages or ask store clerks and managers for more product information. When dealing with the packaged stuff, however, all that information is right there on the package. Which brings us to our first shopping skill: reading labels.

PACKAGED STUFF

Let's start by decoding that jargon on the label. Begin with the back of the product. Here you'll find the nutrition facts panel, which includes a listing of the %DV (percentage daily value) of sodium found in one serving. The amount of sodium per serving is listed in milligrams (mg). The %DV currently is based on a daily sodium intake of 2,400 mg per person, which is 100 mg more than the USDA's upper recommended limit. Keep in mind that the can, bag, or package usually contains more than one serving, so if you plan to eat or use more than a single serving, make sure to multiply those sodium numbers to calculate the true total.

Next, scan the ingredient list. Of course, you'll want to look for words like *salt*, *sodium*, and *Na* (the chemical symbol for sodium). But also look for sneakier sodium contributors:

+ baking powder

+ baking soda

+ monosodium glutamate (MSG)

+ sodium benzoate

+ sodium citrate

+ sodium nitrate

On the front of a package, you'll find other key terms to help you decipher the sodium content in a product, including:

+ **No Salt Added** These products contain no sodium chloride. The sodium content, if any, will come from the natural sodium found in the ingredients.

+ **Sodium-Free** These products have less than 5 mg of sodium per serving and contain no sodium chloride.

+ **Very Low Sodium** These products contain 35 mg or less of sodium per serving.

+ **Low Sodium** These products contain 140 mg or less of sodium per serving.

+ **Light in Sodium** This term means that the sodium level in the product has been reduced by at least 50 percent per serving from its original level or a competitor's product. So, if that product started with more than 500 mg of sodium per serving, then you're still talking about 250 mg of sodium per serving.

+ **Reduced (or Less) Sodium** This term means that the sodium level in the product has been reduced by 25 percent per serving from the original or a competitor's product. So, if that product started with more than 500 mg of sodium per serving, then you're still talking about 375 mg of sodium per serving.

Keep in mind that miscellaneous items, like spices and over-the-counter medications, may also contain sodium. Also, some items, like balsamic vinegar and dry pastas, will differ in sodium content, depending on the brand. A simple turn of a bottle will tell you what's sodium-free and what is not. If you're unsure, here's a general rule of thumb: Whether it is a bag of chips or bottle of vitamin D tablets, if a product does not provide nutritional information, skip it and look for one that does give you the information.

One of the most amazing aspects of the grocery store is that the items change with great frequency. New seasons bring new produce. New health trends mean new products in the snack, freezer, and dairy aisles. So looking at labels, every label, is very important. Even when it seems impossible that a product could be a low-sodium choice, you should always turn the package around and see. Over the years, a simple glance led me to discovering no-salt-added pickles, low-sodium deli meat, and low-sodium Swiss cheese. Be a vigilant label reader and you might find some unexpectedly low-sodium products.

FRESH STUFF

Now that we've tackled the packaged stuff, let's talk about the fresh stuff—mainly, what you'll find at the meat and fish counters.

A big, surprising issue: Beware of "brine." When it comes to poultry (and even beef, pork, fish, and shellfish), some manufacturers plump proteins with salty solutions before they hit the store, increasing the sodium of chicken, for instance, by up to 500 percent.

Avoid items with "broth," "percent solution," "enhanced," and even "natural flavoring" listed in the small print. Look for "air-chilled" and "no water added" to identify products that are free of brine and plumping. When in doubt, read nutritional information, talk to your butcher, and use your sodium know-how—for example, natural chicken should be around 70 mg of sodium per 4 oz [115 g]—to make sure no extra stuff was added.

Armed with this information, you can easily detect which whole foods fall on your "do eat" list and which do not. Though it may feel overwhelming at first, just like any other skill (knitting, yoga, cocktail mixing), it gets easier and more enjoyable over time.

A TIP FROM BETH SHANAMAN, RD
If the numbers and percentages on labels make you dizzy, don't break out your calculator. Instead, use this clever trick from Beth Shanaman, a registered dietitian at Northwest Kidney Centers, to make shopping and sodium decisions simple. Ignore the %DV. Read the mg! Think of the recommended limit of 1,500 mg of sodium a day like money. If you have $1,500 to spend, then look at each food as taking money away from that total. Is it worth it to spend $800 (or 800 mg)—more than half of your "budget"—on a single ingredient? Or is it better spent on a total meal?

LESSON TWO: WALK THE AISLES

At first glance, the grocery store is full of food. But you'll find that it's also filled with tools that make low-sodium cooking exciting. Rice cereal and granola offer uses beyond breakfast or midday snacks, and jam can embellish more than just bread. Which leads us to our second shopping skill: Know what the aisles offer you.

CANNED GOODS

From tomato sauce to beans, vegetables, and bouillon, these days the canned goods section carries a huge variety of no-salt-added products. These are pantry staples that, together with frozen vegetables, make throwing together a satisfying weeknight meal as easy as a twist of the can opener. Spend some time in this aisle and remember, even though these items are technically ready to eat, they can always benefit from some extra attention. Add your own spices, oils, herbs, and vinegars to make these foods pop.

DAIRY AND DELI MEAT

For years, I didn't even bother with the dairy and deli meat aisles. Then I found Swiss cheese with only 35 mg of sodium per slice and cottage cheese with only 45 mg per ¼ cup [55 g], and life changed. Now I turn around every packet of bacon, sliced turkey, and cheese spread just in case I find something new I can enjoy.

FREEZER

For all those who think keeping a low-sodium diet means spending tons of time in the kitchen, I say, head to the freezer aisle. Having starches and vegetables cut and ready to cook means you can make dinner in a matter of minutes. Remember to read the label for hidden sodium in some products.

INTERNATIONAL FOODS

Even your taste buds like to travel. Luckily and surprisingly, this aisle is packed with low-sodium-friendly products like matzo crackers, pickled ginger, hot sauce, nori (a.k.a. sushi seaweed), as well as a variety of dried chile peppers. These will act as great flavor boosters as well as stand-ins for higher-sodium ingredients, like sandwich bread and crackers.

MEAT COUNTER

Just like with fruits and vegetables, try out unfamiliar proteins and cuts of meat. Instead of tilapia, try that strange-sounding monkfish. By learning how to cook different chops, ribs, filets, and even livers, you'll pick up new techniques, flavor combinations, and recipes. All that knowledge will give you the confidence to experiment and substitute ingredients on your own. You'll find yourself buying what looks good or what's on sale rather than what the recipe lists. Remember, you only need a little bit of meat to add a salt-like flavor to your meals, so save that leftover ground pork or a splash of rendered chicken drippings to add a savory kick to your other dishes.

PREPARED FOODS

Most markets now offer prepared soups, sandwiches, and side dishes. Even though you most likely won't find anything low-sodium in this section (yet!), you will find lots of inspiration. Chili macaroni and cheese, lemongrass soup, smashed potatoes with sage, and other interesting concoctions will get those creative wheels cranking for your home-cooked meals.

PRODUCE

Fresh herbs: Get acquainted with fresh herbs. A sprinkle of chopped dill or thyme will make simple dishes special and leftovers taste fresh again. To avoid a big batch going bad, try this trick: Pick out one herb on Sunday and then use that bunch all week long, in your vegetables, in your savory mains, and even your desserts. Use the chosen herb in both traditional and wacky ways, where it belongs and where it has no business hanging out. You'll not only keep those taste buds on high alert (parsley and peas), but you may even discover a new favorite flavor combination (thyme and lime sugar cookies!).

Fruit: When you think of fruit, think of possibilities other than sweet snacks or desserts. Fruit makes a great companion for savory entrées. When roasted or sautéed, fruit adds a surprising layer of flavor to meat, pasta, and side dishes. Cherries, pears, and peaches play well with roasted vegetables. Roasted lemons perk up a simple roasted chicken. Oven-broiled grapes make a rich topping for noodles or provide a twist on traditional bruschetta spread.

Mushrooms: Stock up on mushrooms. They are a rich source of natural umami, with no salt or sodium to speak of. Whether you need to make a quick, earthy stock or increase the meaty oomph of a risotto or stew, mushrooms will help get the job done while maintaining a low-sodium approach.

Try something new: When you see a vegetable or a fruit you don't recognize, add it to your basket, go home and look it up on the Internet, and discover what you can make with it. By learning to use unfamiliar ingredients, you'll become more flexible in your cooking. You'll get more playful as well, confidently substituting what you have on hand (celery root and fennel) for what a recipe lists (onions and potatoes). Most important, you'll start surprising your palate, which is the easiest way to keep yourself from missing the salt. So grab that scary looking thing and give it a go!

SNACKS AND CEREALS

Salt-free potato chips, tortilla chips, and wheat flakes make great snacking staples in your kitchen cupboards and office desk drawers. They also make great swaps for bread crumbs, whether you're topping a casserole or coating a chicken breast. Buy some for midday or game-day cravings, and then keep some on hand for last-minute bread-crumb emergencies.

STORING AND SAVING HERBS

Herbs can be hard. Herbs can be soft. And when not stored properly, herbs can go bad. But with good storage technique (and a few tricks), you can make those herbs last.

I like to place soft herbs (a.k.a. any herbs with a soft stem) in a canning jar or a glass with a bit of water to keep them fresh. Basil keeps best at room temperature and the others (like mint, parsley, and cilantro) keep well in the refrigerator. Just make sure to change out the water every few days and they should stay perky for about a week. When kept like this, they also look mighty nice on your counter when you're prepping dinner or hosting a party. You can also store soft herbs by wrapping the stems in a damp paper towel, placing in a plastic bag, and then into the refrigerator. Because soft herbs bruise easily, only rinse them right before you use them. A quick plunge into a bowl of water will do the trick. Then dry them with the help of a dry cloth or paper towel.

For hard herbs (like rosemary and thyme, or any herbs with woody stems), keep them fresh by wrapping them in a damp paper towel, placing in a plastic bag, and, putting them in the fridge.

Although you can extend the life of harder herbs by drying them upside down in a warm, dry place, another handy way to preserve them is by chopping them up, putting them in ice-cube trays, and covering them with olive oil or leftover salt-free broth. Once frozen, wrap the herb cubes in plastic wrap, put in an airtight plastic bag, and then return to the freezer.

Pop out the cubes when making a simple vegetable sauté or as the base of your next soup, sauce, or pesto. If you want to freeze softer herbs, purée them first in the blender with a little garlic and onion, and follow the same procedure for freezing and storage.

MAX FALKOWITZ
TALKS CHILES

....

*Before becoming a national editor at SeriousEats.com, Max Falkowitz was simply
a hunter—a spice hunter. He's responsible for the Spice Hunting articles on the website,
where he explores the world of flavor beyond salt and pepper (although he dug into that,
too), educating fellow eaters on how to find and use different seeds, blends, and
pastes to their cooking advantage. Here, he guides us through a lesson on one of
low-sodium's most robust flavor-makers: chiles, fresh and dried.*

Modern supermarkets might offer dozens of varieties of fresh and dried chile peppers, but with little information about how they differ. Here are some pointers to help you navigate the selection.

FRESH

Generally speaking, smaller chiles are spicier than larger ones, and green, unripe chiles pack more punch than ripe, red versions. (Noteworthy exceptions include the nuclear-hot orange habanero and Scotch Bonnet peppers.) Green chiles tend toward grassy, pungent flavors, while red, yellow, and orange chiles tend to taste more sweet and fruity. When shopping for fresh chiles, look for smooth, glossy skin and a firm, crisp texture. Old, wrinkled, leathery chiles pack heat but lack a certain fresh flavor. Don't confuse little white notches in chiles, like jalapeños, as signs of age; they're a natural imperfection that's only skin-deep.

DRIED

Chiles are fruit, so it helps to think of dried chiles as raisins, not spices. So, dried chiles should be moist and pliable, indicating that they're fresh and full flavored. The older a dried chile gets, the drier it becomes, and the more flavor it gives up to moisture loss and vaporization of its essential oils. Chiles are typically dried in late summer, so your best bet for fresh dried chiles is late August and early autumn. If all you can find are brittle, papery dried chiles, an all-too-common problem once you move away from the American Southwest, consider visiting a Latin American grocery or ordering chiles online from specialty merchants.

To get the most out of your whole dried chiles, cut them open, take out the seeds, and toast them briefly in a hot, dry pan until they smell aromatic. Then roughly chop them and grind them in a spice grinder or, better yet, soak them in some boiling water or stock for 20 minutes, drain well, and purée them in the blender until smooth. Voilà! You've just made your own fresh chile paste.

LESSON THREE: MAKE FRIENDS

You are now a low-sodium master of the aisles and the products on the shelves. With everything you've learned, you're a grocery-store expert. You know what low-sodium items you love and where to find them. With all this knowledge, it's time to (charmingly) pass it on. Get to know the people who stock the shelves and the person behind the meat counter. Which brings us to shopping-skill number-three: Say hi.

It's that easy. Say hello to the people who work in the store. Strike up a conversation with the butcher or the bagger. Ask them how they like to cook pork butt or if they've tasted the plump strawberries that just arrived. Let them know how much you love the low-sodium steak marinade on their shelves. Or tell them about the stuffing you're making with the salt-free bread they carry. And before you know it, they'll be trading their kitchen secrets, showing you the latest low-sodium items on the shelves, and saying hi, too.

Here's what's really wonderful about this whole "relationship with your grocery store" thing. Let's say there's a brand of salt-free potato chips, sodium-free baking powder, or low-sodium turkey meat that you heard about. You can now ask your new buddy, the store manager, to carry it for you. The worst they can say is no and the best they can do is start a whole low-sodium aisle. And wouldn't that be fabulous?

You never know how many other people shopping in this same store need low-sodium items. If you're nervous about being forward, remember, getting chatty is good. By starting the conversation with a "Hi!" you'll make sure others start to enjoy the grocery store as much as you do.

LESSON FOUR: WHERE TO SHOP

Now that you know how to shop, let's talk about where to shop. Your closest market may be down the block or an hour's drive. You may have multiple kinds of markets to choose from or just one grocery store in town. Whether you make a special monthly trip, shop daily, or make your purchases with the help of the Internet, there are plenty of places where you can purchase fresh, healthful, low-sodium ingredients.

BUTCHER SHOPS

Nothing beats the personal interaction you get with a real butcher. Ask questions about the meat or fish, how it was processed, and how to cook it. Best of all, if you're looking for something really specific (heritage, brine-free turkeys or thinly sliced pork belly), most butchers are more than happy to take special orders.

FARMERS' MARKETS

If you want the freshest produce, look no farther than your local farmers' market. Use websites like the USDA Farmers Market Directory (search.ams.usda.gov/farmersmarkets) or Eat Well Guide (eatwellguide.org) to find the one closest to you. (Eat Well Guide even has a trip planner, so you can find sustainable foods while you're on the road!) Download apps, like Farmstand, that will find a market near you. Or try Eat Wild (eatwild.com) to discover a list of local farms and ranches in your area offering grass-fed meat and dairy. Use your time with the farmers to learn more about unusual produce as well as which fruits and vegetables are in season. So remember, if the market requires a special trip, make that trip special.

HEALTH FOOD STORES

Health food stores will be your best bet for specialty products (in addition to the Internet). Many health food stores have bulk bins for grains, flours, nuts, and dried fruit, so you can purchase and try small amounts of new ingredients before diving in with a big bag of the stuff.

INTERNATIONAL MARKETS

Just like exploring new countries, taking a trip to an international market will introduce you to new foods (like lychee or dragon fruit), unique flavors (bonito flakes and tamarind paste), and unfamiliar products (black garlic and paneer cheese). Be sure to buy items with a label marking them as low in sodium and MSG-free. If no label exists or you feel unsure, look online for the company's website and a consumer help line to find out the nutritional information.

SPICE STORES

Today there are whole stores dedicated to spices, including salt-free spices. Most of them also allow you to pick the amount of spices you want to buy, which, like with bulk-bin items, lets you start small as your palate grows.

THE WORLD WIDE WEB

The easiest way to find low-sodium products is from the comfort of your computer. A quick Google search or the URL of a company's website will let you order your favorite pantry staples at the click of a button. Or further research the nutritional and processing information, if you're having trouble finding it on the label.

5

DIY

Finding Lower-Sodium
Solutions

We have flown to the moon. Crossbred apricots with plums. Developed self-driving cars. Anything is possible. This applies to low-sodium cooking as well. The next time you come up against a high-sodium-food stumbling block, do not despair; channel that same innovative and DIY spirit.

Throughout this book, I talk a lot about creativity as a secret weapon in low-so cooking, and it's time that we hone this skill. Because whether you crave Canadian bacon or get stuck in a food rut, it's always possible (and sometimes best) to take matters into your own hands and DIY a low-so solution. In this chapter you will learn to make over recipes, make up recipes, and make everyday meals taste fantastic—all on your own.

By the end of this book, you'll not only be able to put many of the foods you love back into your life but you'll also start seeing your low-sodium diet less as an ingredient "handicap" and more as the ultimate creative license. You'll infuse standard recipes with more spices and spunk. You'll teach humble ingredients (like cucumber) new tricks (cucumber baguettes!). You'll become a resource for friends with other special diets, and you'll even make salt-free bacon. In sum, with fine-tuned DIY skills, you'll be low-so unstoppable.

FINDING LOW-SO SUBSTITUTES

If there is something you miss eating, turn on those creative engines; you have the power and the tools to give any dish a successful low-sodium makeover.

In my first book, I outlined my formula for "salt-free-ing" any recipe. Of all the steps, finding the right low-so substitute takes the most effort. This is why I've created a list of my favorites for you to reference when you make over recipes on your own. While many of the substitutes will look or taste different from the original ingredient, give even the craziest-sounding ones a chance. Often, they will not only satisfy cravings, but also increase the flavor and nutritional value of a recipe, and sometimes even cut down on prep time.

If you find something missing from this list, however, remember to use the Internet, television, the cookbooks on your shelf, and the grocery store for inspiration. Look to other special diets, too. If you need to replace prepared wheat-based products, check out Paleo and gluten-free resources; if you need to replace something cheesy, look to vegan and dairy-free cookbooks and blogs; if you need to replace cured meats, look to vegetarian and raw diets for easy stand-ins.

Test these substitutes and then keep adjusting until you really like what you're eating. Does the dish need more texture? Add something crunchy. Are all the ingredients green? Add something bright and colorful. Do you miss the salt? Add a spritz of lime, some chopped fresh herbs, or a spice you've never used before. Over time, you'll not only have a low-so success story, but a DIY signature dish—one created with your own flavors, your own spin, your own personality.

ANCHOVIES

If you want to make a Caesar dressing, a fishy pizza, or seafood pâté, replace the high-sodium anchovies with lower-sodium canned sardines.

BACON

Using sliced pork belly, you can make a salt-free alternate bacon that looks and tastes insanely similar to the heavenly salty stuff. My genius sister-in-law is 100 percent responsible for this recipe (see Salt-Free Bacon, page 93). Thanks to her perseverance and many trials, she figured out how to get that crispy texture and smoky flavor your taste buds want, without the salt.

BACON, CANADIAN

When making your next eggs Benedict, skip the pork and instead layer poached eggs and creamy hollandaise over rounds of roasted sweet potatoes or beets; grilled peach or nectarine halves; or a thick slice of heirloom tomato. Give it an extra bacon-like flavor with a blend of oil and the spices used in Salt-Free Bacon (page 93).

BAGELS

Get a doughnut pan and use it to make fake baked low-sodium bagels using a savory batter. You can use a spice mix (like the one in Everything Waffles, page 211) for seasoning.

BREAD AND BUNS

According to the Centers for Disease Control (CDC), bread is one of the top sodium culprits, with 80 to 230 mg of sodium per slice. When you consider breakfast and sandwiches and snacks before dinner, this can quickly add up throughout the day. So while no-salt-added bread exists (and when it's toasted, it isn't half bad), use this as an excuse to think outside of the bread box. Wrap your next sandwich in corn tortillas or sturdy leafy greens. And for burgers, use large cabbage leaves or a grilled portobello mushroom.

BREAD CRUMBS

When you don't have low-sodium bread at home, there are several options for a quick bread-crumbs substitute. For meatballs and burgers that need extra bulk, replace the bread crumbs with finely chopped cauliflower, ground salt-free tortilla chips, cooked rice, or cooked quinoa. For casseroles and baked pastas, top with crushed nuts. Or mix finely chopped broccoli with oil and a little cornmeal. Then broil for the final 3 to 5 minutes of cooking until browned and crispy.

BROTH

When a recipe calls for this high-sodium ingredient, whip up some quick mushroom broth. After only 30 minutes of boiling dried or fresh fungi, you'll end up with an earthy stock filled with natural salt-free umami flavor. The broth is perfect as a low-sodium base for soups, stews, and stuffing. But if you want that traditional flavor, use chicken bones (or meat) and aromatics (like herbs, onions, and garlic) to make a big batch of broth from scratch. For easy use, freeze 2- to 4-cup [480- to 960-ml] portions in individual airtight containers. Or, boil some chicken on Sunday for workweek lunches and use the boiling liquid as broth, refrigerating or freezing as needed.

BROTH SUBSTITUTES

Most of the time, when a recipe calls for broth, I just use water and a lot of spices in its place. But if you are looking for more oomph, use a combination of water and the following easy flavor enhancers.

Fresh vegetable leftovers, like corn cobs, fennel fronds, or chard stems: Boil in water for 30 minutes and use in any recipe that calls for a vegetable broth.

Jam and dried fruit: Use water in place of broth and add 2 or 3 Tbsp apricot jam or ¼ to ½ cup [85 to 170 g] chopped dried peaches or apricots to the pot for extra flavor. Works well for pulled chicken and pork, Moroccan- and Indian-inspired stews and curries, and anything with tomatoes.

Orange juice: Replace the broth with half citrus juice and half water. Works well for risotto, chili, pulled pork, and chicken.

Red or White Wine: Replace the broth in a recipe with water and add ¼ to ½ cup [60 to 120 ml] wine. Red's deep, earthy flavors add richness to meaty pasta sauces and beef stews. White's extra acidity helps brighten risottos or slow-cooked chicken or pork.

Tomatoes (no-salt-added sauce or fresh-cut tomatoes): Replace the broth with half water and half tomato sauce or a large juicy chopped tomato. Works well for curries; Moroccan- and Indian-inspired stews; pasta sauces; and pulled pork, chicken, and beef.

CRAB DIP, CRAB CAKES, AND LOBSTER ROLLS

Impersonate high-sodium crab and lobster meat with other low-sodium fish. Cook, shred, and spice tilapia and snapper for dips. Make cakes out of salmon and cod. And fill homemade low-sodium buns with chunky halibut and your own spiced-up mayo for a take on New England's famous fish sandwich.

CRACKERS

You can find round rice crackers with 0 mg of sodium at the grocery store. For emergency appetizer situations, I always have matzo crackers on hand. They even work for nachos if you need them to. But anything crispy will do when you need something for your spreads. Cucumbers and apples make a satisfying wheat-free substitute.

CREAMY CHEESE

When your pasta or quesadilla needs something creamy to bring it all together, try puréed butternut squash or pumpkin; puréed cauliflower; yogurt or mascarpone; low-sodium ricotta or low-sodium cottage cheese (look for brands with less than 60 mg of sodium per ¼-cup [55-g] serving).

CREAMY SAUCES

Puréed pumpkin, butternut squash, or cauliflower makes a tasty sauce for faux mac 'n' cheese or casseroles. And puréed corn is awesome for chicken pot pie filling and as a dairy-free enchilada sauce.

DINE-OUT DRESSING

Make a simple vinaigrette by mixing olive oil, vinegar, and citrus (see The MacGyver Vinaigrette, page 119), plus spices of your choice in a small jar. Put the jar in a resealable plastic bag and take it with you to the restaurant.

HOT DOGS

Replace traditional high-sodium franks with roasted carrots or try low-so and vegetarian "squash dogs." Buy hot dog–shaped zucchini or squash and halve lengthwise. Add your own low-so marinade and spices, and grill on the flat side of the vegetable. Put the squash halves back together and nestle into a bun (if you can handle the sodium in bread). Otherwise, wrap in a lettuce leaf and top with low-so versions of typical hot dog fare (onions, mustard, low-so pickles).

INSTANT PIZZA DOUGH

Today, you can buy low-sodium pizza dough in the grocery store and online. But when you don't have it in your pantry, use toasted corn tortillas as a flatbread-like substitute or the crust from quick and crispy Chickpea-Flour Pizza (page 94). You can also make fresh dough and spreads from scratch (see page 257). Or go a totally different route by making potatoes, eggplant, zucchini, or winter squash and then topping them with red sauce, seasoned ground meat, and other low-sodium pizza fare.

MAYONNAISE

Most mayonnaise contains more than 100 mg of sodium per 1 Tbsp, so a hearty slather can quickly become a high-sodium event. Here are a few low-sodium options. Soy-based yogurt is quite low in sodium and has just the right creaminess for coleslaws, chicken salads, and sandwich spreads. Sodium-free silken tofu, when blended with salt-free garlic powder and other tasty spices, makes an easy homemade option. Certain hemp seed oil–based mayonnaise products have only 5 mg of sodium per 1 tsp and have been showing up on grocery store shelves lately. Or make Sauce Gribiche (page 166) and call it a day.

MILK

Most milks, including nut, hemp, and soy, can contain upward of 100 mg of sodium per 1 cup [240 ml]. This may fit within most people's dietary limits, but it can quickly add up throughout the day. If you're looking for a lower-sodium switch, coconut milk (now in handy cartons) works well for cereal, curries, and even your morning cup of joe.

OLIVES

When your next pasta, Greek salad, or cheese plate calls for the tang of olives, look no farther than baked or pickled grapes and Pickled Cherries (page 249) to take their place. They're not salty and they aren't olives, but they'll add a fun and unexpected twist to traditional olive-rich dishes.

PARMESAN CHEESE

Take a page from vegan friends and get your hands on nutritional yeast, a deactivated yeast that is sold in health food stores as flakes or in powder form. Sprinkle it on popcorn, mix it into this year's Thanksgiving mash, or knead it right into homemade pizza dough for a familiar zesty kick.

PICKLES

Amazingly, the flavor we associate with pickles is not just salt; it's really the vinegar and strong spices. You can take any quick pickle recipe, lose the salt, and replace it with other flavors, vinegars, and produce to create a low-sodium version of your own with the zing you crave. When the pickles are gone, repurpose the juice in your next vinaigrette, coleslaw, or egg salad.

QUICK PIE CRUSTS

In place of high-sodium prepared pie crusts, simply crumble matzo crackers (or sodium-free cookies) and mix with salt-free butter, sugar, and warm baking spices like cinnamon, pumpkin pie spice, and cardamom. Or make mini tarts shells using coconut flakes (see Macaroon Custard Tarts, page 225). Or savory quiche crusts with grated potatoes (see Mini Hash Brown Quiches, page 208).

SAUSAGE

Simply mix ground meat (turkey, chicken, pork) with salt-free seasonings, form into patties, and brown. Or use aluminum foil to roll the seasoned meat into a sausage shape and then bake and slice. Or skip the shaping and just brown the seasoned meat in a pan and sprinkle on pastas and eggs.

SHREDDED CHEESE

To give your bowl of chili or plate of quesadillas that "stringy cheese" texture, add in grated carrots or zucchini ribbons, or grated butternut squash (see Lemon Chicken Orzo, page 172).

SOUR CREAM AND CREAM CHEESE

Unlike most sour-tasting dairy products, Greek yogurt gives you the tang without the high sodium, averaging 60 mg per 6-oz [170-g] container. It makes a perfect topper for tacos, spread for crackers, or creamy base for dips.

SOY, MISO, AND TERIYAKI SAUCES

A simple mixture of molasses plus rice wine vinegar plus salt-free garlic powder makes a nice stand-in for soy sauce. For a thicker sauce, try adding dark berry jam and/or molasses.

STEAK SAUCE

Make a quick sauce by boiling jam plus salt-free garlic powder and a splash of apple cider vinegar or balsamic vinegar in a saucepan for a few minutes over medium-high heat, stirring constantly. Turn the heat to low, and let the mixture reduce until it reaches a thickness of your liking. Then pour it over steak. You can always add some chopped tomatoes or a little no-salt-added tomato sauce for extra umami.

TOMATO SAUCES

There's good news and great news. The good news? Canned no-salt-added tomato sauce exists and there are many brands to choose from. Puréed pumpkin or sweet potato can be used to add easy and flavorful creaminess to homemade pasta and pizza sauces. The great news? It's easy to give these ready-to-eat sauces some kick with your own herbs and seasonings. Start with a salt-free tomato (or pumpkin) base, and then give it a tasty makeover of your own creation.

DENISE WOODWARD
TALKS TACOS

....

We all have our simple, go-to, weeknight meals; a bowl of rice, a big plate of pasta, an egg frittata with random vegetables in the fridge. While these dishes are easy, eating them over and over again can get pretty boring. It's refreshing to switch things up, not just for your taste buds but for your creativity muscles, too. Which is why these weeknight staples are the perfect canvas for flavor experiments. Each week, you should try something different and unexpected. And to get you started, Denise Woodward of ChezUs.com wants to talk tacos.

Tacos have become a staple in our home because not only are they easy to make but they're as versatile as a recipe can be. All that's required is a creative approach and hungry eaters! I start most of my taco recipes by using fresh, seasonal ingredients along with a basic concept—a protein, some onion, garlic, herbs, and tortillas. The toppings and seasonings are really what makes a taco a totally great taco. Following are a few of our favorite combinations.

BANH MI PORK
Pork tenderloin rubbed down with Chinese five-spice powder, then grilled and sliced, plus shredded napa cabbage, grated carrots, homemade hot sauce, sour cream, and a squeeze of fresh lime juice all served on corn tortillas.

GRILLED LIME CHICKEN
Chicken marinated in fresh lime juice and grilled, diced Fresno chiles, and chopped cilantro, served on corn tortillas with pineapple-corn salsa.

GRILLED SALMON
Salmon fillet strips lightly seasoned with olive oil, lemon zest, and black pepper, then grilled, with diced cherry tomatoes, thinly sliced purple cabbage, and mustard or horseradish-spiked Greek yogurt on flour tortillas.

GREEK STYLE
Browned ground lamb, chopped oregano, diced tomatoes, thinly sliced romaine lettuce, sliced roasted red peppers, and Greek yogurt tzatziki sauce wrapped in a corn tortilla.

VEGETARIAN
Cooked black beans with diced butternut squash, diced jalapeños, cucumber-tomato salsa, and cooling sour cream or yogurt served on corn tortillas.

RECIPE MAKEOVER MAD LIB:
THE CASE OF THE SOS MEATBALLS

If you're nervous about giving recipes a low-so twist, let's practice on paper before heading to the pots and pans.

Remember Mad Libs? The short stories with a handful of adjectives, verbs, and proper nouns missing? Your job was to fill the empty spaces with words of your choosing. It was silly and fun. And it's the perfect way to practice your low-so makeover skills. With salt, spices, and most of the other ingredients missing from the recipe, your job is to fill in the blanks. It's totally okay to be creative. Actually, it's encouraged. So let's give it a go. And when you're finished, you'll have your first low-so recipe to try.

It's 5:30 pm and you just found out that PROPER NAME OF FRIEND is in town and coming over for appetizers and drinks in an hour. With guests! Okay. Breathe. You've got this. Luckily, you already picked up a fresh ½ lb [230 g] of TYPE OF GROUND MEAT from the store on the way home and you also have some fresh TYPE OF HERB from the neighbor's backyard. Everything you need for last-minute meatballs.

How are you going to make this dish sing, and sing fast? Open that fridge! Ah, perfect! You have garlic, onions, and an egg on hand. And there's a bunch of TYPE OF VEGETABLE for added flavor, color, and healthful good stuff. For spices, your cabinet is full of options. Tonight, try something daring, with a dash of TYPE OF SPICE, TYPE OF SPICE, and TYPE OF SPICE. And of course, a few generous grinds of black pepper for good measure.

Now preheat the oven to 400°F [200°C]. Line a large baking sheet with parchment paper for easier cleanup.

Throw three peeled cloves of garlic, a quarter of an onion (roughly chopped), a handful of the herb, and ¼ cup [30 g] of the vegetable (chopped) into the food processor (or blender) and pulse until you get a fine dice. Add ½ cup [55 g] of leftover cooked GRAIN and pulse again until combined. Transfer the mixture to a medium bowl. Then add 1 beaten egg, the ground meat, and the spices. Use your hands to mix everything together. Pinch off some of the meat mixture and roll between your palms, making golf ball–size meatballs (12 to 14). Place them on the prepared baking sheet with some space between them and bake for 20 to 25 minutes, until cooked through and browned. The center of the meatballs should read 160°F [70°C] on a meat thermometer.

But you're not quite finished. You can't serve meatballs without sauce, right? Luckily you have a TYPE OF FRUIT jam in the fridge. Mix ¾ to 1 cup [255 to 340 g] of the fruit jam and 2 Tbsp of SOMETHING WITH BITE, LIKE BALSAMIC VINEGAR, LOW-SODIUM HORSERADISH, OR LOW-SODIUM MUSTARD. Season with some spices and stir until combined. Transfer the sauce to a small pan. Bring to a boil and then turn the heat to medium-low. Cook, stirring frequently, until the sauce starts to thicken, about 10 minutes. Pour the sauce into a few small dipping dishes.

When the meatballs are ready, transfer them to a clean serving dish. Sprinkle with some of the herb for a pop of color. Lay out small plates, toothpicks, napkins, the sauce, and, of course, those drinks.

Ding dong! Pat yourself on the back. Happy hour is ready and your guests have arrived. Now share that terrific dish you created on the fly.

NOTE: Pescatarians, use ½ lb [230 g] cooked fish in place of the ground meat. Use two forks to break the fish apart into small flakes and use as you would the ground meat. Vegetarians, use 1 cup [260 g] no-salt-added, ready-to-eat beans. Drain the beans and pulse in a food processor until chopped and chunky. Use the beans as you would the ground meat.

SALT-FREE BACON

As one blog reader put it, this is the Holy Grail of low-sodium cooking. To get your meat bacon-thin, ask your butcher to slice the pork belly for you or look for pre-sliced pork belly (it may be called "shabu-shabu pork") often found at Asian grocery stores. You can also try cutting your own: Chill the pork belly in the freezer until firm (not frozen), about 20 minutes, and use a sharp knife to cut thin strips ⅛ in [4 cm] thick.

You can find liquid smoke at your grocery store, or substitute a mixture of 2 tsp molasses, 2 tsp apple cider vinegar, and 1 pinch of smoked paprika.

MAKES 16 TO 18 BACON SLICES   **TIME** 1 HOUR, 30 MINUTES

1 lb [455 g] pork belly, sliced ⅛ in [4 mm] thick

2 Tbsp plus 2 tsp maple syrup

4 tsp liquid smoke

2 tsp smoked paprika

1 tsp ground cumin

1 to 2 tsp freshly ground black pepper

Preheat the oven to 200°F [95°C]. Cover two or three baking pans with aluminum foil and put wire cooling racks on top. Line a plate with paper towels and set aside.

Use kitchen shears (or a very sharp knife) to remove the top, thick layer of skin on the pork belly. (Whether you buy whole or sliced pork belly, it usually still has a layer of skin on it.)

Place the pork belly slices on the racks in the prepared baking pans, being careful not to crowd.

In a small bowl, stir together the maple syrup and liquid smoke. In a separate bowl, combine the paprika, cumin, and pepper. Using a pastry brush, coat both sides of the pork belly slices with the maple syrup mixture. Sprinkle the spice mixture on one side of the slices. Roast for 1 hour.

In a large skillet, fry a few bacon slices at a time over medium-high heat until they start to look crispy, about 2 minutes on each side. Using tongs, remove the bacon from the skillet and place on the prepared plate. Repeat until all the bacon is fried. Drain the fat from the skillet as needed between batches. Serve immediately, or store in an airtight container in the refrigerator for up to 5 days or in the freezer for up to 3 months.

CHICKPEA-FLOUR PIZZA

MAKES ONE 10-IN [25-CM] PIZZA   **TIME** 25 MINUTES

1 cup [100 g] chickpea (a.k.a. garbanzo bean) flour

½ to 1 cup [120 to 240 ml] warm water

2 Tbsp chopped fresh herbs (rosemary, cilantro, parsley, or dill)

¼ tsp salt-free garlic powder

¼ tsp freshly ground black pepper

2 tsp olive oil or vegetable oil

SPREAD
HARISSA HOT SAUCE (PAGE 164), ROASTED FIG AND TOMATO SLOW JAM (PAGE 162), FLATBREAD SPREADS (SEE PAGES 259–260)

EXTRA TOPPINGS
FRESH HERBS, RAW CORN KERNELS, COOKED SLICED ONIONS, BROWNED MUSHROOMS

In a medium bowl, using a silicone spatula or wooden spoon, mix the chickpea flour with ½ cup [120 ml] of the warm water, the herbs, garlic powder, and pepper. Slowly add an additional ¼ to ½ cup [60 to 120 ml] water and stir until you have a thick, pancake-like batter. Let sit for 10 minutes.

Preheat the broiler.

If the batter has thickened too much, add a little water to restore the pancake batter consistency.

In a 10-in [25-cm] ovenproof sauté pan or skillet, heat the olive oil over medium-high heat. Pour the batter into the pan and use a clean silicone spatula to spread out to the edge. Cook for 2 to 3 minutes, until the edge begins to brown. Place the pan on the middle rack in the oven and broil for 4 to 5 minutes, until golden brown and set.

Using oven mitts, carefully remove the pan. Spread your chosen spread and extra toppings onto the pizza crust. Return to the oven for 2 to 3 minutes longer, until the toppings are warmed through. Slice and serve.

GABY DALKIN
TALKS AVOCADOS

....

*She may not be on a low-sodium diet, but Gaby Dalkin, founder of
WhatsGabyCooking.com and author of Absolutely Avocados, is an expert
when it comes to awesome food substitutions—of the avocado persuasion.
Turns out, avocados make the perfect swap for certain high-sodium ingredients
and add an element of surprise to simple recipes (like baked goods and even drinks).
So read these avocado tips, use them as a lesson in ingredient potential,
and start seeing your favorite green fruit in a whole new light.*

I've been obsessed with avocados for as long as I can remember. They are hands down one of my favorite things to eat, plus they are loaded with tons of vitamins and minerals and healthful fats that our bodies crave. Ever since writing a cookbook featuring this superfood, I've been using avocados in fun ways to jazz up my meals.

+ **First:** Avocados can be used in place of butter when it comes to baking! Sounds crazy, right? It's not! It's so good and it adds an extra-creamy consistency to whatever you're making.

+ **Second:** Forget the mayo. Replace it with some mashed-up avocado to make a seriously healthful swap. Plus you're adding extra flavor to your sandwich or wrap.

+ **Third:** Use it in a salad dressing. Do you love that creamy consistency of ranch or Caesar dressing? Use avocado to make a creamy vinaigrette, and I promise you'll never miss the store-bought bottled stuff.

+ **And last, but certainly not least:** Use it in smoothies. Avocados lend themselves well to smoothies because they'll take on the flavor of whatever fruits you're using and give you that smooth texture you want.

Bottom line is, avocados are awesome in pretty much anything, even chocolate chip cookies.

GARDENING: THE ULTIMATE DIY

One of the ultimate taste enhancers doesn't come from a bottle or your refrigerator or even the grill. It comes from your own two hands. When you've rolled up those sleeves, put time and energy into making something not just from scratch but from seed, the final product will prove infinitely more enjoyable than anything from plastic wrap or a microwave oven.

Having a garden, of any shape or type, is an awesome addition to your low-sodium tool kit. Before you can say, "But I don't have room for a garden!" let me say this: Even if you only have space for a small herb plant on your windowsill, adding a pinch of basil that you grew will add a pinch of pride to every bite. It's worth it. Plus, the next time you attend a party, skip the flowers and give the host or hostess a colorful bouquet of chard or carrots or anythig fresh from your garden. Now *that's* impressive. Get ready to not just make your own food, but grow it too. And make the most of what Mama Nature provides.

To make more of your space:

+ Consult gardening books and websites for easy solutions for growing edibles almost anywhere.

+ Consult location and seasonal guides so that you plant appropriate herbs and vegetables for your region.

+ Sign up for a community garden plot or volunteer at local and urban farms.

+ Create a garden exchange with neighbors, with each of you planting something different.

···6···

DINE

Eating Well Beyond Your Stove

We don't just eat because food tastes good, we eat because of the social fun that comes with Sunday brunches, Happy Hour gatherings, and romantic evenings spent sharing the same spaghetti noodle.

For anyone with special diet needs, these eating experiences and dining outside the home pose all sorts of new challenges. Mealtime no longer just involves picking the right spice blends or the right ingredients. It means picking the right restaurant, the right menu, and the right approach to ordering. Oh, and maybe the right date partner, too.

Sound overwhelming? Well, just like when you dine by yourself or in your home, by having some creative tools in your pocket (literally) and solid knowledge in your head, you can successfully order out and make memories at tables besides your own. In other words, you will be able to enjoy the social fun of food without always hosting the party or opening your own restaurant.

RESTAURANT RULES + TOOLS

Being able to eat out safely is an essential part of enjoying a low-so life. Both on my blog and in my first book, I outline the basic dining rules that help you avoid high-sodium meals and form great relationships with your favorite restaurants—communication and gratitude are key!

But what about when you want to be spontaneous? When you make last-minute reservations or end up at a restaurant of someone else's choosing, with no time to research or call ahead? With the following tips, it's completely possible to expand your eating experiences and take dining risks, all while staying low-so.

CARRY YOUR CARD

When I land unexpectedly at a restaurant, it can be nerve-racking for both me and the unprepared chef. But by having a small, laminated dietary card in my bag at all times, I am able to eat low-so and on-the-fly. Even without calling ahead, this card lets me give the kitchen all the information they need to feel inspired instead of scared. It is divided into two sections, what to avoid and what to use. It also includes my other personal food needs (I am allergic to salmon and nuts). By handing it to the waiter, I can order effortlessly and pass on my food needs to the chef without any misunderstandings or mistranslations.

USE OPENTABLE.COM

This website lets you make reservations online as well as read reviews and peruse menus. It also lets you save your list of dietary needs in your account. That way, when you book a table last minute, your virtual dietary card will be automatically passed on to the staff, so they know how to best prepare for your arrival, even if that's happening in 30 minutes.

BE DARING

Even when low-so dining seems impossible, creativity plus determination equals possibilities. So when you do end up unexpectedly at, say, a pizza restaurant with friends, don't settle for a glass of water. Ask to speak with the manager. Explain your situation and your dietary needs, and see what he or she can do for you. Who knows—your low-so dish may be so good that it ends up on the menu. The same rules apply for restaurants where communication can be difficult. If you have a friend with you who speaks the language, great. If not, use the technology tips on page 139 and let your phone translate your dietary card, ask questions about the menu, and order for you.

FRESH IS BEST

If you do have a choice between grabbing a meal at a fast-food joint or a sit-down restaurant, go with the second option. A restaurant that cooks-to-order will more likely have fresh ingredients on hand and be able to prepare a low-sodium dish. However, be aware that even "nice" restaurants may use sodium-filled packaged vegetables and legumes such as beans, corn, tomatoes, and spinach, especially when the ingredients are not in season. Always ask a server if vegetables are fresh or from a package or can. And remember best bets for unsalted food or easily adjusted dishes usually include:

+ Vegetable-heavy salads (ask for dressing on the side)

+ Eggs, made to order (try fried, scrambled, or poached)

+ Fresh fish (not breaded or seasoned)

+ Steaks (unseasoned and not pre-marinated)

+ Pasta (cooked in unsalted water)

+ Fresh vegetables (grilled, steamed, or sautéed)

CHECK YELP

Filled with user-generated reviews, this website helps you discover which restaurants will be flexible and friendly when it comes to your dietary needs. Use keywords like "low-sodium" or "allergy," and "accommodating" to search for restaurants willing to make special changes for you.

TAKE OVER THE KITCHEN

Not literally, of course. But with your cooking know-how, you can convert any menu options from none to not-too-shabby. For example, let's say, at first glance, it seems you can only eat a simple green salad. But using your own creativity, you may be able to customize that lettuce with other flavor-packed ingredients found on the menu (citrus, avocado) or textural additions (poached egg, nuts). Think of the menu as a key to what they have available in the kitchen.

TRAVEL SPICE

Pack a little flavor in your bag. Put a mixture of your favorite basic spices/herbs in a spice jar and keep it with you. That way, you can enhance even the simplest meal.

PULL THE ALARM

Sometimes even with all your low-so tricks and communication skills, you may be served food that tastes salty. Don't eat it out of embarrassment or to be polite. Put the fork down, and have a friend give it a taste. If it's agreed the order just doesn't seem right, send it back. Honestly, it's better to be upfront, get something you can eat, and deal with a potentially disgruntled waiter than to have health complications.

BEYOND THE TABLE

There are endless ways to have memorable food experiences besides dining at a restaurant or a friend's house. If you want to be spontaneous but skip the restaurant, go on a farm tour or a berry-picking adventure, or set aside an afternoon to stroll around a local farmers' market selecting foods for lunch or dinner at home. These activities will make the before-dinner prep work the best part of the meal.

MENU IQ

Whether you make a reservation ahead of time or find a spot last-minute, you must understand the words on a menu to make smart, low-so dining choices. And while you may have mastered the more obvious salty keywords—like *brined*, *cured*, and *pickled*—use this list to avoid less-common, trickier terminology. Remember, anytime you come across something unfamiliar, just ask your waiter for more information. The more you understand professional cooking lingo, the more sodium-savvy you will be.

AU GRATIN This term refers to a baked dish (most famously with potatoes) that is traditionally topped with seasoned bread crumbs and cheese.

BATTERED AND BREADED These terms usually mean ingredients have been coated in bread crumbs or a batter, which most likely has been salted and seasoned.

BLACKENED OR CRUSTED These terms usually refer to a (typically salty) spice blend that gets rubbed on fish or meat before being cooked.

CHARCUTERIE This refers to cured, smoked, and preserved meats as well as sausages.

CONFIT This is a culinary technique in which meat is cooked and preserved in its own fat. The process often begins by seasoning the meat with salt.

EN CROUTE Here, an ingredient (such as salmon) will get wrapped and baked in a pastry crust, which often contains the hidden sodium.

FLEUR DE SEL This is a very rare, expensive, fancy sea salt.

FRICO This is a cracker made from baked Parmesan.

JUS A sauce that often accompanies meat (or meaty sandwiches) made from pan drippings that get deglazed with (most likely salted) stock.

MARINATED This term means the ingredients—meats or vegetables—have previously been soaked in a seasoned liquid.

ROE Hard or soft, black and red, roe refers to tiny fish eggs. Although raw roe is quite low in sodium (26 mg sodium per 1 oz [30 g]), most roe gets salted, including the more familiar caviar.

SALATA This is the Italian word for "salted."

TAPENADE This paste-like spread usually contains pureed or finely chopped olives, capers, and sometimes anchovies, as well as salt.

SPECIAL-DIET DATING

Dining out on first dates can present anxieties: What should I wear? Where will we go? And if you're on a special diet, there's one more consideration: How and when will you tell your date about your food needs?

I won't pretend that this subject isn't a big deal. And bringing up your special diet at a first meal together can mean getting into deeper topics. Like everything else with a special diet, it took time (and many dates) to learn how to date *with* dietary needs. I quickly found out, though, that by being honest, I didn't scare my suitors away. It forced me to be authentic, which is, no doubt, essential for building a relationship.

Eventually, I made my dietary needs a part of the first meeting. I figured, if someone couldn't handle it, no worries, on to the next one. But if they could, what better indicator of a good teammate for dates (and dinners) to come. For dinner-dating stumbling blocks, I simply knocked them down with these solutions, one at a time.

PICK THE RESTAURANT

Make a list of all the spots that will serve you and serve you well. When choosing a place to meet, take charge and book a reservation at one of your fail-safe spots—it's a sign of independence.

ORDER SMART

Use that trusty laminated dietary card for a smooth ordering experience as well as to demonstrate your ingenuity.

SPILL THE BEANS

Don't shy away from discussing food needs or health issues. Show off your strength and bravery. Use this opportunity to start teaching your date about your low-so life and expertise.

MAKE A DATE

Plan a "practice" dinner date with a friend or a loved one, and invite your special diet to come along. The more you make your food needs part of your meals and your relationships, the more second nature it will become. And the better you'll eat, love, and be loved.

PLAY CHEF

Sometimes it's easiest to skip the reservation and bring the restaurant home, with you and your date as the chefs. First, choose a recipe (or two!) to cook together; something hands-on such as Broccoli Gnocchi with Lemon Cream Sauce (page 235) or Baked Dim Sum Dumplings (page 231) will provide entertainment, interaction, and potential for adorable flour fights. Then, head to the store or market to gather ingredients. Put on some music, pour some wine (or mock-tails), and see what kind of wonderful magic (and dumplings) you two can make.

ALEJANDRO FOUNG
TALKS FIRST DATES

....

I once met a boy named Alejandro. According to his mother, he'd always been a self-proclaimed "trier of new things." Which was really good for me. Because, very quickly, I fell in love with this boy. And even though my health and dietary needs posed challenges, by being honest (and enthusiastic) with him from the start, he adopted a similar attitude and approach to my low-sodium life. He saw all obstacles as opportunities to think beyond limits, get creative, and simply try new things.

I remember pretty clearly the first time I learned about Jess's dietary restrictions. It happened while sitting in a park on our first date and she told me about her salt-free needs. After returning home and reflecting on what I was going to do for a second date, my first thought was, "Jeez, this is going to be difficult. If I can't eat with her, what am I going to do with this girl?" But I put on my thinking cap and got to work. Step One was embracing the challenge head-on. I decided to cook. I planned a quick meal at home—chicken thighs with yellow curry and pepper, a side of bok choy, a drizzle of sesame oil—followed by a game of Scrabble. Although I lost at Scrabble, I sure won with the easy home-cooked meal.

Even though the dinner was simple, we were both impressed that with the right ingredients, two spices, and sesame oil, we could create something delicious and salt-free. And since that first meal together, I have fallen deeply in love with salt-free flavors (and Jess). Eight years later, I've noticed my palate has greatly expanded and I pick up on far more nuanced flavors in my food.

While I still enjoy a good higher-sodium meal, like dim sum, cheese plates, and chorizo, I would never go back to my heavy-handed days of salting everything and anything without a thought. In fact, I'm still working on the same carton of kosher salt from 2007. Much like I hope you find with this book, in meeting Jess, I discovered a new and greater sense of taste.

GUEST BEST PRACTICES

Potlucks, picnics, and dinner parties—people love a good excuse to gather around food. But if this scenario causes you worry, consider this: It's your perfect opportunity to not only involve friends in your special diet, but also to show them just how flavorful low-sodium food can be. Depending on your relationship with the host or hostess, following are some ideas for how you could do just that.

TIPS APPRECIATED

Your relatives and best friends most likely already know about your dietary needs and may even be eager to try their hand at making special food for you. When you send that RSVP, ask if you can bring a dish or two. If they want to make everything themselves, including a meal for you, offer to help by sending recipe suggestions and other low-sodium resources.

SPECIAL DELIVERY

For the host and hostess who wish to prepare a low-sodium meal, give them a bit of help by bringing special low-sodium products with you or by sending them ahead with the help of one of the many grocery delivery services available (see page 137).

TAKE A COURSE

To avoid having the busy host or hostess make an entire special meal for you, offer to bring a few smaller dishes. Easily transportable low-sodium appetizers and family-style sides will not only fill you up but will taste equally delicious to others. May I suggest bringing Hickory-Smoked Fish Spread (page 228), one of the Kale Salads for Different Seasons (page 182), or Cardamon Cake with Coconut Whipped Cream (page 193) to your next friendly gathering?

FILL YOUR PLATE

If you hate feeling left out or like a nuisance, coordinate with the host or hostess to find out what's on the menu. Then make your own low-sodium version to bring with you. When it is dinnertime, ask for an empty plate, fill it with your food, and eat with everyone else.

GIVE A GIFT

For those events when you don't know the host or hostess very well, bring along an edible gift, like a jar of Toasted Pepita Mix (page 176), Pickled Cherries (page 249), Date Caramels with Crunchy Chocolate Coating (page 205), or Avocado Green Goddess Dressing (page 168) and a basket of fresh vegetables from your D.I.Y. garden. Everyone loves food gifts. Then, when they put your gift out for everyone to enjoy, you'll get a guaranteed low-sodium bite to eat.

··· 7 ···

GO

Making Meals Work
When at Work

You've got big things to do, big people to meet, big adventures to undertake. As soon as you walk out the door every morning, you're on the move. While that busy calendar makes life exciting, it also poses a bit of a challenge for your low-sodium diet: How do you stay satisfied and low-so while on the go?

With a little prep and creativity, your food routine and an active lifestyle don't have to conflict. Quick breakfasts, work lunches, and emergency snacks can all be eaten and enjoyed on a low-sodium diet, and made in as much time as it takes to get your morning coffee or afternoon takeout. There's no need to cheat on your low-sodium ways or, worse yet, wake up an hour early to make lunch every day.

MORNING MEALS

Breakfast may be the most important meal of the day, but it can also quickly tip the sodium scale. With more than 500 mg of sodium, a single bagel can equal one-third of the recommended daily sodium intake. And that's not counting the cream cheese (120 mg of sodium per 2 Tbsp), smoked salmon lox (over 500 mg of sodium per 1 oz [30 g]), or nonfat latte (yes, milk contains more than 100 mg of sodium per 1 cup [240 ml]).

But that doesn't mean you should skip breakfast or start grinding your own sausage meat every morning (although that would be all sorts of amazing). By ditching the processed treats—muffins, microwave oatmeal, breakfast energy bars—and replacing them with fresh whole ingredients or homemade versions, it's easy to fuel up on good food while cutting back on the sodium. Here are some ideas.

YOGURT

Ranging from 0 to 100 mg of sodium per 6-oz [170-g] serving, depending on brand and type, yogurt makes a great canvas for low-sodium morning snacks. Plus, it's portable (throw a container into your work bag), storable (keep a few in the refrigerator at work), and found almost anywhere you go (airports, drugstores, gas stations).

With simple additions, transform your yogurt from sweet to savory and keep your taste buds surprised throughout the week. Yogurt can be eaten all day long, as a spread on low-sodium crackers or bread, a dip for vegetables, and a dressing for salads. Use the following suggestions for your yogurt snack bags. Then mix up creations at home, on the bus, or at your desk.

MEDITERRANEAN MORNING:

Plain Greek yogurt + dill (fresh or dry) + shredded cucumbers

THE TROPICS:

Plain coconut yogurt + toasted coconut + chai spice

CARROT CAKE:

Lemon soy yogurt + shredded carrots + raisins + pepitas + cinnamon

COCOA NUTS:

Plain soy yogurt + peanut or sunflower butter + low-sodium chocolate chips

MATZO AND RICE CRACKERS

If you want to bite into something, skip the high-sodium bagels and breads and reach for lower-sodium options like matzo and rice crackers. Top them with something sweet (yogurt, honey, nut or seed butters) or something savory (egg salad, hummus, guacamole), and get the crunch you're looking for.

BREAKFAST TORTILLAS

Corn tortillas are a major low-sodium staple in my house. They provide a sturdy foundation for quick snacks to bigger meals, like tacos. For breakfast, they make a great bread substitute for morning treats, especially if you're a fan of avocado toast. Use them cold or crisp them with a quick toast in a hot pan or 1 minute in the microwave. Then fill with one of the following spreads for a substantial wake-up call.

GOT A SECOND:
Toasted tortilla + half avocado, mashed and spread + red pepper flakes + fried egg

GOT TO RUN:
Toasted tortilla + half avocado, sliced + yogurt + red pepper flakes

GOT TO GREEN:
Toasted tortilla + half avocado, mashed and spread + shaved zucchini + red pepper flakes

OATMEAL

I grew up on instant-oatmeal packages. As simple as rip, heat, and eat, the hardest part of breakfast was deciding whether I wanted berry or maple flavor. But the flavored versions in these packages tend to be high in sodium—one packet of a common brand of Cinnamon Spice has 250 mg per serving. So let's make our own instant oatmeal instead. It's as easy as bag it, microwave it, and devour it. And you can always prepare a big batch on Sunday and store it in canning jars or airtight plastic bags for the week ahead.

Start with DIY Oatmeal on page 111 (or you can buy premade, plain, no-sodium-added oatmeal) and then experiment with flavor combinations of your own, using the suggested additions for inspiration. You have countless ingredients to choose from. You can also add a splash of coconut milk or a dollop of yogurt (Greek, soy, or coconut milk–based) for extra creaminess and flavor.

CHIA SEEDS

Remember Chia Pets? Those ceramic sculptures of dogs and other animals that sprouted green hair? Well, the little seeds responsible for the grassy hair are also filled with major nutrients, like healthful omega-3 fats, fiber, and manganese, as well as phosphorous, protein, and tryptophan (think Thanksgiving turkey coma), so they may help improve your blood pressure and regulate appetite and sleep. These are just a few of the reasons these little seeds have gone from white elephant gift status to superfood stardom.

To get some chia in your diet, start with the white or black seeds (of good quality) and sprinkle them in smoothies, oatmeal, or fruit juice, or mix with jam before spreading on toasted no-salt-added bread or corn tortillas—because they don't have to be ground for you to eat them. My favorite feature of chia seeds is that, when mixed with a liquid like coconut milk and a few other ingredients, they plump up and transform into a gelled, pudding-like snack.

Using a simple equation (1 cup [240 ml] liquid plus 3 Tbsp chia seeds plus spices), you can experiment with a range of flavors—chocolate yogurt, matcha green tea, or even carrot juice—as well as textural additions—crushed nuts, toasted coconut, fresh fruit, or chocolate chips. And remember to pack chia seeds when you travel. Just mix them with yogurt and jam and keep in the mini fridge overnight for an energy-packed snack the next day. See the two chia pudding recipes on page 112 to get you started.

MUFFIN TINS

As we have learned, bread and bready goods are on the CDC's sodium "watch" list. Whether you grab a croissant (with more than 300 mg of sodium per large croissant) or an oat bran muffin (with more than 550 mg of sodium per large muffin), these convenient morning treats can easily equal one-fourth to one-half of the day's 1,500 mg allotment.

Instead of opening your own bakery, just purchase a standard muffin tin. By mixing a few basic ingredients in a bowl, your trusty muffin tin and your oven will do the rest of the work, baking everything from ranch cornmeal muffins to Mini Hash Brown Quiches (page 208) to anything else you dream up. These will keep you satisfied throughout the week without the extra sodium. So make a few batches of morning treats in your muffin tin to grab on your way out the door.

MUGS AND MICROWAVES

For instant gratification, all you need is a microwave-proof coffee mug and some (salt-free) prepackaged ingredients. Then you can make scrambled eggs, banana bread, and even coffee cake from the comfort of your office kitchen. The mug will be hot (really hot, so use oven mitts or a thick towel to take it out of the microwave, and let it cool off), but it will be ready and on your desk in less than 10 minutes. Check out the Internet for some fun microwave and "food in a mug" recipes. See pages 112 and 114 for three of my favorites.

DIY OATMEAL

MAKES 5 SERVINGS   **TIME** 15 MINUTES

3 cups [240 g] quick-cooking oats

SUGGESTED ADDITIONS

Banana Bread: Salt-free
walnuts + banana slices +
honey + cinnamon + yogurt

Cookie Break: Dried cranberries +
chocolate chips + brown sugar +
candied ginger

Japanese Breakfast: Fresh, sliced
shiitake mushrooms + nori strips +
sesame seeds + sliced green onion
+ poached or hard-boiled egg

PB&J: Salt-free peanuts +
honey + fresh berries

Trail Mix: Salt-free cashews + raisins
+ dried cherries + brown sugar

Tropical Sunrise: Toasted
coconut flakes + coconut milk
+ salt-free macadamia nuts +
dried mango or pineapple

Preheat the oven to 350°F [180°C].

Spread the oats in a large baking pan. Toast for 3 to 5 minutes, until the oats start to turn golden. Transfer 1 cup [80 g] of the toasted oats to a food processor (or blender) and blend into a fine powder. In a large bowl, mix the powdered oats with the remaining 2 cups [160 g] whole oats. Divide among five jars or plastic bags (about ½ cup [55 g] each).

To cook, combine ¾ cup [180 ml] water with one ½-cup [55-g] portion of oatmeal in a microwave-safe bowl and heat for 1 minute in the microwave. Or add boiling water to the oatmeal in the bowl, cover, and let sit for 3 minutes. Mix in your choice of additions, and eat.

BANANA CHAI-CHIA PUDDING

SERVES 2   TIME 20 MINUTES, PLUS TIME IN THE REFRIGERATOR

1½ cups [360 ml] unsweetened coconut milk

1 chai tea bag

½ ripe banana

1 tsp vanilla or almond extract

1 tsp sugar

¼ tsp ground cinnamon

3 Tbsp chia seeds

In a small saucepan over medium heat, bring the coconut milk to a simmer and cook for 2 minutes. Take the pan off the heat, add the tea bag, and let steep for 15 minutes. Squeeze the tea bag into the milk and discard the tea bag. Pour the chai coconut milk into a blender. Add the banana, vanilla, sugar, and cinnamon and blend until smooth.

Transfer the mixture to a 2-cup [480-ml], spill-free glass or plastic container. Add the chia seeds and stir to combine. Let the mixture sit for 15 minutes. Stir again. Cover and put the chia mixture in the refrigerator for 2 hours, or up to overnight, before serving.

MINT CHIP-CHIA PUDDING

SERVES 2   TIME 20 MINUTES, PLUS TIME IN THE REFRIGERATOR

¼ cup [7 g] fresh mint leaves

2 tsp sugar

¼ cup [45 g] chocolate chips

1½ cups [360 ml] unsweetened coconut milk

1 tsp vanilla or almond extract

3 Tbsp chia seeds

Put the mint leaves and sugar in a food processor (or blender). Pulse a few times until you have finely ground mint sugar. Add the chocolate chips and pulse again until the chips are roughly chopped.

Transfer the mixture to a 2-cup [480-ml], spill-free glass or plastic container. Add the coconut milk, vanilla, and chia seeds and stir to combine. Let the mixture sit for 15 minutes. Stir again. Cover and put the chia mixture in the refrigerator for 2 hours, or up to overnight, before serving.

MICROWAVE TOSTADA

SERVES 1   **TIME** 5 MINUTES

One 6-in [15-cm] corn tortilla

½ cup [130 g] no-salt-added canned black or pinto beans, rinsed and drained

¼ tsp salt-free garlic powder

¼ tsp ground cumin

¼ tsp salt-free chili powder or red pepper flakes

½ avocado, mashed

2 dollops plain Greek yogurt

1 sprig fresh cilantro, chopped

1 lime wedge

Place the tortilla on a microwave-safe plate and microwave at full power for 1 minute. Flip the tortilla and heat for another 30 seconds. Let cool—it will crisp up as it rests.

In a bowl, mix together the beans, garlic powder, cumin, and chili powder.

Top the tortilla with the bean mixture, avocado, and yogurt. Sprinkle with the cilantro and spritz with the lime before eating.

VARIATIONS: You can use white beans, chopped fresh tomatoes, and shaved zucchini for a Greek tostada. Or go sweet with a mashed banana, yogurt, and a sprinkle of cinnamon and sugar for a churro tostada.

MICROWAVE BANANA BREAD

SERVES 1　**TIME** 10 MINUTES, INCLUDING COOLING

¼ cup [30 g] all-purpose flour

2 Tbsp granulated or brown sugar

¼ tsp ground cinnamon

¼ tsp sodium-free baking soda

⅛ tsp sodium-free baking powder

1 large very ripe banana

2 to 3 Tbsp dried cherries or raisins

1 to 2 Tbsp unsweetened coconut milk or water

Coat the interior of a microwave-safe mug with nonstick cooking spray. Add the flour, sugar, cinnamon, baking soda, and baking powder and stir with a fork. Add the banana, mash it, and stir the mixture until combined like batter. Add the cherries and coconut milk.

Microwave for 2 minutes. Check to see if it is done by sticking a knife into the center. If the knife looks clean when you pull it out, the bread is ready. If not, continue to microwave in 30-second increments until cooked through.

Using oven mitts, remove the hot mug from the microwave. The inside of the banana bread will be hotter than the outside, so let cool for 3 to 5 minutes. Then grab a spoon and enjoy, straight from the mug.

VARIATIONS: Switch things up. Add shredded carrots, zucchini, or chopped salt-free nuts. Or go savory by ditching the banana, dried fruit, and coconut milk and substituting 1 avocado and some of the spices from the Everything Waffles (page 211), like caraway seeds, poppy seeds, dried onion flakes, and salt-free garlic powder.

WORK LUNCH

When I worked in an office, I usually brought my lunch with me. Grabbing a quick sandwich or bowl of soup at a café meant way too much sodium for my diet. I often used leftovers to get me through the day. While eating something twice can be nice, it can also get boring. So here are some other lunch ideas that take very little time to prepare, whether you do the work on the weekend, the night before, or as you leave in the morning.

REFRIGERATOR SALAD BAR

Armed with lots of fresh ingredients and a few spill-proof containers or canning jars, it's easy to set up a salad bar in your home or office refrigerator. With leafy greens, raw vegetables, cooked grains, an assortment of proteins, and textural additions, you can quickly mix up ingredients throughout the week. To be time efficient, do the basic prep work on the weekend and remember to go bigger at dinner so you have leftovers for lunch—like adding a little extra pasta to the pot, buying a slightly larger roast beef, and boiling a half dozen eggs rather than just two or three.

Purchase bento boxes or other airtight containers. Get spill-free jars for your dressings. Use the following ideas to get your salad bar started. Then get to mixing and matching, and making lunch low-so easy.

THE GRAINS (make extra for dinner to use for lunch)

+ Cooked couscous

+ Cooked no-salt-added rice or pasta noodles

+ Cooked quinoa

+ Cooked rice (brown, white, black, mixed); you'll find no-salt-added microwave rice, too

THE PROTEINS (keep it simple with canned beans or go big with pulled pork)

+ Canned, no-salt-added beans (add your own salt-free spices)

+ Cooked lentils (make from dried lentils at home and add salt-free spices)

+ Corn-Broccoli Burgers (page 201)

+ Curry Tofu Fries (page 217)

+ Firefly Falafel with Herb Yogurt (page 147)

+ Hard-boiled eggs (see page 166)

+ Hickory-Smoked Fish Spread (page 228)

+ No-salt-added deli meat

+ Quickie Shredded Chicken (page 117)

+ Roast Beef and Mustard Seed Carrots (page 189)

+ Speedy Five-Spice Pulled Pork (page 118)

+ Sunday Chicken with Roasted Roots and Fruits (page 223)

THE VEGETABLES (cut down on time by cutting veggies into small bits or thin slices, and enjoy them raw)

+ Broccoli stem slaw (find it packaged or make your own)

+ Finely chopped or sliced kale

+ Grated, raw zucchini and carrots

+ Leafy lettuces

+ Peas, edamame, and corn kernels (fresh or frozen, thawed)

+ Peeled and sliced or diced cucumbers

+ Riced broccoli and cauliflower (florets finely chopped)

+ Shaved Brussels sprouts

THE FRUIT (because they belong in salads, too)

+ Cherry tomatoes

+ Cubed papaya

+ Fresh berries

+ Pomegranate seeds

+ Sliced avocado

+ Sliced mango

THE DRESSINGS (make a few to use throughout the week)

+ Avocado Green Goddess Dressing (page 168)

+ Peach-Jalapeño Sauce (see page 255)

+ Lemon Tahini Dressing (page 170)

+ The MacGyver Vinaigrette (page 119)

+ Sauce Gribiche (page 166)

+ Carrot–Sweet Onion Dressing (page 169)

THE EXTRAS (because a little bit of color, surprise flavors, and texture make a salad better)

+ Chili Polenta Fries (page 216)

+ Cubed jicama or Dill Oil Jicama "Fries" (page 217)

+ Dukka Spice Mix (page 188)

+ Fresh berries

+ Fresh herbs

+ Lime or lemon wedges

+ Oven-roasted chickpeas

+ Salt-Free Bacon (page 93), crumbled into bits

+ Toasted coconut

+ Toasted Pepita Mix (page 176)

+ Toasted unsalted nuts or seeds

+ Whole seeds, like caraway, coriander, mustard, and celery

QUICKIE SHREDDED CHICKEN

You can replace the spices in this recipe with 2 Tbsp of any salt-free spices or blends. You can also add some salad dressing or Roasted Fig and Tomato Slow Jam (page 162) for extra flavor. Be sure to save the leftover cooking liquid to use like broth in a pot of beans, stew, or rice to be made later in the week.

MAKES 4 SERVINGS   **TIME** 30 MINUTES

2 tsp ground cumin

2 tsp sweet paprika

½ tsp salt-free garlic powder

½ tsp ground mustard

½ tsp salt-free chili powder or red pepper flakes

¼ cup [60 ml] orange juice

¼ cup [60 ml] no-salt-added tomato purée or apricot jam

2 Tbsp apple cider vinegar

1¼ lb [570 g] boneless, skinless chicken breasts or thighs

In a small bowl, stir together the cumin, paprika, garlic powder, mustard, and chili powder. Set aside.

In a large lidded saucepan or Dutch oven over medium-high heat, add the orange juice, tomato purée, vinegar, and half of the spice mixture and stir to combine. Add the chicken and enough water to cover. Cover the pan, bring to a boil, and cook for 5 minutes. Turn the heat to low and simmer, with the pan covered, until the chicken easily pulls apart with the tug of two forks, 18 to 20 minutes.

Transfer the chicken to a medium bowl and use the two forks to shred the meat. Add in the remaining spice mixture and ½ cup [120 ml] of the cooking liquid and use a fork to mix.

Store in an airtight container in the refrigerator for up to 4 days.

SPEEDY FIVE-SPICE PULLED PORK

Braising small pieces of pork takes the meat to tender quickly, making this recipe a go-to for weeknights when you crave big flavor.

MAKES 4 SERVINGS   **TIME** 1 HOUR

1 Tbsp vegetable oil

½ small yellow onion, diced

1 lb [455 g] pork tenderloin, fat trimmed and cut into 4 equal pieces

1 tsp salt-free Chinese five-spice powder

½ tsp salt-free garlic powder

¼ tsp freshly ground black pepper

1½ cups [360 ml] water

¼ cup [60 ml] apple cider vinegar

1 Tbsp apricot jam

1 tsp honey

In a medium heavy-bottomed lidded saucepan or Dutch oven over medium-high heat, warm the vegetable oil. Add the onion and pork and cook, stirring the onion frequently and turning the pork pieces, until the meat is browned on both sides, about 5 minutes.

In a small bowl, add the five-spice powder, garlic powder, pepper, water, vinegar, apricot jam, and honey and stir to combine. Add the mixture to the pan, bring to a boil, and cook for 5 minutes. Cover the pan, turn the heat to medium-low, and braise until you can pull the pork apart with two forks, about 30 minutes.

Transfer the pork to a medium bowl and leave the pan of cooking liquid on the stove uncovered over medium-low heat. Use the two forks to shred the pork. Add the pork back to the pan and let the liquid reduce, stirring occasionally, for 12 to 15 minutes.

Store in an airtight container in the refrigerator for up to 4 days.

THE MACGYVER VINAIGRETTE

Sometimes the only thing you can find to eat while dining out is a salad. A plain, dressingless, boring salad. But hold on to your fork for a moment. Because those greens need not go bare. Dress them with an impressive vinaigrette made from simple ingredients you can find pretty much anywhere—from hospital cafeterias to airports to food courts to any establishment that serves food. Which is why I call it the MacGyver Vinaigrette. That dude could seriously make anything from nothing, and you can, too.

The math for the MacGyver Vinaigrette is simple: 1 part acid + 3 parts oil + 1 emulsifying agent + extra flair = a vinaigrette. For the specifics, try the following, whether you make your dressing at home or on the go.

ACID
Try a squeeze of fresh lemon, lime, or orange juice to provide the tang, or use vinegar (just be sure it's 0 mg sodium).

EMULSIFYING AGENT
The egg yolk from a hard- or soft-boiled egg, honey, mashed avocado, or low-sodium prepared mustards will do the trick. This element is optional, but it will make your dressing thick and luscious and clingy.

OIL
Be sure to try different kinds of oil (like nut, avocado, and coconut), but olive oil will be the easiest to find while out and about.

EXTRA FLAIR
Try adding berries, fresh herbs, spices (black pepper or red pepper flakes are the easiest to find, especially if there's pizza on the menu), and tomatoes (which are plump with umami).

To mix the dressing together, a lidded jar and an aggressive shake will work best. A jar is probably the most convenient and portable method, as long as you don't mind carrying a small glass jar in your bag or purse. (Perhaps put it in a resealable plastic bag, just in case.) The dressing will stay emulsified for about 30 minutes. When at home or in a kitchen, you can use a food processor or the drip-and-whisk method to emulsify the ingredients. Or when you're really in a pinch, just pour the different ingredients—acid, oil, emulsifying agent, flair—on the salad separately and use your fork to mix it up.

SIX LOW-SO WAYS TO SANDWICH

Bread may be one of the high-sodium culprits, but that doesn't mean you have to avoid sandwiches forever. Bread makers and salt-free bread recipes make it possible to create low-sodium loaves at home. If you are looking for something more time efficient, try these bread replacements for a quick way to wrap up that midday meal.

CUCUMBER BAGUETTES

Cut a cucumber in half lengthwise and use a spoon to remove the seeds in the middle. Treat the cucumber halves like an open-face baguette sandwich, and top with yogurt and grated vegetables, Hickory-Smoked Fish Spread (page 228), or a simple mix of mashed avocado and herbs. Layer on some low-sodium deli meat, pulled chicken, thinly sliced vegetables, or a chopped hard-boiled egg (see page 166). Wrap each in plastic wrap and put in a resealable bag.

COLLARD LEAF LAVASH

Remove the hard stem from the center of two collard leaves and paint the inside of both leaves with sticky spread, like homemade hummus, thickened Lemon Tahini Dressing (page 170), or mashed avocado. Place one leaf over the other, making one oval-shaped leaf "lavash" (a thin, round flatbread). Place the wrap fillings—like cooked quinoa, zucchini matchsticks, bean sprouts, sliced green onions, chopped jalapeño—on one end of the leaf lavash. Then, just like rolling a burrito or sushi, fold the top and bottom parts of the leaves inward while you tightly roll the wrap up. While holding the wrap, carefully cut it in half. To keep it together, transfer the collard lavash onto plastic wrap

or foil, put the two halves back together, tightly wrap it up, and pack it in a resealable bag.

NORI WRAP

For hikes, airplane rides, or desk lunches, I love making nori (toasted seaweed) rolls. Like the collard wraps, you want to start with something sticky to act as the glue—slightly warm rice is best, but magical mashed avocado will also work. Spread the rice or avocado all over the nori sheet. Put the fillings on the nori sheet as you did with the collard wraps. Wrap the nori over the filling and over itself until you reach the other side. Tightly wrap it up in foil and pack it to go in a resealable bag.

LETTUCE SPRING ROLLS

Make a party out of lunchtime by packing up some butter lettuce leaves; Lemon Tahini Dressing (page 190), Orange-Ginger Sauce (see page 218), or homemade salt-free peanut sauce; julienned carrots and cucumbers; and any other fillings, like the shrimp from the Carrot Vegetable Noodle Salad with Spicy Shrimp (page 199) or Curry Tofu Fries (page 217). When it's time to eat, get spring-rolling.

JICAMA BUNS

If you happen to see jicama at your market, grab one (hint: it looks like a well-fed turnip). You can use this unassuming root to add texture to salads and guacamole, and you can even make sliced jicama into crunchy vegetable "fries" (see page 217). But things are about to get even more awesome. Instead of cutting jicama into the conventional sticks or cubes, cut it into rounds to make a crunchy, flat bun. Compose an open-face sandwich with the jicama "bun" and your choice of spreads and toppings, just like those cucumber baguettes.

HOMEMADE LOW-SODIUM BREAD

Of course, we all occasionally crave the real thing, not just really creative replacements. So I wanted to be sure to give you a few salt-free bread recipes to try: Super-Simple Sandwich Bread (page 149), Easy Focaccia (page 238), or Mei Mei's Green Onion Pancakes (page 151), which you can use like a pita wrap.

Since I didn't cover the whole world of bread, be sure to check the low-sodium, salt-free baking books available. And try revising salty bread recipes (challah!) you find as well.

GENMAICHA MICROWAVE SOUP

If you miss the ease and taste of instant noodles, then your office microwave is about to become your best friend, again. With a few ingredients (raw and dried) and a microwave-safe container, you can prepare a warm soup in minutes, while keeping the sodium, the prep work, and the spills to a minimum.

How? The trick is in tea. Yes, tea! Specifically a bag of genmaicha, which is green tea combined with roasted brown rice to create a savory, umami-filled drink. It can also double as a low-sodium, portable broth.

Simply pack a portable container with some noodle bowl fillings, like the ones in the ingredient list below, which you might find already prepped in your Refrigerator Salad Bar (see page 115).

SERVES 1   **TIME** 10 MINUTES

1 genmaicha tea bag

Boiling water

Cooked meat

Cooked no-salt-added rice noodles

Cubed firm tofu

Fresh or thawed frozen peas, edamame, or corn kernels

Peeled and thinly sliced carrots or zucchini

Spices: pinches of red pepper flakes, salt-free garlic powder, freshly ground black or white pepper, whole coriander seed

Thinly sliced bok choy

Thinly sliced fresh shiitake mushrooms

About 10 minutes before you want to eat lunch, put the tea bag in a big cup of just-boiled water to steep. Steep the tea bag for 5 to 8 minutes. Carefully squeeze the tea bag to get out all of the flavor, then discard.

In a microwave-safe bowl, combine your remaining ingredients with the tea. Heat in the microwave for 90 seconds. Test the temperature of the soup and continue heating in 1-minute intervals until it reaches your desired temperature. Enjoy.

VARIATIONS: Powdered sodium-free chicken, beef, and herb bouillon also make a great broth for on-the-go use. But these products replace the sodium chloride with potassium chloride, so be sure to check with your doctor or nutritionist before using.

IN THE DRAWER

It's important to stock up on low-sodium staples, not just in your home but at your office, too. By having a few nonperishable edibles and a few basic cooking tools on hand, you can whip up a low-so lunch or snack whenever you want.

EDIBLES

+ Canned (or boxed) no-salt-added beans

+ Chia, quinoa, oats (in jars)

+ Dried fruits and vegetables

+ Low-sodium tuna fish

+ Matzo crackers

+ Microwaveable rice

+ Olive oil and vinegar, in small spill-free bottles

+ Salt-free chips

+ Salt-free mug mixes

+ Salt-free popcorn

+ Salt-free spices and spice blends

+ Tea

+ Unsalted nuts and seeds

TOOLS

+ Can opener

+ Microwave-safe bowls and mugs

+ Spoon, fork, knife

And just a quick word from management: It's totally cool to "gift" cooking utensils to your office, like a small rice cooker, which will give both you and your coworkers more options for preparing meals at the office. You could also be in charge of organizing a little spice and grain cabinet. Or go a step beyond and sign up your company (or a group of like-minded coworkers) for a regular farm-to-office food delivery or CSA service, so you always have fresh fruit and vegetables on hand.

And if you miss the tradition of sharing the lunch hour with coworkers, start a monthly potluck. Surely someone else in the office eats vegan, Paleo, nut-free, or even low-sodium. So reach out to the cubicles next to you. Use shared Google Docs to plan your potlucks, making notes of the ingredients and dietary needs. And enjoy lunch hour together.

···8···
ENTERTAIN
Hosting and Holiday Tips

t's time to undo one of the biggest low-sodium myths of all: Salt-free food is not meant to be shared with others. This is just plain wrong.

Over the years, I've hosted plenty of brunches, Thanksgiving with all the fixings, and even a six-course New Year's Eve feast for forty. Sunday night dinners with friends occur on a weekly basis. And simply put, meals at my home are an occasion not to be missed. Now it's time to fill your low-so table with eager guests, too.

Even though it seems unlikely, as someone with special dietary needs, you actually make the ultimate host or hostess. First, you are naturally more prepared and more inclined to make adjustments for other people's allergies and eating habits—which these days, seem to include just about everyone. And while you may fear that your low-so ways exclude you from the world of social dining, you'll find that they make you and your meals more inclusive of everyone else's habits.

Second, as a low-sodium cook, you will make most of your meals from scratch, with fresh ingredients, interesting spices, and exciting combinations that many people have not tried before. These features automatically make your food better than takeout. And because you now know that presentation counts just as much as the food itself, you will wow guests with your use of color and sauces and snappy details. Who wouldn't want to eat with a person who cooked like that?

So instead of hiding your low-so diet or apologizing for it, get ready to show it off. From last-minute dinner parties to big holiday gatherings, the following tips will help you keep your sodium in check while still serving meals to be remembered.

THROWING A PARTY WITHOUT LOSING YOUR MIND

Low-sodium food is meant to be shared. It is made for entertaining. It's perfect for any gathering or celebration. And here's how you can throw a great party that keeps the flavor high and both the sodium and stress low.

ONE POT, INDIVIDUAL PORTIONS, EARLY PREP

Keep things simple. The key to good entertaining is making sure you aren't at the stove the whole time your guests are in your home. That means making one-pot dishes or letting your oven do most of the work for you. Or choosing recipes that you can make ahead of time, serve at room temperature, or simply heat right before the doorbell rings. With individual portions, you can add saltier ingredients (like cheese or cured meats) for guests. When you do want to try something daring, give yourself plenty of practice and time, as well as a backup plan.

DON'T MAKE EVERYTHING

While fresh is best for low-sodium cooking, use a shortcut for some of the ingredients. This might mean buying presliced garlic or using canned beans, bottled marinades, or premade dips for your guests. I give you my blessing. Just make sure that your time-saving purchases are low-sodium and salt-free, if *you* plan to eat them.

DO MAKE A SHOPPING LIST

Even if you think you will remember what you need, you will probably forget something for your menu. To be safe, write down a list—on your phone, on a piece of paper, whatever works for you.

BRING IN THE NOISE, BRING ON THE FUN

Entertaining is not just about food. It is about the whole environment you create for your guests. You don't have to get a degree in Martha Stewart craftiness or splurge on new plates. But there are many simple ways to charm your guests and elevate the mood during prep. How about putting out arrangements of fresh flowers and playing music. Or giving simple appetizers a little extra zip with some of the following ideas:

+ Choose colorful and uncommon vegetables, like purple cauliflower, romaine hearts, or chili-spiced rainbow carrots, for your crudité platter.

+ Use a vegetable peeler to add stripes to cucumber edges before slicing each cucumber into cracker-size shapes. Or use a teaspoon to scoop out the seedy centers of thick slices to make mini cucumber cups, to then fill as you wish.

+ Forget the bread and use sturdy fruit, like sliced apples, firm nectarines, or even dried apricots as the canvas for savory dips and spreads.

+ Mix toasted nuts and seeds with salt-free popcorn and fun spices (cumin, chipotle, dill) for a tasty bar snack.

+ Roll Cauliflower-Nut "Ricotta" (page 196) in crushed, toasted nuts or spices for a fun take on mini cheese balls.

- Make your own herbed butter or herb-infused oil to slather on Easy Focaccia (page 238).

- Make ice cubes colorful by adding fresh berries or herbs to the water before freezing.

GIVE YOUR GUESTS SOMETHING TO DO

Whether your friends man the drink station or help stir a pot, when they feel involved they'll enjoy the finished product that much more. For something really fun, arrange jars of fresh herbs on the table in place of flowers so guests can choose and sprinkle on their own.

KEEP DESSERT SIMPLE

Unless baked goods hit your entertaining sweet spot, dessert is a great place to go the simple route. That doesn't mean you can't make those final bites yourself or add your own special touch, but you don't have to make a three-layer cake or ice cream from scratch (unless you want to). For simple sweet endings, try one of the following.

Crumbles: All you need is a baking dish, enough fresh, ripe fruit to fill the baking dish, and the topping. For the topping, use a combination of flour, unsalted butter, and sugar to sprinkle on top. Play with the types of flour you use (almond, wheat, oat) as well as the kind of sugar (honeycomb and candied ginger) and fat (coconut oil). Try also adding chopped unsalted nuts, coconut flakes, or crushed coffee beans. And feel free to add spice, herbs, and citrus for a flavor boost. Then just put it in a moderate oven (375°F [190°C]) for 30-ish minutes until the fruit is juicy and fork-tender and the top is browned and crispy. Serve with ice cream.

Kitchen Cupboard Chocolate Bark: Line a 9-by-11-in [23-by-28-cm] baking pan with parchment paper. Melt some chocolate and pour it into the pan. While still warm and soft, sprinkle with toppings (crispy rice cereal, coconut flakes, salt-free nuts, dried fruit, chopped mint, candied ginger, cayenne pepper). Store in the refrigerator for up to 3 days. Lift out the parchment, and break the bark into pieces.

Pancake Cakes: Make mini pancakes on the stove. Use whipped cream or Greek yogurt to frost one pancake, top with macerated berries, and add another pancake. Continue until you've built mini, three-layered cakes for your guests. Garnish with some fresh mint or lemon zest. You can even make the pancakes (kept at room temperature, covered in foil) and whipped cream (refrigerated) ahead of time, and assemble them after dinner.

Parfait: Whipped cream, yogurt, chia jams, fresh fruit, granola, honey-coated nuts, honeycomb—the hardest part of a parfait is picking the ingredients. Once you've made your choices, layer the items in glass cups or bowls or even champagne flutes. Or let your guests make their own.

Whipped Cream, Brown Sugar, and Berries: Put the fresh berries in a large bowl, and place the whipped cream and brown sugar in small separate bowls. Tell your guests to dip some berries in whipped cream and brown sugar. And here's the ultimate party trick: Fill a cold canning jar halfway with chilled heavy whipping cream. Close tightly. Tell one of your guests to shake for 5 minutes. And ta-da, you have whipped cream as well as great entertainment. Also, you can give each guest a jar of their own chilled cream to shake and an array of additions to choose from—like shaved chocolate, colored sprinkles, ground cinnamon, and maple syrup—for a DIY whipped cream bar and a sweet parting gift. Is there anything better than that?

MAKE FEASTS FLEXIBLE

When entertaining guests, I never want someone's plate to be empty or their palate to be unsatisfied. I also don't want to make several versions of dinner for every guest with different dietary needs and desires. So I am a big fan of flexible feasts.

These are meals made of small bites or multiple elements where everyone can choose their own food adventure—like a salad bar, but a lot more fun and flavorful. With a spread of colorful options at their fingertips, everyone builds the exact dish they desire; a concept that not only keeps everyone happy, but adds to the entertainment value of the meal.

You can always provide toppings like cheese or cured meats or even a little bowl of salt for those not on low-sodium diets, if you think their palates might appreciate it. Buy premade spreads and sauces for these guests, too. As long as you keep all the individual elements simple, flexible feasts will not add time or cost to your meal.

To practice, here are some ideas to get you started for any meal of the day and any occasion.

BRUNCH: Set up a parfait bar with fresh fruit, dried fruit, nut-free granola, toasted coconut, chocolate chips, and yogurt in soy, coconut, and Greek varieties. Let guests build and layer. If you're feeling brave, try offering a savory version, too, with cucumbers, olive oil, and herb pesto or hot sauce.

LUNCH: Let guests wrap their way with a DIY spring roll bar. Set the table with traditional rice wrappers as well as grain-free options like butter lettuce leaves and nori sheets. Then provide cooked rice or quinoa, thinly sliced carrots, peppers, and cucumbers, avocado, tofu, and cooked shrimp for people to fill and roll as they wish.

DESSERT: Everyone loves a good old-fashioned float. And to satisfy any sweet tooth, turn your counter into an old-fashioned soda shop with a diet-friendly twist. Provide a mix of fizzy, fruit-flavored sodas (all-natural is best), non-dairy ice creams or sorbets, whipped cream, sprinkles, and fresh fruit. Following are some combination ideas to get you started.

Apple Pie: Vanilla Coconut or Almond Milk Ice Cream + Sparkling Cider

Sunny Citrus: Lemon Sorbet + Sparkling Lemonade

Tea Sparkler: Green Tea Coconut Ice Cream + Ginger Ale

DINNER: Personally, I think polenta, tacos, and pizza are three of the easiest meals to turn into flexible feasts. And that's because they all taste great with almost any combination of toppings and fillings. So try one of these menus at your next dinner evening gathering:

The Dinner Party: Polenta with Lamb Chops, Harissa, and Lemon Fennel (page 252)

The Casual Fiesta: Jerk-ish Fish Tacos with Sauce, Slaw, and Salsa (page 255)

The Group Effort: Flatbread with Four Mix-And-Match Spreads (page 257)

THE HOLIDAY TABLE

The holidays are my favorite time of year. The aromas of cinnamon and cloves fill the air, twinkling lights fill the streets, parties fill the calendar, and tradition fills our plates, minds, and bellies. But because of brined turkeys, cheesy mashed potatoes, and other seasonal favorites, the holidays also mean high-sodium foods.

To keep a sense of normalcy, many people trade healthful eating for ease. This can lead to guilt, discomfort, or worst of all, health issues. Which, speaking from experience, isn't so jolly.

So this year, let's all promise to stay on the low-sodium plan. And, with the right approach, avoid risky nibbling. The following tips will keep you satisfied, whether you dine at your own home or at someone else's. And by involving others in your healthful eating habits, you will find that you not only eat better this holiday season, but even inspire others to make a few food resolutions of their own.

HOSTING THE HOLIDAYS

To conquer high-sodium holiday traps, start by doing your homework. Whether it is the honey-baked ham, Tanta's tamales, or that traditional pecan pie, your favorite dishes often include ingredients you may need to avoid. But instead of taking these recipes off the menu, solve the sodium issue by putting nontraditional ingredients back in.

BRISKET

Sodium Culprit: Canned broth; canned tomato products (paste, sauce, ketchup).

Swap: Brisket can be luscious and juicy, or it can be dry, dry, dry. The trick to keeping it moist is a slow roast and a lot of sauce. But to keep that sauce low in sodium, you have to switch up the ingredients. Start with no-salt-added tomato products or even other puréed vegetables (like cauliflower or pumpkin). Then enhance with bold flavors, like red wine, orange juice, apricot jam, and horseradish. Add unexpected spices, like ancho pepper, salt-free chorizo spice blend, and cinnamon as well. And smother your brisket so it has no chance of drying out.

CASSEROLES

Sodium Culprit: Canned soups; bread crumbs; cheese; and crispy onion things.

Swap: You can go the path of making your own low-sodium mushroom soup, your own low-sodium bread crumbs, and your own low-sodium fried onion things. But I personally like keeping my holiday sides as fresh and vibrant as possible, to counter the richness of everything else. So I skip the casserole and make flash-sautéed beans, maple-roasted squash, or glazed carrots instead. Embellish with herbs (like parsley, rosemary, thyme, or dill), thinly sliced shallots, citrus zest, and chopped nuts (like hazelnuts, walnuts, or pistachios). Or if you like crispy things, bake up some hash browns for a crunchy topping.

GRAVY

Sodium Culprit: Canned broth; salted butter.

Swap: The point of gravy at the holidays is to add extra moisture and savory flavor to your poultry and potatoes. So yes, you can make your own silky low-sodium gravy by making your own stock. But this is also an opportunity to switch things up by serving a warm Dilly Chimichurri (page 163), a warm Carrot–Sweet Onion Dressing (page 169), or Curry Mushroom Gravy (see page 203).

HAM

Sodium Culprit: A salty cure.

Swap: Skip the honey-baked ham and chose an uncured cut of pork to star as your main dish. Think beyond the traditional and use pork chops, pork loin, or even a slow-cooked pulled pork. Make a sweet and smoky jam glaze to mimic the hams of holidays past. Or go wild and pair your pork with an unusual salt-free spice blend (like Chinese five-spice) or an unusual sauce (like the spicy Harissa Hot Sauce on page 164).

MASHED POTATOES

Sodium Culprit: Ready-to-eat potato mix; cheese; salted butter.

Swap: First, be sure to start with fresh potatoes (or whatever root vegetable you plan to use). Then, add flavor by mixing in bright additions, like an herb pesto, roasted peppers, or a combination of yogurt and Dukka Spice Mix (page 188).

PIE

Sodium Culprit: Graham cracker crust.

Swap: If you want a traditional-tasting pumpkin pie without making cookies from scratch, try using low-so

ice-cream cones, or take inspiration from raw and Paleo cooks and use nuts to create the crunchy shell. Fill macaroon tarts (see page 225) with pumpkin pie filling. Or skip the classics (and the crust) altogether and make Cardamom Cake with Coconut Whipped Cream (page 193). Replace the toasted coconut flake topping with more holiday-appropriate candied nuts or bright pomegranate seeds.

SMOKED FISH

Sodium Culprit: A salty cure.

Swap: Make your own hickory-smoked fish (see page 228) instead.

STUFFING

Sodium Culprit: Prepared bread; broth.

Swap: If you can't find no-salt-added bread, use Super-Simple Sandwich Bread (page 149). Or, even easier, make cornbread to replace store-bought loaves. But if you don't mind tossing the crumbs, try a wild-rice stuffing instead. Then stud that stuffing with a combination of fresh herbs, sautéed mushrooms, Pickled Cherries (page 249), and pomegranate seeds or cranberries to boost color and flavor.

TURKEY

Sodium Culprit: Brine.

Swap: When you buy your bird, make sure to find one that is brine- and solution-free. Communicate with the grocery store staff or buy from a butcher to ensure your turkey is fresh and not pre-seasoned or plumped. Then use the Low-So Turkey tips on page 132 to keep things juicy.

LOW-SO TURKEY

If you are on a low-sodium diet this holiday season, don't settle for plain chicken breast. Instead, choose from the following methods to produce a seasoned and juicy turkey fit for any Thanksgiving feast.

Flip It Over: Most recipes call for the turkey to be cooked breast-side up. If you turn it to the other side, however, all those cooking juices will drip down around the breast meat, basically basting it for you. If you choose this method, though, just know that your bird may not achieve that award-winning golden hue—although, a glaze at the end and a quick broil will ensure your bird is a stunner. And best of all, you and your guests will enjoy slices of moist turkey breast for dinner and for leftovers.

Break It Apart: All the parts of the turkey are done at different times, which is why it is so darn difficult to keep the white and dark meats equally juicy. If you don't mind skipping the big "carving moment," break the bird into pieces before you put it into the oven, removing the breasts when they reach 145°F [63°C] and the legs and wings at 165°F [74°C]. Or you can butterfly the turkey by removing the backbone and flattening it in a large roasting or baking pan. This will expose the legs to more heat, helping them cook faster (so the white meat doesn't have to wait as long). Because both methods lower the risk of dry meat as well as the time needed to cook it, be sure to check the thigh meat temperature earlier than usual. Depending on the size of the bird, you might have it out of the oven in just a few hours.

Cool It Down: Harold McGee is a culinary genius. When it comes to Thanksgiving turkey, he offers a brilliant suggestion: Use ice packs. Yes, ice packs, to cool the breast meat before it cooks in the oven. While the legs and wings warm up to room temperature, the breast will chill and lower in temperature. When you finally cook the turkey (without ice packs), the breast will cook more slowly than the dark meat.

Lift the Skin: Before you put any salt-free rub on that turkey, lift the skin from the meat at the openings at the top and bottom of the bird. This will allow the skin to remain thin and crispy as it cooks and will also let you rub flavor and moisture directly onto the meat under the skin (see the following paragraph).

Grease It Up: Just because you can't use brine doesn't mean you can't use juicy liquids. Now that you have pockets between the skin and the meat, feel free to fill them with an oil- or butter-based rub, a homemade marinade, or even slices of citrus. This will help keep the meat moist and flavorful as it cooks. As the liquids collect at the bottom of the pan, put them to work as well. Use a ladle to bathe the bird in its juices every 30 to 45 minutes.

Set It Upright: If you get a small enough turkey, you can use the ultimate method for golden poultry: Beer cans. Set your mini turkey upright on a half-emptied can of beer, and the fat will drain off and away from the meat, keeping the skin crispy. The beer will also continually release steam inside the turkey, theoretically keeping the white meat juicy and moist. Make sure the bird is stable in the roasting pan and use a poultry stand for bigger turkeys.

DINING AT SOMEONE ELSE'S TABLE

Because many holiday meals will occur outside of your home, safely share in holiday feasts while sticking to your diet by using the tips on page 105 and adjusting with seasonal ingredients and recipes. And remember, whether it's Thanksgiving or any old Thursday, hosts want their guests to be happy and full. If they find you with an empty plate, they will probably feel terrible that they didn't provide anything for you to eat. So speak up and come up with a solution. Your hosts will be glad you did.

FIND INTERNATIONAL INSPIRATION

Here's the ultimate, foolproof way to overcome "missing the salt" in holiday dishes: Forget the traditions of your childhood and borrow recipes from around the world to serve to your guests. From fish to fried chicken, traditional menus from other countries offer a range of unexpected ingredients and flavors to play with. Your holiday feast will no longer compete with memories from the past but will make new ones instead.

To get you started, introduce one of the following international dishes to your holiday table. And remember, while you can always make these recipes to the letter, you can also use them as inspiration for cross-cultural combinations. Give typical American holiday ingredients (sweet potatoes, turkey) an international twist (tamales, stuffed cabbage).

AUSTRALIA AND NEW ZEALAND

Instead of puddings and pies, take inspiration from the countries down under and make a lighter berry pavlova instead. Add seasonal flavors—like pumpkin spice or crushed chestnuts—to Pavlova Whoopie Pies (see page 261) and serve with tart cranberries and pomegranate seeds.

GREECE

Avgolemono—a thick, creamy soup made from chicken broth, lemon, rice, and egg—starts off the Christmas dinner in Greece. Try a classic recipe or play with Lemon Chicken Orzo (page 172) to create a version of your own.

ITALY

Christmas Eve in Sicily and southern Italy means the Feast of Seven Fishes. Which means you can replace honey-baked ham and brined turkey with shrimp and linguine or Dukka-Spiced Salmon Patties (page 187).

JAPAN

Instead of turkey, fried chicken (specifically of the KFC variety) takes center stage during Christmas Eve, proving so popular that people have been said to place orders months ahead of time. But instead of ordering a bucket of wings, use the Coconut "Panko" Pork Tonkatsu (page 218) to make a crispy chicken (or fish) dish for your table.

MEXICO

Although made all year-round, traditional *posole rojo* makes an appearance on the Christmas Eve menu in Mexico. So this year, add color (and spice) to your holiday feast, and replace creamy squash soups with Green Pea Posole (page 239).

And don't forget to mix and match your menu with dishes from other holidays, too, like latkes in place of mashed potatoes, a kugel-inspired stuffing, a Kwanzaa-inspired roasted squash and peanut soup, or a Chinese New Year duck to help ring in January 1.

···9···

CONNECT

Make Your Low-So World
Better, Easier, and Bigger

When it comes to trying out the latest tech gadgets, I tend to drag my heels. Sure, I have a blog. But I'll be honest, computers scare me. And I'm always a few steps behind the latest phone upgrade, the latest app, and the latest operating system (I'm not even sure what that means). So if you avoid Facebook or iAnything, just know that I'm in your corner.

As someone born, raised, and never leaving the Bay Area, though, I'm surrounded by people in the forefront of all things tech. Even though the constant influx of new products can feel overwhelming, with encouragement (and IT help), I've come to see how tools from the virtual world make real life with a special diet a lot easier, specifically in three challenging areas: socializing, managing time, and traveling.

Let's plug in and see what technology can do for you, your busy schedule, and your much-needed vacation.

DOT-COMS AND COMMUNITY

Nut allergies, gluten-free eating, or a low-sodium diet—everyone with a new food limitation fears the same thing: Losing out on the social experiences associated with eating.

Whether attending last-minute dinners for friends, participating in potlucks, or going on dates, having special food needs makes staying full and satisfied at these events more difficult, and it also makes feeling involved a lot harder, too. Without being able to take a bite of someone else's pizza or having the confidence to share your own low-sodium version, it's easy to feel left out. But thanks to the Internet, it can be easy to overcome feeling like an outsider. By linking to others with similar food needs, you'll not only find a supportive community online, but also the confidence to create one offline as well.

INTERNET ACCEPTANCE

Once upon a time, in the age of actual libraries and bookstores, special-diet guides lived in the health section while everything else food-related lived in the glorious cookbook section. They were two separate worlds, divided.

But once dot-coms entered the picture, the lines began to blur. Recipes for vegan pâté and Paleo cauliflower pizza crusts showed up on special-diet blogs as much as on highly regarded culinary sites. Soon the separation between special diets and food became ancient history. Today, everyone and every diet is welcome at the virtual table.

Which brings me to the best part of this virtual culinary world: Participation! Passive perusing will lead to lots of inspiration, but don't forget to add your own low-so ideas to the ever-growing virtual shelves. Whether you use photo-sharing sites or chat on food forums, you, too, can add to the catalog of culinary information. Maybe even start a blog of your own. For something personal, use Skype or Facetime to host a virtual low-so dinner party or cooking lesson. With the Internet, you never go low-so alone.

NEED HELP? TRY TWITTER, FACEBOOK, AND YELP

Looking for a restaurant in Seattle to make you a memorable low-sodium dinner? Have questions about going to college with a special diet? Wondering where to buy salt-free pickles? Then it's time to get social. Sites like Twitter, Facebook, and Yelp give you immediate access to a huge population of people with similar needs. With just a click, you can start your own low-sodium support group on Facebook, ask the Twitterverse how to correct a cooking disaster, or consult Yelp for diet-friendly dining recommendations. Tap into this web of support and find your special-diet social network at the touch of a button (or two).

IMMEDIATE ACCESS

Now that you feel included and connected, let's discuss how the Internet helps you overcome a second special-diet challenge: Time. Or, more specifically, time management. A common fear associated with low-sodium diets is the number of minutes and hours needed to make meals from scratch—from buying groceries to mastering new cooking skills. But again, thanks to our good pal technology, there are ways to make these low-so tasks more efficient and enjoyable.

BUY ONLINE

You're ready to get cooking. You're inspired, you're excited. But you have one small problem. As far as kitchen tools go, you have a toaster, a wooden spoon, and something that kind of resembles a baking dish. Whether this baking dish can safely go into the oven is currently up for debate. Clearly you need to do some shopping for supplies before you can delve into that first recipe. But since you're such a busy person, you're as short on time as you are on matching silverware.

Thanks to online shopping, you can get all your errands done on the commute to work or even during your lunch break. Shop at the virtual locations of your favorite stores and have all the goods delivered to your door. If you're looking for budget-friendly options, don't forget to check sites like Craigslist and eBay for good deals on often-expensive equipment. Or if you want to splurge, treat yourself to one-of-a-kind dishware and serving trays from sites like Etsy.com.

GET IT DELIVERED

When searching for specialty low-sodium items like cheese, salsa, or bread, don't waste your time with a grocery-store road trip. With a quick Google search, you can buy low-sodium products online and have them shipped directly to your home. It may be a bit pricier and you may have to buy products in bulk, but when you're looking for something to satisfy a craving (like low-sodium cheddar), the extra pennies may be worth it.

Thanks to online companies like Instacart, Google Express, FreshDirect.com, Safeway.com, and Taskrabbit, you can order groceries (and cooking equipment) online and have them delivered, without lifting a finger or getting out of your pajamas. For even more ease, try one of the many meal delivery services and receive professionally developed recipes as well as all the prepped ingredients needed to make them. It's like having a private chef without the big price tag. Just make a special note of your dietary needs.

SAVE MINUTES AND MONEY

From menu planning to electronic coupon clipping, mobile apps will make your next trip to the market efficient and budget-friendly. Get alerts about sales; search for nutritional and allergy information; even scan and bag items as you walk the aisles. Keep up with the growing number of grocery store apps and easily cut down on your bill and time at the store.

DIETS AND DEPARTURES

Dietary limitations don't have to take the spontaneity or flavor out of your adventures. Nor do they have to add stress to well-deserved R&R. With a little help from the Web, anyone with special dietary requirements can travel the world *and* have a satisfied and full tummy no matter where the journey takes them.

PLAN SMART

RESEARCH

Before looking at the weather for the week, use the Internet to research the food and culture of the city (or country) you plan to visit. Check out travel blogs to explore the cuisine, what's typically on a menu, and how the dishes are traditionally prepared. That way, you can smartly navigate a menu according to your dietary needs. And get Googling. Map out the nearest grocery stores before you go, so you can stock up on low-so provisions as soon as you land.

SHOP AHEAD

If you are staying somewhere for a while, you can always send pantry favorites, like canned beans and chips, via mail to your accommodations. But if that gets expensive, email the concierge a grocery list instead and see if he or she will do a little pre-arrival shopping for you. Or try one of the food delivery services mentioned on page 137 to stock up your room when you arrive.

SNACK HACK

For unexpected layovers, long plane rides, and getting unexpectedly lost, it's best to keep SOS snacks and utensils on hand. Use Pinterest and food blogs for easy-to-pack and nonperishable treat ideas such as roasted chickpeas or granola bars. Shop online to purchase tiny can openers, sporks, and collapsible containers for spontaneous cooking or picnicking.

FORGET THE VIEW, GET A KITCHEN

When searching for hotels, look for spaces with small kitchenettes. If your hotel doesn't have those options, remember you can always ask for a refrigerator and a microwave oven to be placed in your room for no to minimal cost. Better yet, skip the hotel and rent, through VRBO or Airbnb, options that provide access to spaces with kitchens or kitchenettes. That way, you can prepare fuller meals if you need to and make snack packs for day trips.

USE FRIENDS, REAL AND VIRTUAL

If you can stay with a friend, you've struck travel gold. Their kitchen, pantry, and stove are now yours, guaranteeing you safe and satisfying meals when you want. But even when you travel without a friend to visit, that doesn't mean a helpful hand is far away. Use those social media tools (see page 136) to ask locals about diet-friendly eateries and grocery stores.

EXPLORE

Part of what makes traveling magical is immersing oneself in the culture—and by culture, I mean cuisine. So trade that museum tour for a food tour. By bus or on foot, these excursions often wind through the streets of a city while providing lots of interesting historical tidbits and culinary inspiration to take back home as a souvenir. Look online for these opportunities wherever you travel or use the Internet to make up an edible tour of your own.

NO ENGLISH, NO PROBLEM

If you plan to travel abroad where the language sounds a lot different from that in your hometown, don't fret. There really is an app for everything—including speaking foreign languages. With a simple photo, some mobile apps will translate phrases found on signs, menus, and, yes, your laminated dietary card. Better yet, other apps will translate a word or phrase from your language to the native language, out loud, in real time. This means *you* may not be able to order in Portuguese, but your phone now can.

PACK SMART

EMERGENCY BITES

For plane rides, layovers, and long afternoons of travel, it's important to have SOS snacks with you, in your bag, at all times. My favorites include low- or no-sodium granola bars, unsalted nuts and seeds, berries and dried fruits, and individual nut butter packets.

CARRY ON

For longer trips, pack that suitcase with heartier, nonperishable items that lie flat and will last without refrigeration. I personally like items with more bite to them, like rice crackers, corn tortillas, sodium-free dried soups (that need only hot water), no-salt-added boxed beans (no can opener necessary), and microwaveable rice, popcorn, and polenta. Don't forget to pack some DIY Oatmeal (page 111) and the dry ingredients for Microwave Banana Bread (page 114), too.

MAKE A TRAVEL TOOL KIT

Just like your toiletries, it's easy (and life changing) to pack travel-size cooking utensils. Fill small, spill-free containers with oil, vinegar, and spice blends. Look to camping stores for tiny can openers, sporks, and collapsible containers (or lidded canning jars) for spontaneous picnics.

GO RAW

Take a tip from stove-free foodies and stock up on prewashed, packaged vegetables. Whether you snack on snap peas or chopped kale, softened in a microwave, you can keep eating green while on the go.

KIDDIE MENU

If things get dire, don't forget about the baby aisle. That's right, blended baby food and dry snacks are nutrient-rich, low in sodium, and, these days, tasty. Especially the fruit blends. So pack a few squeeze packets or puffs to go, just in case.

··· to ···

SHARE

Culinary Karma and
Getting Others Involved

Low-so does not need to, nor should it, be a solo adventure. When you share a low-sodium success story with a friend or a family member or a friendly stranger, you have an opportunity to make a big impact— for yourself and for all the other people living with low-sodium diets or other health-related restrictions. Think of it as community service in the most delicious sense.

With your help and openness, you will teach others about creative cooking solutions. You will inspire them to get into their own kitchens and maybe overcome their own lingering food fears. And you will equip them with the confidence they need to feed you and feed others. So when you worry about speaking up, remember that you are not being an inconvenience; you are becoming an influencer. When you proudly share your low-sodium ways, you not only help yourself live better, but you help others live better, too.

A LESSON IN CULINARY KARMA

I'll never forget my honeymoon to New Zealand. There were mind-blowing hikes on glaciers, bungeed leaps from bridges, casual swims with dolphins, and, of course, nights spent sleeping under shooting stars. The most memorable part of the trip did not come from our event-packed itinerary, however. It came from the discovery of gluten-free options in every restaurant as well as the smallest convenience stores. And (gasp!), even gas stations.

Regarding gluten-free diets, New Zealand seemed even more ahead of the trend than my progressive San Francisco neighborhood. After weeks of sighting gluten-free items in the most unexpected places, I found myself dining at a tiny pub in a tiny town, where I spied a huge menu of wheat- and gluten-free options. I was moved to ask the question that had nagged at me all along: How did they come to be so gluten-free friendly?

The answer was life changing.

According to the owner, one of the local women needed to eat gluten-free. As a regular customer, she also wished to continue enjoying her local restaurant. So instead of hiding her needs, she began bringing a personal stash of gluten-free products with her, to be used by the kitchen to make her dishes. A simple solution to the problem, but brave and novel, nonetheless.

With each item she brought in, she not only enabled herself to eat well, but she educated the owners about her food needs and how to accommodate them. And once the restaurant realized how many other customers shared in her diet, gluten-free dishes became mainstays on the menu. Ultimately, they even got a whole separate menu of their own.

While I cannot speak for the entire country of New Zealand, or remember the name of this restaurant, or speak to the truth of the story I was told, here's the big lesson: By making her food needs heard, this one woman made big changes for herself as well as a whole community of gluten-free eaters and even visitors from abroad. Well practiced at making adjustments, the chefs didn't hesitate when asked to create a flavorful low-sodium dinner for yours truly. So think of her when you feel nervous to make a special request. As the old adage goes, one person can change the world. Or at least a menu.

THE HANDS THAT FEED YOU

Now that we have explored the merits of sharing your food needs with others, let's chat about how to do that, in the most charming way possible.

FIND THE OWNER

Whether you want your local grocer to carry a certain brand of low-sodium tomato sauce or you dream of being able to order a sandwich from your neighborhood deli, the first step starts with getting yourself to said store and finding the owner or manager. Head over during a slow time of day (not lunch hour or dinner time), or even call ahead to see if you can arrange an in-person meeting. Then, get chatting.

Share your story—the whole story—of why you keep a special diet. Let them know your food wishes (order pizza, order a sandwich, keep a special stash of favorite low-sodium items). If you're a regular or live down the block, make sure to mention it. Loyalty counts a lot.

Next, turn it back to them and ask what you can do to help make these accommodations easy and possible (like make dinner reservations early in the evening versus during the later rush hours, provide your own pizza sauce or bread, bring in the names and numbers of your favorite low-sodium suppliers).

Finally, see what kind of deal you can drum up. The worst thing that can happen is that they say no to your requests, while the best result is that you may pave the way for yourself and others to eat at your favorite joints.

TEACH FRIENDS TO COOK

Here's another fun truth about learning to cook low-sodium food: You may very quickly become one of the most adventurous and fearless cooks you know. You'll find that your enthusiasm for all things food will quickly rub off on your friends. Invitations to your house for a meal will not be met with skepticism but excitement. In their eyes, you will become a master of the kitchen. And you'll quickly become the go-to source for culinary inspiration (and answers to cooking questions).

I still giggle when friends hover above the bowl as I prepare a salad, asking me about each ingredient, exclaiming that they never thought to mix those things together or use that particular spice. Or when I arrive at someone else's party to find a stressed host, with an incomplete shopping list or the wrong ingredients, asking me for a recipe remedy or an ingredient substitution. Whoever thought that I, the one with the dietary limits, would become a cooking resource for others?

But it makes sense. Because when you are always working around a missing ingredient, you gain great confidence in thinking on your feet. You learn how to work with what you have or find taste enhancers in unexpected places. And you'll quickly discover that your dietary limits do not exclude you from the world of food and social interactions; they actually put you at the center of them. If you let them.

MAKE FRIENDS WHO MAKE FOOD

Thanks to researchers, we have scientific data that proves eating with others makes us happier and healthier. Beyond creating memories over a big pot of lamb stew, sharing meals actually leads us to choose better food, make healthier choices, and motivate others to do the same. It's the best kind of peer pressure.

You may find that because it's budget friendly or just plain fun friendly, your pals will start to choose cooking together over silently watching a movie, spending big bucks at a restaurant, or shouting over loud music at a bar.

You may also discover that, thanks to all those cooking shows on TV, a lot of your friends have fallen in love with their kitchens, too, and are inspired to experiment and tinker on their own. That they're excited to take on new cooking challenges. This is where things get really fun. With your positive attitude and creative food, you may even move them to take on low-sodium cooking. So if someone wants to give it a try, don't turn them down. They may discover new dishes and spices that you never thought to try. It's fun for them. It's tasty for you.

I'm fortunate that I have a lot of fearless friends and family and know local chefs who not only find great joy in cooking, but specifically in cooking low-sodium food for me. They love to tackle salty challenges and then share the delicious results. In the spirit of sharing, I want to pass along their recipes and hopefully inspire you to build your own circle of generous food-makers.

FRIENDS WHO MAKE FALAFEL

I've found that because of my low-sodium food needs, I tend to form close relationships with the host, waiters, and kitchen staff of a restaurant. This not only ensures that the food I eat is safe for me, but ends up making the eating-out experience more personal. So get ready to add chefs to your list of best buddies. Once you find restaurants that happily cater to your needs, you'll eat there often, and you'll feel like you're eating with friends.

Firefly in San Francisco is one of those places for me. We stop in weekly for a bite and to say hello. Each time we eat with them, they use their freshest ingredients to create something low-sodium and stunning. I'm delighted to share one such recipe (see page 147) by chef Haley Sausner, in hopes of inspiring some new friendships of your own.

FRIENDS WHO MAKE BREAD

I knew from the first date with my husband that he was the guy for me. But what I didn't know then was that with him came a family of low-sodium adventurers who constantly take on my challenges as their own. For example, his sister's boyfriend is an incredibly skilled self-taught baker who makes me special salt-free bread loaves all the time, like the Super-Simple Sandwich Bread on page 149. Which is now yours to make, too. I've given instructions for mixing the dough by hand; but you can also use a stand mixer with a dough hook.

TEN WAYS TO USE BREAD BEYOND SANDWICHES

Now that you have fresh loaves of low-sodium bread, you can make a huge variety of bread-based dishes you may have previously avoided. Following are suggestions to get you started. Search online for recipes and instructions. Add your own dishes to the list. And remember to use the salt-free-ing skills you learned earlier (see page 84) to make them fit within your low-sodium and other dietary needs.

+ Make "egg in a hole"

+ Make French toast

+ Make panzanella salad

+ Make bread pudding—sweet or savory

+ Make (and freeze) bread crumbs

+ Make PB&J bread cake by layering square or round slices with salt-free peanut butter and fresh fruit

+ Make Tuscan bread soup

+ Make stuffing

+ Grill (or toast) bread and cover with pesto for bread pizzas

+ Feed the birds

FRIENDS WHO MAKE SOUP

Once a month or so, I get a text out of the blue from my friend Visra. "When are you home today? I have a soup for you," it says. And a few hours later, containers filled with slow-cooked lentils, star anise–spiced beef stews, and a variety of other creations arrive on my doorstep. Visra, who's just slightly bigger than her stockpot, keeps to a weekly tradition of making stock, from scratch, with leftover bones, without salt. Then she turns that savory base into a soup that warms your worries away. One of my favorites is called Comfort Soup, and the recipe is on page 150 so you can make it for yourself, a friend who's sick, a friend who's a new parent, or anyone who deserves a soup surprise. Freeze what you don't eat for nights when you need an edible hug. To make your homemade soup simpler, spend a slow weekend night making the stock from this recipe. It only takes 30-ish minutes. Refrigerate it, or freeze. You'll have the base for a quick, savory soup or stew any day of the week.

FRIENDS WHO MAKE PANCAKES

When I was just beginning to dive into my low-sodium diet, a few of my friends also began to get more acquainted with their kitchens. One friend was Mei, a genius at many things, who eventually transformed her casual dinner parties into a full-fledged, award-winning food-truck business and restaurant in Boston. Uh, right . . . overachiever. At her wedding, Mei catered all the food, including roasting a whole pig. She also made sure I had a low-sodium version of everything on the menu, from pickles to BBQ sauce to that roasted pig. And the pancake on page 151.

Cut the pancakes into triangles and serve with a drizzle of Carrot–Sweet Onion Dressing (page 169) or Orange-Ginger Sauce (see page 218). For dinner, keep the pancakes whole and serve with a fried egg or Duck à la Foung (page 152), shredding the duck meat and skin and offering one of the sauces on the side.

FRIENDS WHO MAKE DUCK

Let's talk about my father-in-law. He loves to make his own spice blends and rubs and then test me to see if I can name all the flavors. He also loves buying the largest piece of steak he can find and seeing if I can eat it all. Basically, he loves to feed me. And he specifically loves feeding me foods I thought I would never eat again. Like Peking duck, from scratch. And while I usually get to enjoy this treat on Chinese New Year, the recipe is on page 152, for any time of year. Serve with Mei Mei's Green Onion Pancakes (page 151) and Orange-Ginger Sauce (see page 218).

For low-sodium duck, make sure to get a bird that has not been brined. If you purchase a frozen duck, factor in the extra time needed to thaw it, which should be done in the refrigerator inside a large container with a lid, to keep things clean and sanitary.

TESTING OIL TEMPERATURE WITHOUT A THERMOMETER

Frying foods at home used to make me nervous. Mostly because I didn't want to deal with the aftermath mess. And I didn't know how to test oil without a thermometer.

But frying foods doesn't have to be intimidating (or messy). While a thermometer will give you an exact temperature, you can also test the oil with a wooden spoon. Place the end of the spoon into the oil. If you see small bubbles crowd around it, then the oil is ready to go.

As for post-frying, do not toss oil into your drain. Allow it to cool and then put it into a disposable container and discard.

FIREFLY FALAFEL WITH HERB YOGURT

MAKES 12 FALAFEL   **TIME** 45 MINUTES (PLUS 24 HOURS FOR SOAKING)

¼ cup [45 g] basmati rice

½ cup [100 g] dried chickpeas
or garbanzo beans

1 garlic clove, peeled

1 cup [35 g] roughly chopped
fresh baby spinach

½ cup [70 g] peas, fresh
or thawed frozen

¼ cup [7 g] roughly
chopped fresh cilantro

¼ cup [7 g] roughly
chopped fresh mint

2 green onions, root ends
trimmed, thinly sliced

¼ cup [60 ml] lemon juice

2 Tbsp olive oil, plus
more for frying

HERB YOGURT

1 cup [240 ml] plain Greek yogurt

1 garlic clove, minced

2 Tbsp minced shallot

½ cup [70 g] diced English cucumber

1 tsp finely chopped fresh cilantro

1 tsp finely chopped fresh mint

Zest of ½ lemon

Soak the basmati rice and dried chickpeas in 4 cups [960 ml] water for 24 hours before you wish to make the falafel. Or if you're in a pinch, put them in a small lidded saucepan, cover with water, bring to a boil over medium-high heat, and cook for 5 minutes. Remove from the heat, cover, and let sit for 1 hour. Drain the rice and chickpeas.

In a food processor, pulse the basmati rice, chickpeas, and 2 Tbsp water until the mixture forms a chunky paste. You want your falafel batter to remain firm and textured (not runny) so it holds its shape. Add the garlic, spinach, peas, cilantro, mint, green onions, lemon juice, and olive oil. Pulse until well combined. Use a spatula to scrape the sides of the bowl as needed.

Line a baking pan with paper towels. Add ½ in [12 mm] olive oil to a medium sauté pan or skillet and heat over medium heat. Form round falafel patties 2 in [5 cm] wide and ½ in [12 mm] thick (about ¼ cup [60 ml] batter) and, when the olive oil is hot, add them to the pan in batches, being careful not to crowd. Cook until crispy and browned on one side, 3 to 5 minutes. Flip and cook for another 3 to 5 minutes. Transfer the patties to the prepared baking pan. Repeat until all the falafel patties are cooked, adding oil to the pan and adjusting the heat as needed.

To make the herb yogurt: In a small bowl, stir together the yogurt, garlic, shallot, cucumber, cilantro, mint, and lemon zest until well combined.

Serve the falafel patties warm or at room temperature with the yogurt sauce on the side.

SUPER-SIMPLE SANDWICH BREAD

MAKES 2 LOAVES   **TIME** 2 HOURS, 30 MINUTES

2 cups [480 ml] warm water

⅔ cup [130 g] sugar

1½ Tbsp active dry yeast

¼ cup [60 ml] vegetable
oil, plus 1 tsp

5 to 6 cups [600 to 720 g]
white bread flour

In a large bowl, mix the warm water with the sugar until dissolved. Mix in the yeast and allow it to rest and get bubbly, about 10 minutes.

Add the ¼ cup [60 ml] vegetable oil to the yeast mixture and stir. Add the flour, 1 cup [120 g] at a time, mixing it together with a spatula. When the dough starts to come together, transfer it to a lightly floured work surface. Knead the dough until no lumps are present, about 10 minutes. Don't worry, it will start out flaky and then will get smooth and elastic.

Wash and dry the large dough bowl. Transfer the dough ball back to the bowl and pour in the 1 tsp oil. Use your fingers to coat the bottom and sides of the dough with the oil. Cover with a warm damp towel and allow the dough to rise until doubled in size, about 1 hour.

Preheat the oven to 350°F [180°C].

Remove the dough to a lightly floured work surface and cut it in half. Transfer the dough to two greased 9-by-5-in [23-by-12-cm] loaf pans. Using your hands, spread the dough so it reaches the sides of the pans. Cover the pans and allow the dough to rise for 30 minutes.

Put the loaves on the middle oven rack and bake until golden brown, 30 to 35 minutes, rotating the pans 180 degrees halfway through baking. Transfer the loaves in the pans to a cooling rack. When cool, remove the loaves from the pans.

Cool and store in an airtight plastic bag for up to 3 days. To freeze the second loaf, wrap it tightly in plastic wrap or put it into a paper bag, and then place in an airtight bag with as much air removed as possible. Thaw the bread in its wrapping to prevent moisture from forming on the loaf.

VISRA'S COMFORT SOUP

SERVES 4   **TIME** 1 HOUR, 15 MINUTES

SOUP STOCK

7 cups [1.7 L] water

2 lb [910 g] pork bones or
1 chicken carcass from Sunday
Chicken (see page 223)

2 medium daikon radishes, peeled

15 fresh cilantro stems, no leaves

3 garlic cloves, peeled

Pinch of freshly ground
white pepper

3 cups [210 g] shredded
green cabbage

PORK MEATBALLS

¼ cup [7 g] fresh cilantro leaves

4 garlic cloves, peeled

2 green onions, root ends
trimmed, thinly sliced

1 lb [455 g] ground pork

Pinch of freshly ground
white pepper

1 tsp ground coriander

2 Tbsp chopped cilantro leaves

2 Fresno or jalapeño chiles,
deribbed, seeded, and cut into
¼-in [6-mm] slices (optional)

To make the Soup Stock: Put 6 cups [1.4 L] of the water in a large soup pot or Dutch oven and place over medium-high heat. Add the pork bones, cover, and bring to a boil. Turn the heat to medium-low and simmer for 20 minutes. Meanwhile, cut the daikon into rounds 1 in [2.5 cm] thick and bind the cilantro stems with kitchen twine or a heat-safe rubber band. Add the daikon, cilantro stems, garlic, pepper, and remaining 1 cup [240 ml] water to the pot. (You can also wrap the cilantro stems and garlic cloves in a little square of cheesecloth and tie the bundle with some kitchen twine, also known as making a sachet. Plop the aromatic bundle into your soup pot and tie the loose twine end to your pot handle.) Cover and cook for 10 minutes. Using tongs or a slotted spoon, remove the bones, garlic, and cilantro stems. Stir in the cabbage, cover the pot, and cook for an additional 10 minutes.

Meanwhile, to make the Meatballs: Add the ¼ cup [7 g] cilantro leaves, garlic, and green onions to a food processor (or blender) and pulse until the mixture is finely minced. Transfer the mixture to a medium bowl. Add the pork, pepper, and ground coriander. Mix with your hands until well combined. Pinch off 1-Tbsp-size pieces of the meat mixture and gently roll between your palms, forming small balls.

Bring the stock back to a gentle boil over medium-high heat. Use a slotted spoon to carefully lower the meatballs into the stock. Stir gently and cook for a final 10 to 12 minutes, until the meatballs are cooked through. Serve the soup warm, garnished with the chopped cilantro leaves and sliced chiles (if desired).

MEI MEI'S GREEN ONION PANCAKES

MAKES 4 LARGE OR 8 SMALL PANCAKES   TIME 1 HOUR

2 cups [240 g] all-purpose flour

1 cup [240 ml] boiling water

3 or 4 green onions, root ends trimmed, thinly sliced

4 tsp black sesame seeds

2 Tbsp sesame oil

In a medium bowl, using a wooden spoon or silicone spatula, mix together the flour and boiling water until you are able to form the mixture into a dough ball.

When cool enough to handle, pinch off one-fourth of the dough and cover the rest with a damp towel. On a lightly floured work surface, roll out the dough ball with a floured rolling pin into a flat circle about 6 in [15 cm] wide. If the dough is too sticky to handle, add a little more flour to the work surface. Lightly sprinkle one-fourth of the green onions and 1 tsp of the sesame seeds on the dough and gently press them into the dough with your hand.

Tightly roll up the dough to make a cigar shape. Press the ends and seam closed and gently roll and stretch the dough into a longer snake shape about 12 in [30.5 cm] long. Coil the snake in a spiraled circle, and press the end into the coil. Roll the dough out again into a flat circle about 6 in [15 cm] wide. This double rolling technique means that the yummy green onion bits will be sandwiched between several thin layers of dough. And it's okay if the snake splits and green onion slices come spilling out—it's part of the appeal. Repeat with the remaining dough until you have four large green onion pancakes. Set aside.

Heat 1½ tsp of the sesame oil in a large sauté pan or skillet over medium-high heat. Add one green onion pancake to the pan at a time, cooking until crispy and browned on both sides, 5 to 6 minutes per side. Place on a paper towel–lined plate. Repeat these steps, adding 1½ tsp sesame oil to the pan each time, until all the pancakes are browned and crispy.

To store, stack the pancakes between parchment or wax paper in an airtight bag and refrigerate for up to 4 days. Reheat in a 400°F [200°C] oven for 5 to 7 minutes for sandwiches.

DUCK À LA FOUNG

SERVES 4 TO 6   **TIME** 2 HOURS, 45 MINUTES (MOSTLY ROASTING TIME)

One 5-lb [2.3-kg] duck, neck and giblets removed

1 Tbsp whole coriander seeds, ground with a spice grinder or mortar and pestle

2 tsp salt-free garlic powder

2 tsp ground cumin

2 tsp freshly ground black pepper

1 Tbsp orange juice

Remove the top rack from the oven and put the other rack in the middle. Preheat the oven to 425°F [220°C]. Line a roasting pan with aluminum foil (or better yet, use a foil roasting pan that you can later discard). Place a roasting rack in the roasting pan.

Pat the duck dry with a paper towel and place it on a cutting board. Using a sharp knife, cut off excess fat at the neck and cavity areas. Use kitchen shears to remove the wing tips, or leave them on if you like extra-crunchy wings. With the knife almost parallel with the skin, make small slashes all over the duck skin, cutting into the fat but being careful not to go through to the meat. This will allow the fat to drip out and off the duck, leaving the skin to get crispy.

In a small bowl, stir together the coriander seeds, garlic powder, cumin, and pepper with the orange juice. Rub the spice mixture all over the duck, front and back.

Place the duck on the roasting rack, breast-side down, and roast for 30 minutes. Remove the duck from the oven and lower the oven temperature to 375°F [190°C]. Using two sets of tongs or big serving forks, carefully tip the duck, allowing the liquid and fat from the cavity to drain into the pan. Then flip the duck so it is breast-side up. Continue to cook until the meat is tender and the skin is crispy, about 1 hour and 20 minutes. A meat thermometer placed in the leg joint should read 175°F [80°C].

Transfer the duck to a cutting board and let rest uncovered for 15 minutes before carving. Cut the duck into pieces or shred the meat to serve.

GIFTS OF HEALTH

During holidays and birthdays, a magical exchange happens: We give people lists of items we want and they give them to us to enjoy. It's an act of love and generosity. And if you live with a special diet, it's also the perfect opportunity to stock up on items that will help you eat well and with ease.

But remember, while these suggestions are for you, they also make great gifts for your loved ones, too. By giving others your favorite low-sodium spices, sauces, and other secret weapons, they'll be better outfitted to cook for you. As well as discover new ways to make food tastier, easier, and more exciting.

FOR THE BEGINNER

If you're starting a low-sodium diet and stepping into your kitchen for the first time, your loved ones are in luck. Whether they buy you measuring spoons, pots and pans, or an electric mixer, you need it. Use sites like Amazon or Pinterest to find the products you love, and then make lists (with links!) so people can purchase them. If you're looking for budget-friendly options, include goods from eBay and Craigslist as well.

FOR THE ARTISAN

List your favorite specialty products for your shelves and pantry. For grocery-store items, provide family and friends with brand names and even the store aisle where the product can be found. And for Internet-only products, provide links.

FOR THE HOME COOK

Make sure the kitchen is the happiest place in the home by adding simple pleasures, like radios and iPod docks to keep you grooving. Have mini vacuums and chemical-free cleaners handy to keep you calm when messes happen.

FOR THE BOOKWORM

Get the gift of inspiration with a pile of new cookbooks and food-magazine subscriptions. And remember, even if the literary resource isn't low-sodium specific, it can still provide plenty of ideas and instruction that will increase your confidence and creativity in the kitchen.

FOR THE SHOPPER

Don't discount the power of a gift card. When it comes to being on a special diet, these prepaid presents mean fresh ingredients from favorite grocery stores and farms, home delivery services, and artisan products. To make this gift even more special, your holiday elf can include a favorite recipe or a date night for you to enjoy the goods together.

FOR THE TIME-SAVER

The right gadgets can make you feel like you have a personal sous chef in the kitchen. Hand blenders, rice cookers, bread makers, and even ice-cream makers cut down on the time and energy needed to make flavorful foods. Items like slow cookers will even make dinner while you're out of the house. Easy to clean and easy to use, these utensils make from-scratch as simple as ordering out.

FOR THE ENTERTAINER

You eat with your eyes as much as your mouth. So for the enthusiastic host or hostess, there's no better gift than colorful napkins, plates, and serving ware. For something extra special, search on Etsy for tableware ideas or custom orders.

FOR THE MOVER AND SHAKER

Special diets don't need to stop you in your tracks. With beautiful bento or tiffin boxes, mason jar mugs, spill-free storage containers, and small fabric coolers, you can take your homemade food wherever you go. To work, to the football game, and even on an airplane; have airtight containers, will travel.

FOR THE EXPERIMENTER

Take your cooking to the next level with hickory chips, dehydrators, doughnut pans, mandolines, baking scales, and other chef-worthy tools. These items make any DIY project doable and will help you make over your favorite recipes at home, or even create new classics of your own.

FOR THE KIDS

Give little foodies everything they need to take charge of the kitchen and their diet needs. Aprons, kid-safe cutlery, and a colorful stepping stool will enable them to take part in the prep work. Bento lunch boxes as well as colorful allergy labels and tattoos (by Safety-Tat) ensure that they will eat well and safely beyond the home. Bookmaking websites offer the creative guidance for writing a cookbook of their very own.

··· 11 ···

TASTE

The Six Low-So Cooking Commandments
and Recipes

We have arrived. The kitchen.

This is where the magic happens. This is your place to experiment. This is where you get to put everything you've learned into play—all those spices and oils, the pots and pans, and the stacks of cookbooks; all the inspiration you picked up from restaurant menus, dishes served at other people's parties, and ingredients you've discovered while exploring cultures beyond your home.

This chapter is greater than the sum of its recipes. I introduce my Six Low-So Cooking Commandments—a total of six simple guidelines that will help you make more from less sodium every time you step into your kitchen. Each of the six recipe groups offers meals for every time of the day, breakfast to dessert, and even bigger gatherings and celebrations. You may notice they've been referenced throughout the book to help you bring each low-sodium lesson from the page to your tables.

But unlike the real commandments, nothing is set in stone. I encourage you to follow the guidelines, but I also give you my blessing to break free from the directions. Adjust the spices, use what vegetables and herbs you have on hand, and make the recipes your own! Before you dive in, here are a few words about the recipes.

COOKING TIME

I've included estimates in each of the recipes for how long it might take you to make each dish. If you're new to cooking, though, or if you have never peeled a butternut squash (see page 45), it may take you a little longer. Don't get discouraged. The more you cook a dish, or cook in general, the faster you will get. You'll eventually be able to cook several dishes at once, without burning them. So take your time and don't watch the clock the first time around. And don't fear long cooking times. Make a special date to get to know these more involved dishes. Most of the longer cooking times are not spent actively cooking—the biggest chunk of minutes (or hours) usually takes place in the oven or the fridge, freeing you to do other things. Just check in once in a while with your pot or pan so nothing burns or boils over.

MIX AND MATCH

Feel free to combine elements from different recipes to create a new dish. Really, do it. In the following pages, you'll learn to make polenta, roasted chicken, and a lot of dressings, just to name a few. These are building blocks for any dish you dream of. And while they are paired with other components or include suggested serving combinations, they're pretty darn flexible and interchangeable.

STARTING FROM ZERO

All the recipes use fresh, whole ingredients. Other than an occasional dollop of yogurt or jam or coconut milk, you will not find anything packaged or processed, not even canned beans or tomato paste. That's because I want to start everyone at zero—zero salt and zero processed ingredients. This approach makes room for a lot of natural flavor. From there, cut corners when you need to, like using frozen hash browns instead of freshly grated potatoes, or precut, no-salt-added frozen vegetables, or salt-free spice blends. Or, if you're not on a low-sodium diet, go ahead and add that sprinkle of salt. By starting at zero, you have ultimate flexibility and control of the sodium content in your food, for whatever your health needs and for whomever you feed.

SODIUM COUNTS

The recipes in this chapter will help teach you how to make fresh, flavorful, balanced food without salt or processed ingredients; they are not meant to serve as a specific, nutrition-based plan. If you'd like to calculate the total sodium in a dish or the other nutritional contents, I highly suggest using nutritional calculators provided by sites like the USDA SuperTracker (www.supertracker.usda.gov) and MyFitnessPal (www.myfitnesspal.com/recipe/calculator). Make sure to also consult professionals and adjust recipes accordingly to fit specific health needs.

That's it. You're officially ready to roll. Set the table, tie on your apron, trust your palate, and let the seasons be your compass.

SIX LOW-SO COOKING COMMANDMENTS

THOU SHALT
USE NATURAL FLAVOR

The best place to begin your low-sodium cooking adventures is with the natural flavors found in the ingredients themselves. Before reaching for the spice rack, boost a dish with fresh herbs, umami-filled mushrooms, and a burst of citrus. By employing the oven, the grill, and the blender, you can give even the most unassuming of ingredients (ahem, lettuce) a taste transformation. Use these recipes as the starting point for your own experimentations. You'll discover the sweet, salty, bitter, sour, umami, and smoky tastes your food has to offer.

THOU SHALT
USE COLOR AND TEXTURE

It's time to channel your inner artist and start playing with a range of ingredients that add visual and textural appeal to every meal—especially those dishes that are all the same color or consistency. If something looks or tastes bland, you'll find that a pop of green herbs, a sprinkle of red paprika, or the crunch of toasted nuts will fix the issue. Even broiling a pan of sauced noodles until the top layer gets crispy will give a simple pasta or casserole a welcome crunch. It's that simple. Go ahead and dig into Mother Nature's palette of colors and textures, accessorize your meals, and mix things up for your mouth and eyes.

THOU SHALT
STEAL

When it comes to cooking, stealing is totally acceptable behavior. Whether you take ideas from other cultures or other special diets, the tricks you'll learn will liven up dishes of your own design. Sometimes, these food substitutions even make recipes healthier or more time-efficient than the original version. So add an element of surprise to your table—skip rice and use cauliflower instead; give gravy a curried makeover; and create candy out of dates. If it's bad to steal, I don't want to be good.

THOU SHALT
REINVENT

Today, we live in a world where kale can be chips, bananas can be ice cream, and butternut squash can stand in for the cheese in mac 'n' cheese. So if your favorite food or convenience items are too high in sodium, hope is not lost. It's just time for an ingredient swap.

By reinventing recipes and replacing high-sodium ingredients with creative low-sodium stand-ins, you can enjoy your favorite dishes again. Yes, they may look or taste a little different from the original. But because you're being creative, you'll find that they're enjoyable in a whole new way.

THOU SHALT
BE BRAVE

Have you ever done something that seemed totally impossible at first? Hiked to the top of a mountain? Completed a marathon? Got to work on time on a Monday morning? From small victories to huge accomplishments, we've all felt the powerful rush of pushing ourselves beyond what we thought was possible. Sometimes it's not pretty (like Monday mornings) but once you know you can do it, it gets easier. And when you hear that little voice say, "You can't do that!" you'll be more likely to say, "Oh, yes I can!"

That's what this section is about. Bravery. Conquering cooking fears and pushing aside the culinary roadblocks that keep you from trying the scary things. It's about proving to yourself that you have the skills to make pasta or baked dumplings or ice cream from scratch. So the next time a seemingly difficult technique or recipe catches your eye, you won't shy away. You'll dive in, with confidence, even when a dish sounds complicated. Low-sodium cooking only gets better with a sense of adventure, and you'll find that after making those "hard" recipes once or twice, you'll soon tackle them without instructions, by memory and by feel. Transforming you from a timid cook into a fearless chef, willing and able to conquer any mountains (or croquembouche) no matter how intimidating.

THOU SHALT
WOW

Your final lesson in low-sodium cooking is all about showing off. No more apologizing for your low-sodium food. It's time to be dang proud of it. Whether that means hosting dinner parties or giving edible gifts, your low-sodium creations deserve to be shared with others. They don't have to be difficult, and they don't have to be fussy. You now have all the skills you need to make simple, fresh, low-sodium food worthy of second helpings. You'll find that you not only wow your friends and family, but you also might teach them something new. Start with these recipes for low-sodium bragging success. Then create some go-to showstoppers of your own. Because there ain't no party like a low-sodium party.

ROASTED FIG AND TOMATO SLOW JAM

Start with the natural umami found in tomatoes and the natural sweetness in figs. Intensify those flavors by a gazillion with the help of the oven. Add a bit of sour from balsamic. And get a jam, sauce, or spread that needs to be slathered over slices of fresh nectarines or bites of Easy Focaccia (page 238), swirled into a bowl of pasta noodles, or oozed over a juicy steak. You can also replace the figs with a fresh persimmon, roughly chopped and roasted with the tomatoes.

MAKES 1 CUP [250 G]   **TIME** 1 HOUR

24 cherry tomatoes, stemmed

1 Tbsp olive oil, plus 2 tsp

¼ tsp freshly ground black pepper

8 dried black figs

¼ cup [35 g] diced yellow onion

2 tsp molasses

1 tsp balsamic vinegar

¼ cup [60 ml] water

Preheat the oven to 400°F [200°C].

Place the cherry tomatoes in a large baking pan. Add the 1 Tbsp olive oil and the pepper to the pan, and use your hands to toss and coat. Place the pan in the oven and roast until the tomatoes blister and wrinkle, 20 to 25 minutes.

Remove the stems from the figs, cut the figs in half, and place them in a food processor (or blender). Transfer the tomatoes to the food processor and allow them to cool, about 10 minutes. Then blend until mostly smooth—there will still be chunky bits of fig and that's okay.

In a small saucepan, heat the remaining 2 tsp olive oil over medium heat. Add the onion and cook, stirring frequently, until it begins to soften, about 3 minutes. Add the tomato-fig purée, molasses, vinegar, and water and stir to combine. Bring to a simmer and cook for 2 to 3 minutes. Turn the heat to low and cook, stirring frequently toward the end of cooking time, until the figs and tomatoes become a thick sauce, 20 to 25 minutes. Remove from the heat and let cool.

Store in an airtight container in the refrigerator for up to 1 week.

DILLY CHIMICHURRI

This herb-based sauce is best known as a bright topping for rich, savory steaks. It's a winning combination. But just because the equation works, doesn't mean you can't switch things up. Use the basic formula (herbs + acid + garlic = sauce) as inspiration for your own creations, and experiment with the herbs you have on hand. Don't be afraid to play with texture (add creamy yogurt) or pair with other nontraditional dishes, like Dukka-Spiced Salmon Patties (page 187) and Curry Tofu Fries (page 217).

MAKES 1 CUP [240 ML]   **TIME** 5 MINUTES

1½ tsp chopped jalapeño chile

2 garlic cloves

1 medium shallot, quartered

¼ cup [7 g] chopped fresh dill

¼ cup [60 ml] vegetable oil or olive oil

2 tsp apple cider vinegar

¼ cup [60 ml] plain Greek yogurt (optional)

1 tsp lemon juice (optional)

In a food processor (or blender), add the jalapeño, garlic, shallot, and dill. Pulse until the ingredients are minced. Add the vegetable oil and vinegar, and pulse again to combine. Add in the yogurt (if using) and lemon juice (if using), and pulse a few more times until smooth.

Store in an airtight container in the refrigerator for up to 4 days.

HARISSA HOT SAUCE

Most store-bought hot sauces will contain more than 100 mg of sodium per 1 tsp. But you can harness the same heat with the help of dried chiles, fresh chile peppers, and a blender. A homemade hot sauce allows you to play with countless sauce types (and chiles), beyond the tongue-scorching kind. So let's start with harissa, a Tunisian hot sauce—or paste, if you make it thick—that adds a spark to everything it touches; including your eyes, so be careful. When handling chile peppers, I suggest you wear gloves. Once you master this hot sauce, explore other combinations of chiles from all over the world.

MAKES 1¼ CUPS [300 ML]   **TIME** 40 MINUTES

1 or 2 dried chipotle, ancho, pasilla, or guajillo chiles

2 red bell peppers

2 Tbsp lemon juice

¼ cup [60 ml] canola oil

1 tsp ground cumin

½ tsp salt-free garlic powder

½ tsp ground coriander

Put the dried chiles in a small heatproof bowl and pour boiling water over them, just covering them. Let soak for 30 minutes.

Meanwhile, preheat the oven to broil and line a baking pan with aluminum foil.

Cut the bell peppers in half and remove the stems and seeds. Lay the pepper halves in the prepared pan, cut-side down. Broil the peppers until the skin is charred, 15 to 20 minutes. Remove from the oven and, using tongs, put them in a medium bowl. Use the foil pan liner to cover the bowl and let the peppers steam for about 15 minutes. When cool to the touch, use your hands to remove the charred pepper skins and discard. Set the peeled peppers aside.

Drain the rehydrated chiles, and reserve the soaking liquid. Use a knife (and wear gloves) to remove the stems and seeds. Put the chiles and bell peppers in a food processor (or blender), and add the lemon juice, canola oil, cumin, garlic powder, ground coriander, and 2 Tbsp of the chile-soaking liquid (or add more if you want it spicier). Blend until smooth; add a little water, as needed, for the desired sauce consistency.

Store in an airtight container in the refrigerator for up to 7 days.

NOTE: If you make a thicker version of this hot sauce, you can use it in place of tomato paste for curries and stews.

HOW TO PICK A PEPPER

By switching up your dried chiles, you'll give your hot sauce very different flavors. Each type of chile packs a different punch (level of heat), so use this guide, ranging from mild heat to super hot, to pick the best pepper for your own preferred heat level.

aji: mild heat with some fruity flavor

ancho: dried poblano chiles, sweet with mild heat

pasilla: mild in heat with a licorice-like flavor

California: dried Anaheim chile, mild in heat

guajillo: mid-level heat with a tougher skin that requires a longer soak time

chipotle: dried and smoked jalapeño chiles that come in two different levels of heat: *más suave* (more mild) and *muy picante* (very spicy)

Chile de Arbol: bright red, mad hot

SAUCE GRIBICHE

Chicken eggs happen to be yet another source of natural umami. Poached, fried, or scrambled—they make a simple, savory addition to any dish. Here's a new trick: Gribiche! This egg-based sauce dances between a creamy mayonnaise-like dressing and a smooth egg salad, meaning you can use it in a variety of ways. Spread it on crackers. Mix it into a bowl of fresh peas (also rich in umami). Pile it on top of warm, roasted asparagus or cool, sliced radishes. Scoop it into your mouth with a fork. Make this sauce every weekend so you can add umami to your meals all week long.

MAKES ¾ CUP [180 G]   **TIME** 20 MINUTES

1 medium shallot, finely chopped

2 Tbsp apple cider vinegar

2 eggs

1 to 2 Tbsp grapeseed oil or olive oil

½ tsp ground yellow mustard

½ tsp brown or yellow mustard seeds

¼ tsp salt-free garlic powder

¼ cup [7 g] loosely packed, chopped fresh herbs (my favorites: chives, parsley, dill, or celery leaves)

Freshly ground black pepper

In a small bowl, combine the shallot and vinegar. Set aside.

Prepare a small bowl full of ice and water. Put the eggs in a medium saucepan and cover with 1 in [2.5 cm] cold water. Cover the pot and bring to a boil over medium-high heat. As soon as the bubbles are rolling and you hear the eggs knocking, take the pan off of the heat and let the eggs sit, covered, for 8 minutes. Use a slotted spoon to carefully transfer the eggs to the bowl of ice water. When cool enough to touch, remove the eggs from the ice water. Crack each egg and, while holding the egg under running water, peel off the shell. Separate the egg whites from the yolks into two separate bowls.

In the yolk bowl, slowly add the grapeseed oil a few drops at a time, stopping to whisk the mixture with a fork until the oil and yolk combine. Keep adding drops of oil and whisking, until the yolks become thick, smooth, and creamy. (This can also be done in a small food processor or blender.) Add the ground mustard, mustard seeds, and garlic powder and mix until combined. Set aside.

Use a clean fork to break up the egg whites into little bits. Drain the shallot and reserve the liquid.

Mix the egg whites together with the egg yolks for an egg-salad look and feel. Add the shallot, herbs, and a grinding of pepper. Taste the sauce. If you like vinegar, add a bit of the shallot pickling liquid to the mixture.

Store in an airtight container in the refrigerator for up to 4 days.

VARIATION: Keep the yolk "mayo" and the egg white bits separate. Mix the yolk "mayo" into a salad or sliced vegetables. Top with the egg white bits, shallot, herbs, and pepper for a layered look.

AVOCADO GREEN GODDESS DRESSING

I've become obsessed with this dressing. The natural sweetness and creaminess of the avocado mixed with fresh herbs and tangy vinegar means one addictive combination that makes any dish praiseworthy. Massage it into a mix of raw vegetables, like kale or coarsely chopped broccoli. Mix it with raw zucchini noodles. Use it as a dip for rice crackers, or a spread for sandwiches. Swap it in as a sauce for almost any meat dish. You'll be a Goddess convert in no time.

MAKES 1½ CUPS [360 ML]   **TIME** 5 MINUTES

2 garlic cloves, roughly chopped

1 small shallot, roughly chopped

¼ cup [7 g] tightly packed fresh cilantro leaves

¼ cup [7 g] fresh basil leaves

¼ cup [15 g] chopped fresh chives

¼ cup [60 ml] lemon juice

2 Tbsp lime juice

2 to 3 Tbsp olive oil

½ medium avocado

2 tsp apple cider vinegar

Put the garlic, shallot, cilantro, basil, chives, lemon juice, and lime juice in a blender (or food processor) with 2 Tbsp of the olive oil and purée until smooth. Add the avocado and vinegar and blend again until well combined. Add the remaining 1 Tbsp olive oil if needed to get your desired dressing consistency.

Store in an airtight container, with a little water on top to prevent browning, in the refrigerator for up to 4 days. Pour off the water before using.

CARROT-SWEET ONION DRESSING

Remember how the natural sodium found in whole foods is your low-sodium secret weapon? Well, this carrot-based dressing is a perfect example of how to use those higher-sodium ingredients (carrot!) to your flavor advantage. Once you try this recipe, be sure to harness the natural sodium powers of other vegetables, like beets, celery, and artichokes, by making them into dressings, sauces, and drinks, too.

MAKES 1 CUP [240 ML]   **TIME** 20 MINUTES

1 medium carrot, roughly chopped

¼ white onion, chopped

½ cup [120 ml] grapeseed oil or olive oil

1 Tbsp apple cider vinegar

2 Tbsp lemon juice

½ tsp salt-free garlic powder

Fill a small pot with 2 in [5 cm] water and place a metal steamer basket in the pot, above the water. Bring the water to a simmer over high heat and place the carrot pieces in the steamer basket. Cover and steam over medium-low heat until the carrots are tender, about 20 minutes.

Transfer the carrot to a small food processor (or blender). Add the onion, grapeseed oil, vinegar, lemon juice, garlic powder, and 1 Tbsp water and blend. (The dressing will be slightly chunky, so if you want it smoother, add a bit more water or lemon juice.)

Store in an airtight container in the refrigerator for up to 1 week.

LEMON TAHINI DRESSING

Tahini, which is basically sesame seed paste, lends a nutty flavor without the nuts. It is commonly used as a base for hummus, and it also makes a rich and savory dressing for vegetables or noodles—and, as you'll see on page 199, vegetable noodles. If you make it thick, you can use it as a spread. You could try also using black sesame seeds for a different look and flavor. Helpful hint: A store-bought jar of tahini will often come with the sesame oil and the "paste" separated. To mix without the mess, lay the jar on its side (with the lid on) for a little while, until the oil moves from the top to the side of the jar. Use a knife or thick end of a chopstick to stir and blend.

MAKES **ABOUT 1½ CUPS [360 ML]** **TIME** **5 MINUTES**

½ cup [70 g] tahini

2 Tbsp lemon juice, plus
zest of 1 lemon

¼ cup [30 g] roughly
chopped peeled ginger

½ tsp salt-free garlic powder

1 tsp toasted white sesame seeds

¼ cup [7 g] chopped
fresh cilantro leaves

Pinch of red pepper flakes

Combine the tahini, lemon juice, and ginger in a food processor (or blender). Blend until smooth. Add ½ cup [120 ml] water and blend again. Keep blending in water, ¼ cup [60 ml] at a time, until the dressing reaches your desired consistency—thick and creamy like a sauce or runny for a dressing. Add the garlic powder, sesame seeds, cilantro, red pepper flakes, and lemon zest and pulse a few times to combine.

Store in an airtight container in the refrigerator for up to 1 week.

GRILLED LETTUCE SALAD

This salad, generously contributed from Bruce Cole, publisher of *Edible San Francisco*, proves that a little heat and smoke will significantly transform any ingredient. Lettuce is as simple in flavor as ingredients can get, but just a bit of char suddenly adds flavor complexity and visual appeal. So remember, especially during the summer months, if you want an easy way to jazz up a simple dish, throw those unsuspecting ingredients on the grill.

SERVES 4   **TIME** 30 MINUTES

2 heads Little Gem lettuce or romaine hearts

3 garlic cloves, minced

2 Tbsp olive oil or vegetable oil

¼ tsp freshly ground black pepper

Carrot–Sweet Onion Dressing (page 169)

2 to 3 Tbsp minced fresh chives or chopped fresh dill

Prepare a charcoal grill for high heat or preheat a gas grill to high.

Cut the lettuce heads in half, slicing all the way through the root ends. Run under cold water, spreading the leaves apart to rinse out any dirt or debris. Spin dry in a salad spinner or shake dry by hand, and lay cut-side down to drain on a clean kitchen cloth or paper towels.

Put the garlic in a large plastic bag or baking dish with the olive oil and pepper. Toss to combine. Put the lettuce halves in the bag or baking dish and toss to spread the oil-garlic mixture all over the leaves and into the nooks and crannies.

When the coals in your charcoal grill are covered with white ash or your gas grill is at 400°F [200°C], lay each lettuce half cut-side down on the grate, directly over the coals. Cook for 5 minutes. Flip one to check if it is crisped and slightly blackened. If not, return it to the grill and cook for another 2 to 3 minutes. You only grill the cut side of the lettuce.

Once the lettuce is slightly blackened on the cut side, place it on a serving platter or individual dishes. Spoon the dressing over the lettuce and sprinkle with the chives to serve.

LEMON CHICKEN ORZO

Store-bought low-sodium broth or stock can have around 100 mg of sodium per 1 cup [240 ml], depending on the brand. If sticking to a very-low-sodium diet, it's best to make your own with bones and scraps and some time in a pot. But these days, I often skip making the stock or broth ahead of time. I've found that, with the right ingredients and the right recipe, you can make the stock as you cook your meal, like for this dish, which uses chicken thighs, squash, and lemon to create a bright and meaty broth, together in the pot as the orzo cooks. This approach lets you coax out those savory flavors using just one recipe. For those who can handle a little extra sodium, serve with grated Parmesan on the side. And if you don't feel like prepping the butternut squash, swap in 1½ cups [90 g] chopped broccoli florets instead, adding them during the final 5 to 10 minutes of cooking.

SERVES 4   **TIME** 1 HOUR, 15 MINUTES

1½ cups [210 g] peeled, cubed butternut squash

2 tsp olive oil

4 garlic cloves, minced

4 boneless, skinless chicken thighs

Zest and juice of 2 lemons

¼ tsp dried dill

¼ tsp salt-free garlic powder

Pinch of freshly ground black pepper

Pinch of red pepper flakes

1 cup [180 g] orzo

Fresh dill for sprinkling (optional)

Using a food processor with a grater attachment or a box grater (be careful of your fingertips), shred the butternut squash. It will look like shredded Cheddar cheese. Set aside.

In a Dutch oven or large saucepan with a lid, add the olive oil and garlic and sauté over medium-high heat, stirring often, until the garlic turns golden brown, 2 to 3 minutes. Add the chicken thighs and brown, 3 to 5 minutes per side. Add ¼ cup [60 ml] of the lemon juice, the lemon zest, dill, garlic powder, black pepper, red pepper flakes, and 2 cups [480 ml] water and stir to combine. Bring the liquid to a boil and cook for 5 minutes, scraping up any browned bits on the bottom of the pan with a wooden spoon. Turn the heat to low, cover the pan, and simmer until the chicken thighs are tender enough to break apart with the wooden spoon, 6 to 8 minutes.

Add the orzo and squash to the pan, and stir to combine. Turn the heat to medium-low, cover, and cook until the squash softens and the orzo takes on a risotto-ish texture, 15 to 20 minutes. Be sure to stir frequently to keep the orzo from sticking to the bottom of the pan; add another ½ to 1 cup [120 to 240 ml] water, as needed.

Take the pot off of the heat and use tongs or a fork to transfer the chicken to a medium mixing bowl. Use two forks to pull the chicken pieces apart, return the shredded chicken to the pan, and stir. Ladle the chicken orzo into bowls and serve with a sprinkle of fresh dill, if desired, and a sprinkle of the remaining lemon juice.

LEMON ZINGER BARS

Most packaged breakfast bars contain a lot of hidden sodium, more than 100 mg per bar, depending on the brand. But it's easy to make your own morning-friendly treats, packed with healthful and perky flavors. This blend of eye-opening lemon and spicy ginger will put a spring in your step. If you're not a ginger fan, mellow out the "zing" by replacing ½ cup [70 g] of the ginger with chopped dried cherries, dried apricots, or pitted dates for a slightly sweeter taste.

MAKES SIXTEEN 2-IN [5-CM] BARS **TIME** 1 HOUR, 25 MINUTES

2¾ cups [230 g] whole rolled oats

4 pitted dates, chopped

¾ cup [105 g] chopped candied ginger

Juice and zest of 2 lemons

¾ cup [180 ml] warm water

Preheat the oven to 375°F [190°C]. Grease an 8-by-8-in [20-by-20-cm] baking pan or line with parchment paper.

Put ¾ cup [60 g] of the oats into a food processor (or blender) and pulse until the oats form a flour. Pour into a medium mixing bowl and set aside.

Add the dates and ginger to the food processor with the lemon juice and water. Allow the mixture to sit and soften for 30 minutes. Blend until the mixture is smooth.

Add the remaining 2 cups [170 g] oats and the lemon zest to the bowl with the oat flour. Pour in the date-ginger mixture. Stir until well combined, and then pour the mixture into the prepared baking pan. Bake until the edges become golden brown and the mixture feels firm to the touch, 35 to 40 minutes.

Remove the baking pan to a cooling rack. When cool, remove from the pan onto a cutting board and cut into squares. Set the bars on the cooling rack to firm up a bit more, about 10 minutes.

Store in an airtight container or resealable plastic bag for up to 1 week. To warm, reheat in a 375°F [190°C] oven for 6 to 8 minutes or in the microwave for 30 seconds.

TOASTED PEPITA MIX

Giving ingredients a pleasing texture can be as simple as toasting them. And one of my favorite items to crisp up are pepitas, the tasty and tender inner meat of shelled pumpkin seeds. Tossed with spices, including coriander seeds (bonus mouth appeal), they make an easy snack or even a texture-improving topping for soups, mashed vegetables, fish, or other dishes of the "soft" and "velvety" variety. Serve the mix like a bar snack, add a drizzle of honey and combine with popcorn for a party mix, or blend with herbs to make a toasty pesto.

MAKES 1 CUP [120 G]   **TIME** 10 MINUTES

1 Tbsp coriander seeds

1 tsp cumin seeds

1 cup [120 g] no-salt-added pepitas

½ tsp grapeseed oil or olive oil

¼ tsp salt-free garlic powder

¼ tsp sweet paprika

⅛ tsp cayenne pepper

Pinch of freshly ground black pepper

Heat a medium sauté pan or skillet over medium heat. Add the coriander seeds and cumin seeds and toast them until they are fragrant, about 2 minutes, shaking the pan or stirring them frequently with a wooden spoon or spatula. Transfer the seeds to a medium bowl and set aside.

Add the pepitas to the pan and cook, stirring frequently, until they begin turning golden and start to jump in the pan, 3 to 5 minutes. Add the grapeseed oil, garlic powder, paprika, cayenne, and black pepper and stir to combine. Cook for 2 minutes. Add the pepita mixture to the toasted coriander seeds and cumin seeds, stir, and let cool.

Store in an airtight container at room temperature for up to 2 weeks.

RAW BITES

Let's talk appetizers for a moment. They are the opening act for the main dish. Good ones get you pumped up and those taste buds tingling. Which is why they're the perfect items for playing with color and texture—something exciting that says, you like this? Just wait for what's to come. All that sparkle doesn't have to come at the price of long cooking times, however. You can actually create show-stopping appetizers in just a few minutes, using raw ingredients. Give these three a try the next time you need to create a tasty lineup.

NECTARINE GUACAMOLE

MAKES 4 CUPS [910 G]   **TIME** 10 MINUTES

1 yellow nectarine, pitted and diced

2 green onions, root ends trimmed, thinly sliced

2 avocados, mashed

1 cup [140 g] corn kernels, fresh or thawed frozen

1 cup [155 g] halved cherry tomatoes

1 tsp coriander seeds

½ tsp minced jalapeño chile

¼ cup [7 g] fresh chopped cilantro leaves

Zest and juice of 1 lime

Salt-free tortilla chips, raw vegetables, or small, square pieces of sodium-free nori for serving

In a large serving bowl, mix the nectarine, green onions, avocados, corn kernels, cherry tomatoes, coriander seeds, and jalapeño with a spoon or fork until combined. Add the cilantro, lime zest, and half of the lime juice and stir to combine. Taste and add more lime juice, as needed. Serve with chips, vegetables, or nori squares.

VARIATIONS: Roast 2 cups [210 g] diced tomatoes in the oven for 30 minutes and add them to the guacamole for an extra boost of color and umami. You can also substitute 1½ cups [270 g] chopped cucumber when nectarines are out of season.

LIME-CHILI STREET CARROTS

SERVES 4 TO 6   **TIME** 10 MINUTES

6 large carrots, rainbow if possible

Zest and juice of 1 lime

½ tsp salt-free chili powder

Start by peeling the outer layer of the carrots. Trim off the roots and most of the stem, but leave a bit of the stem because it looks quite pretty when you plate them.

Cut the carrots in half, lengthwise, and cut those halves in half lengthwise again. Put the carrots in a deep, square or rectangular dish or large plastic bag and set aside.

In a small bowl, mix the lime zest and juice with the chili powder. Pour the lime mixture over the carrots and mix with your hands until the carrots are coated with all that lime-chili goodness. Cover and keep refrigerated for up to 2 hours. Or place the carrots on a serving platter, or in cups with the stems peeking out the top, and eat right away.

RADISH-AND-ONION YOGURT SPREAD

SERVES 4 TO 6   **TIME** 10 MINUTES

12 large Cherry Belle or
Easter Egg radishes

½ cup [120 ml] Greek yogurt

1½ Tbsp dried onion flakes

¼ tsp salt-free ground mustard

¼ tsp salt-free garlic powder

¼ cup salt-free pine nuts or
walnuts, toasted and crushed

Wash the radishes, trim off the roots (if desired), and leave a bit of the stems. Use a handheld grater or a food processor with the grater attachment to shred four of the radishes. Pat or squeeze to remove excess liquid. Transfer the grated radish to a small bowl and mix with the yogurt, onion flakes, ground mustard, and garlic powder. Set aside.

Cut the remaining radishes in half lengthwise, and then again in half lengthwise (if radishes are large). Place them on a serving platter or large plate.

To serve, use a knife to spread the yogurt mixture on the cut side of the radishes and sprinkle with the pine nuts. Or, let guests spread and sprinkle on their own.

TOASTED RICE PATTIES

At Nojo restaurant in San Francisco, chef and owner Greg Dunmore treats me with a range of low-sodium delicacies from gyoza to *chawanmushi* to chicken-neck yakitori. And even fried pig feet. But my favorite dish? It's the toasted rice patty, the simplest of them all. There are no sauces, fried panko crusts, or other tricks involved. What makes this dish so extraordinary? The textural contrast of the crispy exterior and the pillowy rice center. And when you add a spritz of lemon juice, a sprinkle of nori (dried seaweed) confetti, and some black sesame seeds, you've got a feast for the mouth and the eyes.

MAKES 4 PATTIES   **TIME** 1 HOUR, 15 MINUTES (MOSTLY IN THE RICE COOKER)

1 cup [200 g] short-grain white rice (see Note)

½ sheet sodium-free nori

2 tsp black sesame seeds

1 to 3 Tbsp sesame oil

1 lemon, cut into 4 wedges

Using a fine-mesh sieve placed over a bowl, rinse the rice under running water, stirring it with your hands until the water looks almost clear, 30 seconds or so. Put the rice and 1½ cups [360 ml] water into a rice cooker, cover, and turn on. When the rice is cooked, fluff and let sit on warm, with the lid closed for 30 minutes.

Meanwhile, use scissors to cut the nori into strips ½ in [12 mm] long, like little nori sprinkles. Set aside.

Transfer the rice to a large bowl or baking pan, add the sesame seeds, and stir until combined. Let the rice cool, 10 to 15 minutes. With oiled or wet hands, take one-fourth of the rice and pack it into a tight, hockey puck–like disc, round in shape with a flat top and bottom. This shape provides a good surface area for toasting, which is what you want. If the rice sticks to your fingers too much, put it in a wet towel or in some plastic wrap or use a ring mold placed on top of wax paper to help you pack and shape it. Repeat to make four rice patties. Set aside.

In a large skillet, heat 1 Tbsp of the sesame oil over medium-high heat. Add two of the rice patties at a time, or whatever fits in the pan without crowding. Cook until the bottoms turn golden and crispy, 8 to 10 minutes. Flip and cook the other sides, another 8 to 10 minutes. Continue until all the patties have been toasted, adding more oil and adjusting the heat as needed.

Sprinkle the warm, toasted rice patties with the nori strips and serve with the lemon wedges alongside.

NOTES: Sushi begins with short-grain white rice (now often labeled as "sushi rice" in stores). This type of rice is starchier than long-grain rice, which is what makes it sticky and hold together. So don't try to substitute, because you'll end up with a nice pilaf instead of a pillow of rice. To make sushi and rice balls (*onigiri*), the steamed rice is seasoned with salt (and sugar and vinegar, in the case of sushi). So be aware and make your own sushi and rice balls at home.

If you have time, you can also put the shaped rice patties into the refrigerator until chilled (or overnight) for an extra-crispy crust.

KALE SALADS FOR DIFFERENT SEASONS

Long before kale was a *big thing*, the leaves were often used as a dark green backdrop for party platters of fresh vegetables. Remember that? While we didn't totally appreciate kale for its taste quite yet, people appreciated kale for its good looks and ability to highlight other colorful ingredients. I love using kale leaves for salads for that reason. And yes, I like leaving them raw, too. The sturdy kale leaves easily soften with a little olive oil and lemon, while still retaining their vibrant color. Kale looks (and tastes) great with a range of fruits and vegetables, including orange scalloped squash and summer stone fruit, bright green avocados, golden toasted pepitas, and ruby pomegranate seeds. So use these two recipes as a starting point to explore all things kale. Because kale is pretty much the little black dress of vegetables, you can dress it up for any season. (Note: Because every bunch of kale is different in size, a good rule of thumb is that 24 big kale leaves, without the tough bottom stems, will make approximately 6 cups [360 g] kale ribbons.)

ROASTED SQUASH AND KALE SALAD

SERVES 4 TO 6   **TIME** 1 HOUR

2 delicata squash or
1 medium acorn squash

3 Tbsp olive oil

1 Tbsp honey

24 large lacinato kale
leaves, deribbed

Zest of 1 lemon, plus
2 Tbsp lemon juice

¼ tsp salt-free garlic powder

Pinch of freshly ground
black pepper

¼ cup [30 g] raw no-salt-
added pepitas

¼ cup [40 g] pomegranate
seeds (when in season)

1 fennel bulb

Preheat the oven to 400°F [200°C].

If using delicata squash, cut off the knobby ends and cut each squash in half lengthwise. Use a spoon to scoop out the seeds. Cut each squash in half crosswise into half-moon shapes 1 in [2.5 cm] thick. If using acorn squash, peel the skin, then cut off the ends and set the squash upright on one of the cut ends. Slice down from the top, cutting the squash in half. Use a spoon to scoop out the seeds. Cut each squash half crosswise into half-moon shapes 1 in [2.5 cm] thick. Cut those slices crosswise in half again.

In a medium bowl, combine the squash, 2 Tbsp of the olive oil, and the honey and use your hands to mix everything together. Put the squash slices in a large baking pan in a single layer, and bake until fork-tender, 35 to 40 minutes, turning once halfway through.

Meanwhile, cut the kale leaves into thin ribbons and put them in a salad bowl or onto a large serving dish. Add the remaining 1 Tbsp olive oil, the lemon zest, lemon juice, garlic powder, and pepper. Use your hands to massage the mixture into the kale until it becomes soft, 2 to 3 minutes. Set aside.

Heat a dry, medium sauté pan or skillet over medium-high heat. Add the pepitas and toast, stirring frequently, until they turn golden and begin to pop, 3 to 5 minutes. Add the warm pepitas and the pomegranate seeds to the kale, and use tongs or salad spoons to mix until combined.

Cut the root end from the fennel. Remove any discolored outer layers. Using a mandoline, or really good knife skills, thinly slice the fennel bulb. Add the fennel slices to the kale. Add the baked squash slices, toss again to combine, and serve immediately.

KALE COBB SALAD

SERVES 4 TO 6   TIME 20 MINUTES

2 Tbsp olive oil

Zest and juice of 1 lemon

¼ tsp salt-free garlic powder

2 large avocados, halved and pitted

24 large Lacinato kale leaves, deribbed

1 cup [140 g] corn kernels, fresh or thawed frozen

1 nectarine, pitted and diced

4 to 6 radishes, trimmed and thinly sliced

2 hard-boiled eggs (see page 166), finely chopped

In a large mixing bowl, combine 1 Tbsp of the olive oil, the lemon zest, 2 Tbsp of the lemon juice, and the garlic powder. Scoop out half of an avocado, add it to the bowl, and use a fork to mash it with the other ingredients until you have a creamy dressing.

Cut the kale leaves into thin ribbons and add them to the dressing. Use your hands to massage the dressing into the kale until it becomes soft, 2 to 3 minutes. Taste and add the remaining 1 Tbsp olive oil or more lemon juice if needed. Set aside.

Cut the remaining avocado into ½-in [12-mm] cubes.

Place the kale mixture into a salad bowl or onto a large serving dish. For a traditional composition, starting on one side, put a row of corn kernels, a row of nectarine cubes, a row of cubed avocado, a row of sliced radishes, and a row of chopped hard-boiled eggs. Or use tongs or salad spoons to mix everything together. Cover and refrigerate until ready to serve, up to 3 days.

DUKKA-SPICED SALMON PATTIES

Recipes that involve bread crumbs—from meatballs to casseroles—always pose a sodium challenge because they contain bread (remember the CDC top-culprit list?) and salty seasonings. Some products can equal more than 1,600 mg of sodium per 1 cup [110 g].

By using a nut-based replacement, you can make a low-sodium substitution while enhancing the color and texture of the dish. Enter dukka spice, a blend of toasted nuts, seeds, and spices that can be mixed into yogurt or olive oil as a spread, sprinkled on salads and soups, or folded into your burgers and meatballs in place of seasoned bread crumbs. The chickpea flour in the recipe binds the patties together, while the dukka spice provides the bulk and flavor. Since you can use any salt-free nuts or spices to make dukka, experiment with your own blends for different levels of warmth, nuttiness, and heat.

MAKES 6 TO 8 PATTIES   **TIME** 1 HOUR (MOSTLY CHILLING IN THE FRIDGE)

1½ lb [680 g] salmon fillets, skin on and deboned

1 recipe Dukka Spice Mix (page 188)

2 green onions, root ends trimmed, thinly sliced

¼ white onion, finely diced

¼ cup [7 g] chopped fresh cilantro or basil

Zest of 1 lemon, plus ½ lemon for squeezing

1 egg, lightly beaten

3 Tbsp chickpea flour, or ¼ cup [15 g] panko bread crumbs

Vegetable oil for frying

Carrot-Sweet Onion Dressing (page 169) or Greek yogurt for serving

Preheat the oven to 375°F [190°C]. Line a baking pan with parchment paper.

Place the salmon fillets skin-side down in the prepared baking pan. Bake until the fish turns light pink, 10 to 12 minutes. Transfer to a plate. Once cool enough to handle, peel off and discard the salmon skin. Put a fresh piece of parchment in the baking pan.

Using two forks, flake the cooked salmon into small pieces and transfer to a large mixing bowl. Add the dukka, green onions, white onion, cilantro, lemon zest, egg, and chickpea flour. Stir to combine. Make small salmon patties, 2½ in [6 cm] wide, using about ½ cup [90 g] of the mixture per patty. Place the patties in the prepared baking pan. Cover with aluminum foil or plastic wrap and refrigerate for 30 minutes, or overnight, to help the patties firm up for successful frying.

CONTINUED

DUKKA SPICE MIX

MAKES ¼ CUP [85 G]

TIME 10 MINUTES

¾ cup [90 g] toasted salt-free pepitas, pine nuts, pistachios, or almonds

2 Tbsp white sesame seeds

2 Tbsp coriander seeds

1 Tbsp cumin seeds

¼ tsp salt-free garlic powder

¼ tsp freshly ground black pepper

Heat a medium skillet or sauté pan over medium-high heat. Add the pepitas and toast, stirring frequently, until they turn golden and begin to pop, 3 to 5 minutes. Transfer the pepitas to a small mixing bowl. Add the sesame seeds, coriander seeds, and cumin seeds to the skillet and toast until they become fragrant, about 2 minutes.

Transfer the toasted nuts and seeds to a food processor (or spice grinder). Add the garlic powder and pepper and pulse until the mixture forms a crumbly powder.

Store in an airtight container for up to 1 month.

When ready to cook, line a large plate with paper towels. In a large skillet, heat 2 to 3 Tbsp vegetable oil over medium-high heat until the oil begins to ripple. Carefully put two patties into the skillet and cook until golden brown, 3 to 4 minutes. Flip the patties and cook for another 2 to 3 minutes. Transfer the patties to the prepared plate. Discard any browned bits from the skillet and repeat with the remaining patties, adding more oil and adjusting the heat as needed. Serve warm with a squeeze of lemon juice and a drizzle of dressing.

VARIATION: Want to make a faster version of this recipe for dinner? Simply coat even-size salmon fillets with 1 tsp vegetable oil each. Rub the dukka on top and cook the fillets as directed. Remove the skin and serve whole with lemon wedges or the dressing.

ROAST BEEF AND MUSTARD SEED CARROTS

Let's not underestimate the visual appeal of a giant, juicy hunk of beef and a sauce made from the roasting juices. But to make a meaty meal even more spectacular, pair it with a side that adds crunch and color, like burnt-orange Mustard Seed Carrots. As a side dish to your roast, the carrots offer a toothy bite, thanks to their sturdiness and a surprising pop from the mustard seeds. And as leftovers, the roast beef makes mighty fine sandwiches. Note: Keep in mind that cooking times for the roast beef may vary. Every cut of meat and every oven is different. If using grass-fed beef, start checking for doneness after 45 minutes of roasting to make sure that the meat doesn't dry out.

SERVES 4 TO 6   **TIME** 3 HOURS, 15 MINUTES (45 MINUTES ACTIVE TIME)

1 tsp dried dill

1 tsp salt-free garlic powder

1 tsp freshly ground black pepper

2 to 3 lb [910 g to 1.4 kg] top round beef roast, with ¼-in [6-mm] layer of fat, tied with butcher twine

2 tsp vegetable oil

4 garlic cloves, minced

½ red onion, cut into ½-in [12-mm] slices

12 large cremini mushrooms, cut into ¼-in [6-mm] slices

½ cup [120 ml] orange juice

1 cup [240 ml] water

Preheat the oven to 325°F [165°C].

In a small bowl, mix together the dill, garlic powder, and pepper. Pat the beef roast dry with a paper towel and rub the spice mixture into the entire surface of the roast.

In a Dutch oven or cast-iron skillet, heat 1 tsp of the vegetable oil over medium heat. Add the beef and brown on all sides, 3 to 4 minutes per side. Transfer to a plate and set aside.

In the same Dutch oven, heat the remaining 1 tsp vegetable oil over medium-high heat. Add the garlic, onion, and mushrooms and cook, stirring frequently, for 2 minutes. Add ¼ cup [60 ml] of the orange juice and use a wooden spoon to scrape up the browned bits on the bottom of the pan. Cook until the onion softens, 3 to 5 minutes. Return the meat to the pan and add the remaining ¼ cup [60 ml] orange juice and the water. Cover with a lid or aluminum foil, transfer to the oven, and roast for

CONTINUED

2 Tbsp honey

1 Tbsp balsamic vinegar

¼ tsp mustard seeds

3 garlic cloves, minced

12 large carrots, ends removed, cut in half lengthwise

1 Tbsp olive oil

1¼ hours. Check the meat's internal temperature by inserting a meat thermometer into the center part of the roast. When it's done, the thermometer will read about 145°F [63°C] for medium-rare or 160°F [71°C] for medium. If it's not done, keep cooking, checking the temperature every 10 minutes until the meat has reached your desired doneness.

Meanwhile, in a small bowl, mix together the honey, vinegar, mustard seeds, and garlic. Set aside.

In a large baking pan, place the carrots in a single layer and, using a pastry brush, brush them with the olive oil to coat well. When there are 45 minutes remaining for the roast, place the carrots into the oven to cook alongside.

When the roast beef is cooked to medium-rare (or your desired level of doneness), remove from the oven, transfer to a cutting board, tent with aluminum foil, and let rest for 10 to 15 minutes. Place the pan with the meat drippings, onion, and mushrooms on the stove over medium-high heat and bring it to a boil. Lower to a simmer and cook until the sauce reduces by one-third, 12 to 15 minutes.

Take the carrots out of the oven and brush them with the honey-mustard seed glaze. Return the carrots to the oven and continue cooking for a final 8 to 10 minutes.

Cut the twine from the roast and thinly slice the beef against the grain, making two to three slices per person. Top with a generous spoonful of the mushrooms, onion, and pan sauce, and divide the carrots evenly among the plates. Serve warm.

CARDAMOM CAKE WITH COCONUT WHIPPED CREAM

It may seem impossible to improve upon a moist olive oil cake covered in heavenly coconut whipped cream, but with the addition of toasted coconut flakes and a pinch of saffron you'll create welcome contrast in color and texture that makes this pillowy dessert even dreamier, with warm spices and bright citrus hidden in each bite. If desired, switch things up and decorate the cake with crumbled candied ginger, chopped pistachio nuts, or other nutty toppings you might have in your cupboard.

A day ahead of making the cake, put the can of coconut milk in the refrigerator. This makes the coconut fat, or cream, rise to the top, which will help you separate the coconut water from the pure white cream part for whipping. If your store has "coconut cream," grab it. With no "watery" part, you can use the whole can to make coconut whipped cream. After frosting the cake, keep leftover whipped coconut cream in the fridge, covered, and use it throughout the week for a quick fruit parfait or on top of morning chia pudding or granola.

MAKES ONE 9-IN [23-CM] CAKE   **TIME** 1 HOUR, 30 MINUTES

½ cup [120 ml] olive oil, warmed

2 pinches of saffron threads

1½ cups [180 g] all-purpose flour

2 tsp sodium-free baking powder

½ tsp ground cardamom

Zest of 2 lemons

½ cup [120 ml] full-fat Greek yogurt

3 eggs

⅔ cup [130 g] granulated sugar

Preheat the oven to 350°F [180°C]. Place a medium mixing bowl and whisks from an electric mixer (or the bowl and whisk of a stand mixer) in the freezer to chill. Grease a 9-in [23-cm] round springform cake pan.

In a small bowl, mix the warm olive oil with the saffron and let steep for at least 10 minutes. Remove the saffron threads and set the oil aside. In a medium mixing bowl, add the flour, baking powder, cardamom, and half the lemon zest and whisk together. Set aside.

CONTINUED

**One 13.5-oz [400-ml] can
full-fat coconut milk,
refrigerated overnight**

⅔ cup [80 g] powdered sugar

**1 cup [100 g] unsweetened
shredded coconut, toasted**

In a large mixing bowl, whisk the yogurt with the eggs and granulated sugar. Slowly whisk in the saffron oil until combined. Add the flour mixture and, using a wooden spoon or spatula, stir until combined and smooth. Pour the batter into the prepared cake pan, smooth the top, and bake for 25 to 30 minutes, until a toothpick inserted into the center comes out clean. Set the cake on a wire rack to cool.

Meanwhile, turn the coconut milk can upside down, open, and pour out the thin coconut water until you reach the thick layer of coconut cream. Scoop the coconut cream into the cold mixing bowl. (Coconut water will keep the coconut cream from stiffening when whipped. If this happens, simply call your frosting a "glaze." Remember, if you make a mistake, change the name and no one will know the difference.)

Add the powdered sugar and remaining lemon zest to the coconut cream and whip on medium-high speed until the coconut cream thickens, 5 to 8 minutes. Put in the refrigerator to harden, 30 minutes or up to overnight.

Remove the completely cooled cake from the cake pan and place on a cake plate or stand. Use a knife or angled icing spatula to spread the thickened coconut whipped cream on the top of the cake, then sprinkle with the shredded coconut. Cut into slices and serve.

MAHARAJA-STYLE CURRY POWDER

For sauces, dips, and spice blends, I get a lot of inspiration for low-sodium flavor by looking at the ingredient lists on the back of bottles. When there's something you want to re-create at home, like homemade curry powder, start by stealing ideas from the products that already exist. Then use the Internet or other cooking resources to find extra instructions, if you need them. Don't be afraid to give the recipe a few twists of your own.

MAKES ¼ CUP [75 G]   **TIME** 5 MINUTES

2 Tbsp cumin seeds

2 Tbsp coriander seeds

1 Tbsp fenugreek seeds

1 Tbsp fennel seeds

1 Tbsp brown mustard seeds

1 Tbsp cardamom seeds

1 Tbsp peppercorns

One 2-in [5-cm] cinnamon stick

1 Tbsp dried onion flakes

1 Tbsp ground turmeric

2 tsp salt-free garlic powder

2 tsp red pepper flakes

½ tsp ground cloves

¼ tsp ground ginger

¼ tsp saffron threads (optional)

Put the cumin seeds, coriander seeds, fenugreek seeds, fennel seeds, mustard seeds, cardamom seeds, peppercorns, and cinnamon stick in a medium sauté pan or skillet and toast over medium heat, stirring or shaking the pan frequently, until the spices become fragrant, 1 to 2 minutes. Toast for another 30 to 60 seconds, then pour into a medium bowl.

Add the onion flakes, turmeric, garlic powder, red pepper flakes, ground cloves, ground ginger, and saffron threads (if using) to the bowl and stir to combine. Working in batches, including the cinnamon stick, place the mixture into a spice grinder and pulse until you have a fine powder, and return to the medium bowl. Whisk the mixture together so that the spices combine thoroughly.

Store in an airtight container in a cool, dark place for up to 1 month.

CAULIFLOWER-NUT "RICOTTA"

Low-sodium eaters share something very important with vegan eaters: They need to find tasty replacements for cheese. Luckily, vegan geniuses have already come up with fun ways to mimic cheese, for everything from macaroni (puréed cauliflower or butternut squash) to Parmesan cheese (nutritional yeast). And here's one more: Nut cheese. A blend of creamy nuts, like macadamia and cashews, makes an awesome stand-in for spreadable cheeses, like ricotta.

With vegans paving the way, I decided to make a nut cheese, too—this time with cauliflower and pine nuts, for extra milkiness. It's perfect for stuffed shells, cheese balls, sandwiches, pizza toppings, and spreading on salt-free rice crackers. Try this recipe, then make a nut cheese of your own. Play with different herbs, nuts, and spices.

MAKES 2 CUPS [840 G]   **TIME** 20 MINUTES

2½ cups [275 g] roughly chopped raw cauliflower

¾ cup [90 g] salt-free pine nuts

¼ tsp ground nutmeg

¼ tsp dried parsley

¼ tsp salt-free garlic powder

¼ tsp freshly ground black pepper

¼ cup [60 ml] orange juice

Fill a pot with 2 to 3 in [5 to 7.5 cm] water and insert a steamer basket. Add the cauliflower to the basket, cover, and steam until fork-tender, 6 to 8 minutes.

Meanwhile, put the pine nuts in a medium sauté pan or skillet and toast over medium heat until golden brown, 3 to 5 minutes, shaking the pan occasionally to keep them from burning.

Remove the cauliflower and the pine nuts from the heat and let cool, 5 to 8 minutes.

In a food processor (or blender), combine the cauliflower, pine nuts, nutmeg, parsley, garlic powder, pepper, and orange juice. Process until you have a ricotta texture. Scrape the sides of the bowl with a spatula to get any missed nuts or cauliflower. Add a little water if the mixture is too thick. Pulse again to combine.

Store in an airtight container in the refrigerator for up to 1 week.

CAULIFLOWER RICE, PEA, AND EDAMAME SALAD

While some may balk at the idea of raw food, heat-free cooks definitely know a thing or two about transforming uncooked ingredients into filling meals. Like this trick of giving cauliflower a fine chop in a food processor and turning tough florets into a soft pile of rice-like flecks. They'll add bulk to your salad and soak up your dressing or fill up a roll of seaweed for a rice-free sushi snack, for those on Paleo diets.

SERVES 4　**TIME** 15 MINUTES

1 cup [120 g] frozen shelled edamame

1 cup [140 g] peas, fresh or frozen

3 cups [330 g] chopped cauliflower florets

¼ cup [60 ml] orange juice

¼ cup [60 ml] olive oil

¼ cup [7 g] chopped fresh cilantro or parsley

¼ tsp salt-free garlic powder

¼ tsp dried dill

¼ tsp red pepper flakes

⅛ tsp freshly ground black pepper

1 to 2 Tbsp minced shallot

½ cup [70 g] salt-free pine nuts

Fill a large bowl with ice water. Fill a medium pot halfway with water and bring to a boil. Add the edamame to the boiling water and cook for 4 minutes. Then add the peas and cook for 2 minutes. Drain the edamame and peas and add them to the ice water. Cool, then drain and set aside in a medium bowl.

Meanwhile, add the cauliflower florets to a food processor (or blender) and pulse until they have a crumbly, ricelike texture. Add the riced cauliflower to the edamame and peas.

Pour the orange juice into a small mixing bowl and, while whisking, slowly add the olive oil until well combined. Add the cilantro, garlic powder, dill, red pepper flakes, black pepper, and shallot. Whisk the dressing until well combined.

Put the pine nuts in a small sauté pan or skillet and toast them over medium heat until golden brown, 3 to 5 minutes, shaking the pan to keep them from burning. Pour onto a plate to cool.

If not serving right away, put the cauliflower-pea-edamame salad and the dressing in separate airtight containers and refrigerate overnight, or up to 3 days. When ready to serve, mix the dressing into the salad and sprinkle the toasted pine nuts on top.

CARROT VEGETABLE NOODLE SALAD WITH SPICY SHRIMP

Thanks to gluten-free and meat-free diets, as well as a vegetable peeler, vegetables no longer need to be the sidekick to a dish. They can be the star. They can be noodles, and they can remain raw or quickly sautéed, depending on the time and texture you need. I highly recommended making a bunch of vegetable noodles at the beginning of your week to use for weekday lunches or even quick dinners. Start with this salad and mix and match with other dressings, proteins, and soups for your own vegetable noodle creations. Faux noodle pho? Chicken–squash noodle soup? Spaghetti-squash spaghetti? Let that imagination and the peeler fly.

It's best to use frozen shrimp to be certain of sodium content, because shrimp can sometimes contain extra sodium from brining and the use of salt solutions before hitting the market. For those who do not eat shrimp, replace with Curry Tofu Fries (page 217) cut into cubes.

SERVES 4   **TIME** 35 MINUTES

**5 medium carrots
(rainbow if available)**

¼ to ½ cup [60 to 120 ml] Lemon Tahini Dressing (page 170)

4 oz [115 g] snow peas, washed and trimmed

2 green onions, root ends trimmed, thinly sliced

½ red Fresno chile

½ jalapeño chile, seeded and thinly sliced (optional)

¼ cup [7 g] chopped fresh Thai or regular basil

Use a vegetable peeler to make carrot ribbons or the grater attachment on a food processor or a box grater to shred the carrots. Transfer to a large mixing bowl and add ¼ cup [60 ml] of the dressing. Toss to coat well; taste and add more dressing, if desired. Add the snow peas, green onions, Fresno chile, jalapeño, Thai basil, and cilantro and toss to combine. Set aside.

In a medium mixing bowl, mix the garlic powder, chipotle chile powder, and pepper until combined. Add the shrimp and toss until coated with the spice rub.

CONTINUED

¼ cup [7 g] chopped fresh cilantro

1 tsp salt-free garlic powder

1 tsp salt-free chipotle chile powder or salt-free chili powder

¼ tsp freshly ground black pepper

12 extra-large frozen shrimp with tails, thawed, peeled, and deveined

Coconut oil for frying

¼ cup [30 g] salt-free, chopped peanuts

1 lime, cut into 4 wedges

Heat 1 Tbsp coconut oil in a large sauté pan or skillet over medium-high heat. Add the shrimp in batches, and cook on both sides until nicely seared and the shrimp are pink, about 3 minutes per side. Remove the shrimp to a plate and set aside. Wipe out the pan if it is watery from the shrimp. Repeat with the remaining shrimp until all are cooked, adding more coconut oil and adjusting the heat as needed.

Serve the salad, accompanied by the shrimp, peanuts, and lime wedges in separate bowls and let your guests dish up their own plates.

CORN-BROCCOLI BURGERS

Whether you make Mondays meatless or limit protein intake, don't skip burgers. But do skip the packaged vegetable patties, which can have more than 400 mg of sodium per patty, depending on the brand. Instead, get your fix with a mix of broccoli, corn, and spices. Serve in butter lettuce leaves, on top of a salad, or in between two slices of Easy Focaccia (page 238).

MAKES 10 TO 12 PATTIES   **TIME** 30 MINUTES

1½ cups [135 g] broccoli florets

1 cup [120 g] all-purpose flour

¼ tsp salt-free baking powder

½ tsp salt-free garlic powder

½ tsp ground cumin

¼ tsp red pepper flakes

¼ tsp freshly ground black pepper

1 egg, lightly beaten

½ cup [240 ml] water

2 cups [280 g] corn kernels, fresh or thawed frozen

2 green onions, root ends trimmed, thinly sliced

¼ cup [7 g] chopped fresh cilantro leaves

Vegetable oil for frying

Butter lettuce leaves for serving

Plain Greek yogurt, Dilly Chimichurri (page 163), or Lemon Tahini Dressing (page 170) for serving

Using a knife or food processor (or blender), chop the broccoli florets until they form a crumblike texture. Set aside.

In a medium bowl, mix together the flour, baking powder, garlic powder, cumin, red pepper flakes, and black pepper. Add the egg, water, corn, green onions, broccoli crumbs, and cilantro. Using a spoon or spatula, mix until well combined.

In a large sauté pan or skillet, heat 1 to 2 Tbsp vegetable oil over medium-high heat, making sure the oil is spread over the bottom of the pan evenly. Spoon the batter into the pan (¼ cup [60 ml] batter per patty), making patties 2½ in [6 cm] wide and about ½ in [12 mm] thick. Cook three or four patties at a time, depending on the size of your pan, until crispy and golden brown, 3 to 5 minutes per side. Remove the cooked patties to a paper towel–lined plate. Repeat until all the batter has been cooked, adding more vegetable oil and adjusting the heat as needed.

Serve the warm patties with butter lettuce leaves, and slathered with yogurt. Store leftover patties in an airtight container in the refrigerator for up to 4 days.

CAULIFLOWER STEAKS WITH CURRY MUSHROOM GRAVY

I admit, I was skeptical of cauliflower steaks. I mean, I love cauliflower. It's a culinary chameleon. But steak? Really? Well, it's true. Cauliflower steak makes a "meaty" dish. It won't taste like a T-bone, but with the help of the mushroom sauce, it is substantial and savory. It requires a napkin, a sharp knife, and maybe a side of fries, of the potato or tofu variety. And it's a worthy and healthful addition to your weekly menu. Be sure to save the extra cauliflower for Cauliflower-Nut "Ricotta" (page 196) or Cauliflower Rice, Pea, and Edamame Salad (page 197).

SERVES 2   **TIME** 30 MINUTES

One 1½-lb [680-g] cauliflower

1 Tbsp vegetable oil

2 tsp coconut oil

4 garlic cloves, minced

¼ white onion, diced

1 Tbsp diced seeded jalapeño chile

¼ tsp coriander seeds

2 cups [140 g] sliced cremini mushrooms

¾ cup [180 ml] canned light coconut milk

1 to 2 tsp Maharaja-Style Curry Powder (page 195) or other salt-free curry blend

¼ tsp freshly ground black pepper

¼ cup [7 g] fresh cilantro leaves

Preheat the oven to 375°F [190°C].

Break off the leaves around the base of the cauliflower and set aside. Starting at the top and a little right of center of the cauliflower stem, use a large sharp knife to cut down lengthwise through the stem to make two steaks, each about 1½ in [4 cm] thick. Trim any brown parts off the bottom of the stem.

In a large, ovenproof skillet, heat the vegetable oil over medium-high heat. Add the cauliflower steaks in a single layer and cook until lightly browned, 3 minutes per side. Add the cauliflower leaves to the skillet and transfer the skillet to the oven. Roast for 15 to 20 minutes, or until the cauliflower steaks are fork-tender and golden in color.

Meanwhile, in a medium lidded sauté pan or skillet, heat the coconut oil over medium-high heat. Add the garlic and onion and cook, stirring constantly, until translucent, 3 to 5 minutes. Add the jalapeño and coriander seeds and cook, stirring frequently,

CONTINUED

for another 3 minutes. Begin adding the mushrooms in batches, so as not to crowd the pan, and cook, stirring often, until they brown and become soft, 8 to 10 minutes. Turn the heat to medium and add the coconut milk, 1 tsp of the curry powder, and the pepper. Taste and add another 1 tsp curry powder, if desired. Stir to combine, scraping up any flavorful browned bits from the bottom of the pan. Turn the heat to low, cover, and cook until the sauce thickens slightly, 8 to 10 minutes.

Make a bed of the cauliflower leaves on two plates and put a cauliflower steak on top of each. Cover with the warm curry mushroom sauce and serve sprinkled with the cilantro.

VARIATION: For more bulk, break up 2 cups [220 g] of the remaining cauliflower and pulse in a food processor (or blender) to make cauliflower rice. Transfer to a medium bowl and combine with ¼ cup [7 g] roughly torn basil leaves, 1 Tbsp lemon juice, and a pinch of freshly cracked black pepper. Serve as a base for the cauliflower steaks.

DATE CARAMELS WITH CRUNCHY CHOCOLATE COATING

Date shakes. Date cakes. Recently, dates started taking over the dessert section, which makes sense since they add natural sweetness and a pop of sugary crystals to recipes. Because they're sticky, they act as a perfect binder for granola bars and cookies. And when heated in a pan, they also make a great stand-in for caramel.

Although homemade caramels are generally low in sodium as long as you skip salted butter and salt, this recipe is a perfect example of how easily you can boost the flavor of a dish just by switching up the ingredients—like dates for sugar, coconut oil for butter, and coconut milk for heavy cream. If you want to see what the date hype is about, give this recipe a try and get ready to be impressed. Cover your date caramels in chocolate and chopped candied ginger, crushed nuts, or toasted coconut—or even crumbled Salt-Free Bacon (page 93) for a real low-sodium surprise.

MAKES ABOUT 12 CARAMELS   **TIME** 25 MINUTES (PLUS AT LEAST 1 HOUR, 30 MINUTES FREEZING TIME)

2 Tbsp unsweetened finely shredded coconut

3 Tbsp coconut oil

1 cup [180 g] pitted dates, finely chopped

¼ cup [60 ml] canned light coconut milk

1¼ tsp vanilla extract

1 cup [170 g] dark chocolate chips

½ cup [70 g] chopped salt-free ginger candy (or pistachios, walnuts, or extra toasted coconut flakes)

Put the shredded coconut in a large sauté pan or skillet and toast over medium-high heat until golden brown, 2 to 3 minutes. Watch carefully and stir often to get even color. Pour onto a plate and set aside.

In a small saucepan over medium heat, add 1 Tbsp of the coconut oil and the dates. Cook, stirring occasionally, until the dates melt into a caramel-like consistency, about 5 minutes. Stir in the coconut milk, 1 tsp of the vanilla, and the toasted coconut and cook until the mixture comes together and thickens slightly, 3 to 5 minutes.

CONTINUED

Place a 5-by-13-in [12-by-33-cm] piece of parchment paper on the counter with the long edge facing you. Pour the date-caramel mixture onto the left side of the parchment, about 1 in [2.5 cm] from the edge. Using a spatula, flatten and spread the caramel until it makes a 4-by-4-in [10-by-10-cm] square, about 1 in [2.5 cm] thick. Fold the right side of parchment paper over the caramel square. Place on a cookie sheet or flat plate and put in the freezer to harden for at least 1 hour.

Put the chocolate chips, remaining 2 Tbsp coconut oil, and remaining ¼ tsp vanilla in a small saucepan over low heat. Stir constantly until the chocolate melts, 3 to 4 minutes. Remove from the heat and let cool to room temperature. (You can also melt the chocolate in the microwave, heating for 30 seconds, stirring, and repeating another one or two times until melted.)

Cut the date caramel into 1-in [2.5-cm] squares. Use a spoon or your fingers to dip the caramels into the melted chocolate, and then return them to the parchment paper. Sprinkle the tops with the ginger candy. Place the dipped caramels back into the freezer for at least 30 minutes before serving.

Store in an airtight container in the freezer for up to 1 month. Reserve any leftover chocolate in an airtight container in the refrigerator for up to 1 week and reheat for more dipping fun.

VARIATION: For those that don't need to watch their sodium strictly, sprinkle sea salt on top of the caramels while the chocolate is hardening. For those watching their sodium closely but wanting to spice things up, add a sprinkle of cayenne pepper or salt-free chili powder.

MINI HASH BROWN QUICHES

Ready-to-use pastry dough can contain about 800 mg of sodium per 9-in [23-cm] crust. While you can always make your own dough from scratch, for a faster solution just use grated potatoes. Frozen hash browns are especially convenient. With a little oil and a quick trip to the oven, grated potatoes make a crispy basket to hold any sort of filling—from finely chopped vegetables and whatever herbs you have on hand to browned ground meat (like home-seasoned pork, to fulfill sausage cravings). For an easy breakfast, simply crack individual eggs into the crusts and let the oven take over.

MAKES 8 MINI QUICHES   **TIME** 1 HOUR

2 large Yukon gold potatoes, peeled and grated, or 4 cups [560 g] thawed frozen, no-salt-added hash browns

¼ tsp salt-free garlic powder

¼ tsp freshly ground black pepper

1 Tbsp olive oil or vegetable oil

2 eggs

½ cup [60 g] grated carrot

¼ cup [15 g] finely chopped stemmed kale leaves

¼ tsp dried dill

¼ tsp smoked paprika

2 Tbsp water

Preheat the oven to 375°F [190°C]. Coat eight wells of a standard muffin tin, all the way to the top edges, with nonstick cooking spray.

Put the grated potatoes in a large bowl and mix in the garlic powder, pepper, and olive oil. Using your hands, press the potato mixture into the prepared muffin wells as you would a pie crust, covering the bottom and the sides all the way to the top. Bake until the potatoes turn golden brown and crispy, about 30 minutes. Set the crusts aside, still in the tin.

Meanwhile, in a large glass measuring cup with a pouring spout, whisk the eggs with a fork. Add the carrot, kale, dill, paprika, and water and whisk until combined.

Pour the egg mixture into the potato crusts, filling almost to the top. Return the pan to the oven and cook until the eggs set and are no longer jiggly, about 15 minutes. Serve warm.

VARIATION: When making Mini Hash Brown Quiches for brunch, sprinkle some with Parmesan cheese in the final minutes of baking for those guests who can handle the sodium.

BANANA-ZUCCHINI PANCAKES

Instant pancake mix from a box can contain more than 1,000 mg of sodium per 1 cup [130 g], depending on the brand. Let's go beyond that box and make a mix that requires just a smidge more time. In the end, you'll have puffy pancakes with moist banana bread–like flavor and shreds of healthful zucchini. Make a quick compote by adding fresh berries to the hot pan after you've cooked the pancakes. Add some ground cinnamon and drizzle on top to finish the dish. If you have the grated zucchini ready to go, you can make these pancakes on a lazy Sunday, a busy Monday, or any morning of the week.

MAKES 6 PANCAKES **TIME** 30 MINUTES

1 cup [120 g] all-purpose flour

2 tsp salt-free baking powder

1 large banana, mashed

½ cup [120 ml] canned light coconut milk

½ cup [50 g] grated zucchini

¼ tsp ground cinnamon

1 tsp vanilla extract

Coconut oil for frying, plus more, melted, for topping (optional)

Fresh berries for topping (optional)

Powdered sugar for sprinkling (optional)

In a medium bowl, add the flour and baking powder and stir with a fork to combine.

In a separate medium bowl, mix the banana and coconut milk with a fork until well combined. Add the zucchini, cinnamon, and vanilla and stir again to combine. Add the zucchini mixture to the flour mixture, and stir until it's the consistency of thick pancake batter. It's okay if some banana chunks are visible.

Melt 2 tsp coconut oil in a large sauté pan or skillet over medium heat. When hot, use a spoon to add the batter to the pan, making two to four 3-in [7.5-cm] pancakes at a time, depending on the size of your pan. Cook until the edges of the pancakes start to turn brown and crispy, 3 to 5 minutes. Flip the pancakes and cook another 3 to 5 minutes. Remove the cooked pancakes to a warm plate and cover loosely with aluminum foil to keep warm. Repeat until all the batter is used, adding more coconut oil to the pan and adjusting the heat as needed.

Serve the pancakes warm, topped with melted coconut oil, fresh berries, or a sprinkle of powdered sugar, if desired.

EVERYTHING WAFFLES

If there's one thing I really miss on a low-sodium diet, it's bagels. With more than 600 mg of sodium per typical 4-in [10-cm] bagel, that's too much for me to nosh on. Eventually I realized that what I really craved wasn't the round circle of dough, but the spices in the bagel and the creamy cheese spread. So forget the dough circle and make these square (or round) waffles with a mixture of spices. Cover them in your own low-sodium schmear made of Greek yogurt or even Hickory-Smoked Fish Spread (page 228). Top with sliced red onions, sprouts, avocado, or just a fried egg.

Wrap individual waffles in foil and a plastic bag, and freeze for up to 3 months. Then thaw and re-toast in a 375°F [190°C] oven or toaster oven until warm and crisp, 2 to 3 minutes, for an easy weekday breakfast. And remember, you can also use waffles as a "bread" alternative for sandwiches. Try a Waffle BLT, or a Waffle Club, or Leftover Roast Beef on a Waffle.

MAKES 6 TO 8 BIG WAFFLES   **TIME** 45 MINUTES

¾ cup [90 g] all-purpose flour

½ cup [60 g] whole-wheat flour

1 tsp salt-free baking powder

2 tsp caraway seeds

2 tsp white sesame seeds

2 tsp celery seeds

2 tsp brown mustard seeds

2 tsp salt-free garlic powder

2 tsp salt-free onion powder

1 tsp freshly ground black pepper

In a medium bowl, combine the all-purpose flour, whole-wheat flour, baking powder, caraway seeds, sesame seeds, celery seeds, mustard seeds, garlic powder, onion powder, and pepper and stir to mix. Set aside.

In another medium bowl, whisk the egg yolks with the coconut milk and green onion and add to the flour mixture. Stir until combined.

In a third medium bowl, whip the egg whites until they form soft peaks. Gently fold the egg whites into the waffle batter, being careful not to overmix. You will still see some fluffs of egg whites in the batter, which is okay.

CONTINUED

2 eggs, at room temperature, separated

1 cup [240 ml] unsweetened coconut milk

1 green onion, root end trimmed, thinly sliced

Preheat a waffle iron according to the manufacturer's instructions, on a medium-high to high heat setting, depending on how crispy you want your waffles. Coat the waffle iron with nonstick cooking spray.

Add about ¼ cup [60 ml] batter for the first waffle. Cook until toasted and crispy; after your first try, you may need to cook each waffle longer or increase the heat. Place the cooked waffles on a warm plate and cover loosely with aluminum foil to keep warm. Repeat until you've used all the batter. Serve warm.

VARIATION: Want a wheat-free alternative? Make potato waffles. Simply omit both the flours, baking powder, and coconut milk. Grate a large, peeled Yukon gold potato to make 2 cups [300 g] of shredded hash browns (or use frozen hash browns). Drain the potatoes of their liquid, and mix with the spices, green onion, and a whisked egg. Cook as instructed, using about ⅓ cup [40 g] of batter per waffle and increasing the time as needed for your desired crispness. *Makes 4 waffles.*

FOUR FRIES

Not much can get between me and a potato. Especially of the french-fry persuasion. But for many people with kidney disease, who must not only watch sodium but also potassium, those spuds pose a problem. Fear not, though, because potatoes aren't the only ingredients that can be cut and baked into fries. From parsnips to jicama, there are plenty of options. Pair with Dilly Chimichurri (page 163) or Avocado Green Goddess Dressing (page 168).

CRUNCHY PARSNIP FRIES

SERVES 4   **TIME** 15 MINUTES

4 medium parsnips, root ends trimmed

2 Tbsp yellow medium-ground cornmeal

2 Tbsp vegetable oil

½ tsp salt-free garlic powder

½ tsp dried dill

½ tsp freshly ground black pepper

Pinch of cayenne pepper

Preheat the oven to 400°F [200°C]. Coat a large baking pan with vegetable oil or cover with aluminum foil.

Cut the parsnips into thicker french-fry shapes, about 3 in [7.5 cm] long and ½ in [12 mm] wide.

In a large resealable plastic bag or a big bowl, mix the cornmeal, vegetable oil, garlic powder, dill, black pepper, and cayenne. Add the parsnips. If using a bag, close and shake; if using a bowl, mix with your hands until the parsnip fries are coated with the cornmeal mixture. Transfer the coated parsnips to the prepared baking pan, laying them out in a single layer. Bake until crispy, 20 to 22 minutes, flipping halfway through. Serve warm.

VARIATION: Want a healthful topper for your next barbecue? Use a peeler to make long ribbons from the parsnips instead of fries, yielding about 2 cups [240 g]. Bake as directed until crispy, 8 to 10 minutes. Enjoy them like onion rings.

CHILI POLENTA FRIES

SERVES 4   **TIME** 1 HOUR, 30 MINUTES

3 cups [720 ml] water

1 cup [140 g] yellow medium-ground cornmeal

1¼ tsp salt-free chili powder

½ tsp dried dill

¼ tsp salt-free garlic powder

Olive oil for brushing

Lightly coat an 8-by-8-in [20-by-20-cm] baking pan with olive oil.

In a medium pot, bring the water to a gentle boil over medium heat. Slowly pour in the cornmeal, stirring constantly. Add 1 tsp of the chili powder, the dill, and garlic powder; turn the heat to low; and continue stirring until the polenta is thick and the liquid is absorbed, 10 to 12 minutes. Remove from the heat and transfer to the prepared baking pan, using a spatula to evenly spread the polenta to the edges of the pan; the polenta should be about ½ in [12 mm] thick. Put in the refrigerator to cool, uncovered, for 30 minutes or up to overnight.

Preheat the oven to 450°F [230°C]. Lightly coat a 9-by-12-in [23-by-30-cm] baking pan with olive oil.

Run a knife around the edge of the polenta to loosen it from the sides of the pan. Hold a cutting board on top of the pan and flip, letting the polenta fall out of the pan and onto the cutting board. Brush the top of the polenta with a little olive oil and sprinkle with the remaining ¼ tsp chili powder. Cut the polenta into fry shapes—skinny fries or thick steak fries, whatever you're craving. Place them in a single layer in the prepared baking pan and bake for 10 minutes. Flip and bake for another 10 minutes, until golden brown. Turn on the broiler for the final 2 minutes if you want them extra crispy. Serve warm.

CURRY TOFU FRIES

SERVES 4 **TIME** 45 MINUTES

One 14-oz [400-g] package firm tofu, drained, compressed, and patted dry

3 Tbsp sesame oil

2 tsp salt-free garlic powder

1 tsp Maharaja-Style Curry Powder (page 195) or other salt-free curry powder

¼ tsp cayenne pepper or salt-free chili powder

Preheat the oven to 400°F [200°C]. Coat a baking pan with vegetable oil or line with aluminum foil.

Cut the tofu into french-fry shapes. Spread the tofu fries on the prepared baking pan in a single layer.

In a small mixing bowl, combine the sesame oil, garlic powder, curry powder, and cayenne. Using a pastry brush, paint the tops of the tofu fries with one-half of the seasoned sesame oil. Bake for 20 minutes. Carefully turn the fries, and paint with the remaining half of the seasoned sesame oil. Return to the oven and cook until the tofu fries become slightly puffy and crispy, about 15 minutes longer. Serve immediately.

DILL OIL JICAMA "FRIES"

SERVES 4 TO 6 **TIME** 15 MINUTES

¼ cup [7 g] roughly chopped fresh dill

½ tsp salt-free garlic powder

¼ tsp freshly ground black pepper

¼ cup [60 ml] olive oil

2 Tbsp orange juice or lemon juice

One 1-lb [455-g] jicama

In a small food processor (or blender), combine the dill, garlic powder, pepper, olive oil, and orange juice and pulse until smooth.

Peel and cut the jicama into french-fry shapes, about ½ in [12 mm] thick and 3 in [7.5 cm] long. In a medium bowl or a shallow container, mix the jicama with the dill oil. Cover and refrigerate for 30 minutes, or up to overnight, before serving.

COCONUT "PANKO" PORK TONKATSU WITH ORANGE-GINGER SAUCE AND SUGAR SNAP PEA SLAW

Panko are Japanese bread crumbs, often found in the international foods aisle of the grocery store. They have a slightly nutty taste and a flaky, almost fried texture that typical bread crumbs can't compete with—especially in a traditional Japanese tonkatsu recipe, where it serves as the breading for a deep-fried pork cutlet. Some panko brands only contain 40 mg of sodium per ½ cup [30 g], which may work for some people's diets but may be too high for others. So when thinking of what had a similar nutty flakiness, I realized that a low-sodium substitution existed: Coconut flakes.

SERVES 4   **TIME** 1 HOUR, 30 MINUTES

SUGAR SNAP PEA SLAW

Zest and juice of 2 limes

¼ tsp sugar

4 oz [115 g] sugar snap peas, trimmed and strings removed

½ cup [35 g] finely shredded green cabbage

ORANGE-GINGER SAUCE

1 cup [240 ml] orange juice

One 1-in [2.5-cm] piece ginger root, peeled and minced

1 Tbsp honey or sugar

¼ tsp garlic powder

¼ tsp sesame oil

To make the Sugar Snap Pea Slaw: In a medium bowl, mix together the lime zest, lime juice, and sugar. Cut the snap peas diagonally across the length of the pea pod. Some peas may pop out, which is totally okay; just collect all the cut sections and peas and put them in the bowl. Add the cabbage and toss to combine. Cover and refrigerate for 30 minutes, or up to overnight.

To make the Orange-Ginger Sauce: In a small saucepan over medium heat, whisk together the orange juice, ginger, honey, garlic powder, and sesame oil. Bring to a boil and cook, stirring frequently, for 5 minutes. Turn the heat to low and continue to cook, stirring occasionally, until the sauce reduces by half, about 15 minutes. Set aside.

To make the Coconut "Panko" Tonkatsu: In a small bowl, mix the coconut, sesame seeds, garlic powder, ground coriander, and pepper until combined.

CONTINUED

COCONUT "PANKO" TONKATSU

1 cup [100 g] unsweetened finely shredded coconut

1 Tbsp white sesame seeds

¼ tsp salt-free garlic powder

¼ tsp ground coriander

Pinch of freshly ground black pepper

4 boneless pork chops, about ½ in [12 mm] thick

All-purpose flour for dredging

2 eggs, lightly beaten

Canola oil for frying

¼ cup [7 g] fresh cilantro leaves (optional)

Using a sharp knife, make slashes in the fat on the pork chops. One at a time, place the pork chops into a resealable plastic bag or between two sheets of parchment paper and use a meat pounder (or a heavy skillet) to flatten the chops until they are ¼ in [6 mm] thick. Put the pork on a plate and set aside.

Set up a dipping station. Put 1 cup [120 g] flour in a wide, shallow bowl. Put the eggs in a second wide, shallow bowl. Put the coconut "panko" in a third wide, shallow bowl.

Fill a sauté pan with 1 in [2.5 cm] canola oil and heat over medium-high heat. While the oil gets hot, prepare a pork chop by dredging it first in the flour, then dipping it in the egg, then dipping it in the coconut "panko" crumbs, turning the pork chop until it is completely coated.

When the oil begins to ripple, carefully put the breaded pork chop into the pan. Fry until golden brown, 4 to 5 minutes. Flip and fry the other side for another 5 minutes. Place the cooked pork on a cutting board. Repeat to bread and fry the remaining pork chops.

Cut the crispy pork tonkatsu diagonally into slices. Sprinkle with the cilantro, if desired. Serve with the slaw and orange sauce alongside.

COCONUT "PANKO" FISH

Want a flour- and meat-free alternative to Coconut "Panko" Pork Tonkatsu (page 218)? Try this Coconut "Panko" Fish, which has all the same fixings. While this version calls for halibut, any other firm and fatty fish, like salmon, will work just as well. If you do decide to use a thinner fish, decrease the cooking time. Either way, make sure to get the skin and bones removed.

SERVES 4   **TIME** 1 HOUR

1 cup [100 g] unsweetened finely shredded coconut

1 Tbsp white sesame seeds

¼ tsp cayenne pepper

¼ tsp salt-free garlic powder

¼ tsp ground coriander

Pinch of freshly ground black pepper

1 egg, lightly beaten

Four 6-oz [170-g] halibut fillets, skin and bones removed

¼ cup [7 g] fresh cilantro leaves (optional)

Sugar Snap Pea Slaw (see page 218) for serving

Orange-Ginger Sauce (see page 218) for serving

Preheat the oven to 400°F [200°C]. Line a baking pan with aluminum foil and place a wire rack on top. Coat the rack with olive oil cooking spray.

In a wide, shallow bowl, mix the coconut, sesame seeds, cayenne, garlic powder, ground coriander, and black pepper until combined.

Put the egg in a second wide, shallow bowl.

One fillet at a time, dip the fish into the egg, shake to release extra egg, and dip into the coconut "panko," then set the breaded fish on the wire rack in the prepared baking pan. Repeat until all four fillets are breaded. Coat the fish on both sides with olive oil cooking spray.

Bake until the coconut "panko" turns golden and the fish is cooked through, 12 to 15 minutes. Time will vary depending on the thickness of your fish—thinner fillets will cook faster. To check for doneness, tug at one fillet end with a fork. If it flakes off easily, it's ready.

Place the fish on a serving platter or on individual plates. Sprinkle with the cilantro, if desired. Serve with the slaw and orange sauce alongside.

SUNDAY CHICKEN WITH ROASTED ROOTS AND FRUITS

Which came first, the chicken or the potatoes? Either way, they make an excellent pair. An iconic duo, some might say. But consider altering this combo by adding a few more friends to the party—namely carrots and fruit. The combination brings a sweet, almost caramel-like flavor to the dish, which makes a simple roasted chicken dinner something extra-special. For a seasonal fruit swap, instead of peaches or nectarines, use two tart apples (peeled) and ½ cup [60 g] dried apricots, halved. Save leftover chicken for weekday lunches and the bones for Visra's Comfort Soup (page 150).

SERVES 4   **TIME** 2 HOURS, 30 MINUTES (MOSTLY OVEN TIME)

ROASTED ROOTS AND FRUITS

3 large carrots, trimmed

2 medium Yukon gold potatoes

3 peaches or nectarines, stemmed and pitted

¼ tsp salt-free garlic powder

¼ tsp dried dill

Pinch of red pepper flakes

2 Tbsp olive oil

SUNDAY CHICKEN

One 3- to 4-lb [1.4- to 1.8-kg] fryer chicken, neck and giblets removed

1 lemon, cut crosswise into slices ¼ in [6 mm] thick

1 Tbsp olive oil

Remove oven racks as needed so the roasting pan with the chicken-topped roasting rack will fit in the center. Preheat the oven to 425°F [220°C].

To make the Roasted Roots and Fruits: Cut a piece 1½-in [4-cm] long from the thick end of one carrot. Using this piece as a guide, cut the remaining carrots, the potatoes, and the peaches into similarly shaped chunks. Put the roots and fruits in a large mixing bowl. Add the garlic powder, dill, red pepper flakes, and olive oil and toss until well combined. Set aside.

To make the Sunday Chicken: Using a paper towel, pat the chicken dry. Then use your fingers to gently lift the chicken skin away from the meat, creating little pockets. Slide the lemon slices between the skin and breast meat. While you're at it, place some lemon slices in the main chicken cavity as well. Rub the skin all over with the olive oil, garlic powder, and black pepper.

CONTINUED

¼ tsp salt-free garlic powder

¼ tsp freshly ground black pepper

Place the chicken, breast-side up, on the roasting rack in the baking pan. Bake for 15 minutes, then lower the oven temperature to 375°F [190°C]. Put the roots and fruits around the chicken in the bottom of the pan, or in a separate roasting pan, if you want or need to avoid chicken fat. Cook until the chicken temperature reaches 165°F [74°C] on a meat thermometer, about 1 hour and 15 minutes. If you don't have a thermometer, you can also slice into the thigh near the bone to see if the juices run clear and the meat is white (not pink). If the chicken is not done, cook another 15 minutes and check again. Use a wooden spoon to stir the roots and fruits halfway through roasting.

Transfer the chicken to a cutting board and let rest for 10 minutes. Transfer the roots and fruits to a serving bowl and cover with aluminum foil to keep warm. Carve the chicken as desired, and serve with portions of roots and fruits alongside.

THOU SHALT **REINVENT**

MACAROON CUSTARD TARTS

Just as with the Mini Hash Brown Quiches (page 208), shredded coconut offers a quick and convenient solution to making little pie or tart crusts without the sodium of prepared pastry crusts. While this recipe is meant to mimic those cute little custard tarts you see at pretty much every catered event you've ever been to, you can fill these macaroon crusts with anything. Go simple with jam and fresh berries. Go fluffy with whipped cream or meringue. Or go chocolate with a cocoa and citrus mousse. They're so simple to make, you can try all the options.

MAKES TWENTY 2-IN [5-CM] TARTS **TIME** 1 HOUR

3 eggs, separated, at room temperature

1 cup [200 g] granulated sugar

½ tsp vanilla extract

3½ cups [350 g] unsweetened finely shredded coconut

Zest of 3 limes, plus ¼ cup [60 ml] lime juice

2 Tbsp cornstarch

¾ cup [180 ml] cold water

½ cup [60 g] fresh raspberries

Powdered sugar for sprinkling

Preheat the oven to 325°F [165°C]. Line a baking pan with parchment paper.

In a medium bowl, whisk the egg whites, ½ cup [100 g] of the granulated sugar, and the vanilla together with a fork. Fold in the shredded coconut and all of the lime zest. Make 20 mounds of the macaroon mixture, about 1½ Tbsp each, and place in the prepared baking pan. Wet your hands slightly and use your fingers to create 2-in [5-cm] tart shapes by making a deep indent in the center and high sides. Bake until the edges of the tart shells become golden in color, 18 to 20 minutes. Remove to a wire rack to cool. Leave the oven on.

Meanwhile, in a medium heavy-bottomed saucepan, whisk the remaining ½ cup [100 g] granulated sugar and the cornstarch. Gradually whisk in the cold water. Whisk the egg yolks in a small bowl, and whisk into the mixture in the pan. Over medium heat, whisk the water-egg mixture constantly while bringing it to a boil, 2 to 3 minutes. After the custard is thick and boiling, continue to cook for about 30 seconds, whisking constantly. Remove from the heat and whisk in the lime juice.

CONTINUED

Spoon the lime custard into the center of each tart and up to the brim, about 1 Tbsp per tart, leaving the tarts on the pan. Bake until the custard has set, 10 to 12 minutes. Let the tarts cool for a few minutes in the baking pan before moving to a cooling rack.

Top the custard-filled tarts with fresh raspberries and a sprinkle of powdered sugar to serve.

VARIATION: Need a short cut? Use a muffin tin with greased silicone liners or metal tartlet pans and fill with the macaroon mixture, pressing into the bottom and sides to form the tart crusts. Bake as directed. Skip the custard, and mix orange marmalade with whipped cream. Fill the macaroon crusts with the orange cream once they're fully baked and cooled. Didn't use all that custard? Mix it with berries and whipped cream for tomorrow's dessert, or into your morning yogurt or oatmeal for a decadent breakfast treat.

HICKORY-SMOKED FISH SPREAD

Don't let billowing smoke or the fact that you have to find hickory chips scare you from making this spread. It's actually ridiculously easy to smoke your own fish at home without the extra sodium, and the tasty results are well worth facing your fears. Which is good, because some prepared smoked white fish can have more than 1,300 mg of sodium per 1 cup [220 g], depending on the brand. You'll end up making this insanely good spread so often that it may well become your go-to appetizer. Serve with low-sodium crackers or raw vegetables. Full disclosure: Heating the hickory chips this way will most likely leave burn marks in the bottom of your pot, so use an old pot that you won't mind scruffing up a bit. It will also make the kitchen smoky, so be sure to open up a few windows as well to keep the smoke alarm from sounding.

MAKES 1 TO 1¼ CUPS [220 TO 275 G]   **TIME** 45 MINUTES

8 oz [230 g] tilapia, skinned, deboned, and cut into 2-in [5-cm] chunks

½ to ¾ cup [120 to 180 ml] plain Greek yogurt

½ tsp dried dill

¼ tsp salt-free garlic powder

Pinch of freshly ground black pepper

Pinch of cayenne pepper

¼ cup [7 g] fresh dill (optional)

Place ½ cup [35 g] hickory chips in the center of a tall, heavy pot, wide enough to fit a steamer basket or metal colander. Place a steamer basket in the pot on top of the wood chips.

Line the steamer basket with parchment paper and place the fish chunks on the paper in a single layer. (If necessary, steam the fish in two separate batches.) Cover the pot tightly with a lid or aluminum foil. Turn on the kitchen fan or open a window. Put the pot on the stove and cook over high heat for 5 to 8 minutes. Uncover the pot; if it is filled with smoke, turn the heat to low, replace the lid or foil, and cook the fish until it takes on a golden brown color and the flesh is white and cooked through, about 5 minutes longer. Transfer the fish from the basket to a small bowl. Cover and put it in the refrigerator to cool completely, about 15 minutes.

CONTINUED

Separate the cooled fish from any gelled juices or fat that formed in the fridge; discard the juices and fat. Transfer the fish chunks to a medium bowl and use a fork to break them up. Add ½ cup [120 ml] of the yogurt and the dill, garlic powder, black pepper, and cayenne and mix well until combined. Add the remaining ¼ cup [60 ml] yogurt as needed to obtain your desired spreading consistency.

Store in an airtight container in the refrigerator for up to 3 days.

BAKED DIM SUM DUMPLINGS

If there's a food you miss on your low-sodium diet, don't simply long for it. Try to re-create it at home. When I first started my low-sodium journey, I missed dim sum dumplings madly. While the idea of making dumpling dough initially scared me, after doing a little research I realized all it required was flour, water, and a little time. And by making it a weekend project, you will actually enjoy all the rolling as well as the results. Once they're made, you can boil, steam, pan-fry, or bake them. Freeze the leftovers for a quick dinner or a savory morning snack. Just know that your dumplings may look more like empanadas than the thin-skinned kind you might be used too, especially if you bake them. But take a bite and you won't care.

MAKES 32 DUMPLINGS   **TIME** 2 HOURS

DUMPLING DOUGH

2 cups [240 g] all-purpose flour

1 cup [240 ml] hot water

FILLING

4 tsp sesame oil

4 oz [115 g] ground pork

1 cup [80 g] finely diced stemmed shiitake mushrooms

1 cup [70 g] shredded green cabbage

1 cup [120 g] grated zucchini

2 Tbsp minced shallot

2 green onions, root ends trimmed, thinly sliced

To make the Dumpling Dough: Put the flour in a food processor and with the machine running, slowly pour in the hot water, ¼ cup [60 ml] at a time, until the mixture forms a ball. (Add more water if the dough is too dry or add more flour if it seems too wet.) Once you have the right consistency, simply let the ball tumble around in the processor bowl for 30 seconds. Place the dough in a large bowl. If you do not have a food processor, put the flour in a large bowl and make a well in the center. Add half of the hot water and use a spatula to slowly stir and incorporate the flour. Continue to work the flour into the wet dough, adding more water slowly and as necessary, until it comes together into a pliable ball. Knead the dough on a floured work surface for few minutes, until it becomes soft and springy.

Cover the bowl with a damp towel or plastic wrap, and let the dough rest and rise for at least 30 minutes. At this stage, the dough will keep, refrigerated, for 1 day. Let it rise at room temperature for 1 hour before using.

CONTINUED

1 tsp salt-free Chinese
five-spice powder

½ tsp salt-free garlic powder

¼ tsp red pepper flakes

2 Tbsp sesame oil

To make the Filling: Heat 2 tsp of the sesame oil in a large skillet over medium-high heat. Add the ground pork and cook, stirring often with a wooden spoon, until browned, 6 to 8 minutes. Transfer the cooked pork to a large bowl. Add 1 tsp sesame oil to the skillet and heat over medium heat. When hot, add the mushrooms and cook, stirring often, until browned, 6 to 8 minutes. Transfer the mushrooms to the bowl with the pork.

Add the remaining 1 tsp sesame oil to the skillet and heat over medium heat. Add the cabbage and zucchini and cook, stirring often, until they soften and are browned, 8 to 10 minutes. Transfer the cabbage and zucchini to the bowl with the pork. Add the shallot, green onions, Chinese five-spice powder, garlic powder, and red pepper flakes to the bowl and stir to combine well. Cover the bowl with plastic wrap and refrigerate for 15 minutes, or up to overnight.

Preheat the oven to 375°F [190°C]. Line a large baking pan with parchment paper. (Depending on the size of your baking pan, you may need to use two or make the dumplings in batches.)

Now for the fun. Cut the dough ball into four equal pieces and then, from each piece, make eight 1-Tbsp-size balls. (Math: This makes 32 dough balls total.) On a lightly floured work surface, use a rolling pin or even a tall spice jar to flatten each ball into a 3-in [7.5-cm] circle about ¼ in [6 mm] thick. Fill a small bowl with water.

Put a scant 1 Tbsp of the filling in the center of each dough circle. Dip a finger in the water and moisten the edge of one side of the dough circle, then fold the dough over to the other side and pinch the edges together to form a half-moon shape. Or, draw the sides together toward the top, forming a purse shape, pinching and twisting the dough together to close it. Place the finished dumplings on the prepared baking pan.

Put the 2 Tbsp sesame oil in a small bowl and, using a pastry brush, paint the tops of all the dumplings with the oil. Bake until the dough is crisp and golden, 25 to 30 minutes. Serve warm.

NOTE: Store the baked dumplings in an airtight container in the freezer for up to 3 months. Reheat in a 375°F [190°C] oven for 5 minutes or in the microwave for 1 minute.

BROCCOLI GNOCCHI WITH LEMON CREAM SAUCE

The lesson of this recipe is twofold: First, be brave enough to make your own pasta, and second, be brave enough to totally make over a recipe. Most gnocchi are made with potatoes or ricotta. But I thought, if I am going to take the time to make my own dough, I might as well make it special. And if a potato can transform into pasta, then why can't broccoli do the same? I discovered that it can. Plus, the process of making broccoli gnocchi is not difficult at all (look at the cooking time). Double plus, you'll use an entire head of broccoli, from stalk to tree top—which means the recipe is healthful and not wasteful. When entertaining non-low-so guests, offer grated Parmesan cheese for sprinkling.

SERVES 4 TO 6   **TIME** 1 HOUR, 15 MINUTES

2 cups [240 g] roughly chopped broccoli stems, plus 3 cups [180 g] roughly chopped broccoli florets

2 garlic cloves

½ tsp freshly ground black pepper

¼ cup [60 ml] lemon juice, plus zest of 1 lemon

1½ cups [180 g] all-purpose flour

3 Tbsp [45 g] unsalted butter

½ cup [120 ml] heavy cream

Pinch of red pepper flakes

Line a baking pan with parchment paper or dust lightly with flour.

In a food processor (or blender), combine the broccoli stems, garlic, black pepper, and the lemon juice. Purée until the broccoli mixture is smooth-ish, stopping to scrape down the bowl and adding 1 Tbsp water if needed to loosen. Transfer the purée to a medium bowl. Add the flour, ¼ cup [30 g] at a time, stirring until well combined after each addition. When ready, the dough will feel neither too sticky nor too flaky, just soft and pliable.

With floured hands, shape the dough into a ball. On a lightly floured work surface, cut the dough ball into four even sections. Working with one section at a time, roll out the dough into a long rope about ½ in [12 mm] thick. Use a knife to cut the dough rope into ½-in [12-mm] pieces. Place the tines of a fork on top of each dough piece, one at a time, and pull the fork toward you, gently rolling the gnoccho onto itself, making little grooves. Place the

CONTINUED

finished gnocchi in the prepared baking pan. (At this point, you can dust the gnocchi with flour and put in the freezer. When they harden, transfer to resealable plastic bags and freeze for up to 3 months.)

Bring a pot of water to a boil over high heat. Working in batches, drop the gnocchi into the boiling water. Cook until the gnocchi rise to the top, about 3 minutes. Use a slotted spoon to remove the gnocchi and place in a dry baking pan or on a piece of parchment paper. Continue until all the gnocchi are cooked and well drained.

Heat 1 Tbsp of the butter in a large sauté pan or skillet over medium heat and add the broccoli florets to the pan. Turn the heat to medium-high. Cook, tossing frequently, until slightly softened and browned, 6 to 8 minutes. Tranfer to a large serving bowl and cover with aluminum foil to keep warm.

Add another 1 Tbsp butter to the sauté pan and melt over medium heat. Working in batches, add a layer of gnocchi and cook until browned and crispy, 3 to 5 minutes, shaking the pan continuously so the gnocchi don't stick. Add the cooked gnocchi to the serving bowl with the broccoli florets. Repeat until all the gnocchi are pan-fried, adding more butter to the pan and adjusting the heat as needed.

Heat the remaining 1 Tbsp butter in the sauté pan over medium heat. Add the cream and cook, stirring occasionally, until thick, 4 to 5 minutes. Add the lemon zest and red pepper flakes. Cook for 1 minute more. Pour the cream sauce directly into the serving bowl and stir gently to coat. Serve warm.

VARIATION: Want to keep things lighter? Use olive oil in place of the butter. And instead of the cream sauce, put ¼ to ½ cup [60 to 120 ml] crème fraîche or plain Greek yogurt in the serving bowl while you cook the broccoli. When you add the warm vegetables and pasta, the crème fraîche or yogurt will melt into a sauce. Sprinkle a little lemon zest on top and gently mix.

EASY FOCACCIA

I always thought baking bread was too difficult to attempt. But I've found that, like everything else in cooking, the more you make bread, the simpler it becomes. You don't need a bread maker, just your hands and a pan. After making a few rolls and loaves, you'll understand how dough should feel, and whether it needs more liquid or more flour. Experiment with herbs, spices, and toppings. And when friends decide to come over for dinner, just whip up homemade focaccia (what some call "snacking bread") for them to nibble.

MAKES ONE 9-BY-13-IN [23-BY-33-CM] LOAF   **TIME** 3 HOURS, 15 MINUTES (MOSTLY INACTIVE TIME)

2¼ tsp active dry yeast

3½ cups [420 g] all-purpose flour

2 tsp salt-free garlic powder

1 tsp celery seeds

1 tsp lemon zest

1¼ cup [300 ml] warm water

1 tsp olive oil, plus more for drizzling

In a large mixing bowl, whisk together the yeast, flour, garlic powder, celery seeds, and lemon zest. Add 1 cup [240 ml] of the water and use your hands to mix the dough until it starts to come together. If the dough is too dry, slowly add ¼ cup [60 ml] water until the dough comes together.

Transfer the dough to a lightly floured work surface and knead until it feels smooth and springy. Wipe out the mixing bowl and place the dough back in. Rub the dough with the 1 tsp olive oil. Cover the bowl with plastic wrap and let it rise until it has doubled in size, 1½ to 2 hours. The warmer your kitchen is, the faster the dough will double.

Preheat the oven to 425°F [220°C]. Lightly oil a 9-by-13-in [23-by-33-cm] baking pan.

Transfer the dough to the prepared baking pan and stretch it to reach all the sides of the pan. Let it rise again, 20 to 30 minutes.

Use your fingertips to make indentations in the dough. Drizzle with 1 to 2 Tbsp olive oil. Bake until golden, about 20 minutes, rotating the pan halfway through. Ta-da! Focaccia! Serve warm.

SOUP TO SAUCE

Flexible cooking is an essential skill for making good, low-sodium food. That means creating second-day meals from leftovers, inventing recipes with straggler ingredients from the fridge, or turning simple soups into sauces, like these recipes. By learning to use ingredients and even whole dishes in unexpected ways, you will become more confident to cook off-the-cuff and get creative with what you have in your kitchen.

GREEN PEA POSOLE

MAKES 5 TO 6 CUPS [1.2 TO 1.4 L]   **TIME** 1 HOUR, 30 MINUTES

1 jalapeño chile

1 poblano or Anaheim chile

1 Tbsp olive oil

4 garlic cloves, chopped

1¼ cups [150 g] chopped
yellow onion

½ tsp freshly ground black pepper

4½ to 5 cups [1 to 1.2 L] water

4 cups [560 g] shelled
peas, fresh or frozen

2 chicken thighs, skinned
and deboned

1 cup [140 g] corn kernels,
fresh or thawed frozen

Fresh cilantro leaves, 1 sliced
green onion, 1 diced avocado,
and/or salt-free tortilla chips
for garnish (optional)

Preheat the oven to broil. Line a baking pan with aluminum foil.

Cut the jalapeño and poblano in half lengthwise and remove the stems and seeds. Lay the chiles cut-side down in the prepared pan. Broil until charred; remove the jalapeño after 8 to 10 minutes and the poblano after 12 to 15 minutes. Put into a small bowl. Use the foil to cover the bowl and let steam, about 15 minutes. After they are cool to the touch, remove and discard the charred skin and then roughly chop.

In a large soup pot, warm the olive oil over medium-high heat. When hot, add the garlic and yellow onion and cook, stirring frequently, until they start to brown, 3 to 5 minutes. Add the pepper, 4 cups [960 ml] of the water, and the peas. Bring to a boil and cook for 5 minutes. Turn the heat to low and simmer until the peas have softened, 6 to 8 minutes.

Remove the pot from the heat, add the roasted chiles to the soup, and use an immersion blender to purée until smooth. Add

CONTINUED

the chicken and the remaining ½ to 1 cup [120 to 240 ml] water, as needed. Return the soup to medium-high heat, bring to a boil, and cook for 5 minutes. Turn the heat to medium-low, cover, and cook for another 25 to 30 minutes.

Use tongs to remove the chicken thighs from the soup and place into a medium bowl. Use two forks to shred the chicken and then add it back to the soup along with the corn. Cook for a final 5 minutes. Ladle into bowls, and top with cilantro, green onion, avocado, or chips, as desired, to serve.

GREEN CHILAQUILES

SERVES 2 **TIME** 30 MINUTES

Three 5-in [12-cm] corn tortillas, cut into 6 triangles each

2 Tbsp vegetable oil, plus 2 tsp

¼ tsp salt-free garlic powder

¼ tsp salt-free chipotle chile powder

2 eggs

⅓ cup [40 g] chopped red onion

1 tsp chopped seeded jalapeño chile

2 cups [480 ml] Green Pea Posole (page 239)

¼ tsp smoked paprika

¼ tsp dried oregano

¼ tsp ground cumin

1 sliced avocado, 1 sliced green onion, plain Greek yogurt, fresh cilantro leaves, and 1 sliced seeded jalapeño chile for garnish (optional)

Preheat the oven to 350°F [180°C]. Line a baking pan with parchment paper.

Put the tortilla triangles in a large mixing bowl. Drizzle with 1 Tbsp of the vegetable oil, the garlic powder, and chile powder. Gently mix with your hands until the chips are evenly coated. Arrange the tortilla triangles in the prepared baking pan, and bake until they turn golden in color and crispy, about 10 minutes. Remove the tortilla chips from the oven and let them cool and harden.

Heat a large sauté pan or skillet over medium-high heat. Add 1 Tbsp vegetable oil and swirl to coat the pan. Gently crack the eggs, one at a time, into the pan and cook until the whites are firm and the edges begin to brown and curl, 2 to 3 minutes. If the whites still seem runny or you want a well-done yolk, cover the pan with a lid or aluminum foil. When cooked to your liking, transfer the eggs to a plate, cover with foil, and set aside.

CONTINUED

In the same sauté pan over medium-high heat, add the 2 tsp vegetable oil, red onion, and chopped jalapeño. Cook, stirring frequently, until the onion begins to soften, 3 to 5 minutes. Turn the heat to medium and add the posole, paprika, oregano, and cumin. Bring to a simmer, turn the heat to low, and cook, stirring frequently, until the sauce thickens, about 5 minutes. When the sauce is thick enough to stick to the back of a spoon, gently fold in the crispy tortilla triangles.

Ladle into bowls, and top with one fried egg each, and the avocado, green onion, yogurt, cilantro, or sliced jalapeño, as desired, to serve.

VARIATION: For something easier, cut down on cooking time by using no-salt-added canned tomato sauce instead of the posole. Cook the onion and jalapeño as directed and add the sauce and spices, cooking for another 10 minutes to get all the flavors blooming. Fold in no-salt-added tortilla chips. Instead of frying the eggs, crack them directly on top of the sauce. Cover the pan and cook until the eggs set and the whites turn white, 3 to 5 minutes. You have breakfast for two, or multiply for a big brunch.

ROASTED PEPPER AND BUTTERNUT SQUASH SOUP

MAKES 5 TO 6 CUPS [1.2 TO 1.4 L]   **TIME** 45 MINUTES

1 red bell pepper

2 Tbsp unsalted butter

1 cup [120 g] chopped yellow onion

4 garlic cloves, minced

4 cups [560 g] cubed
butternut squash

¼ tsp salt-free garlic powder

¼ tsp freshly ground black pepper

⅛ tsp red pepper flakes

4 cups [960 ml] water

Preheat the oven to broil and line a small baking pan with aluminum foil.

Cut the bell pepper in half and remove the stem and seeds. Lay the pepper halves cut-side down in the prepared pan. Broil until charred, 15 to 20 minutes. Remove from the oven and, using tongs, put the halves in a medium bowl. Use the foil to cover the bowl and let steam, about 15 minutes. After they are cool to the touch, remove and discard the charred skins. Set aside.

In a large soup pot, melt the butter over medium-high heat. When the butter begins to turn a golden brown color, about 2 minutes, add the onion and garlic and cook, stirring frequently, until softened, 2 to 3 minutes longer. Add the squash, garlic powder, black pepper, and red pepper flakes. Stir to combine. Add the water, stir, and bring to a boil. Turn the heat to low, cover, and simmer for 20 minutes. Remove from the heat.

Roughly chop the roasted red pepper and add to the pot. Using an immersion blender, purée the soup in the pot until smooth. Return the soup to medium-high heat, and bring to a boil. Turn the heat to medium and cook, stirring occasionally, until the soup is reduced to your liking, another 10 to 15 minutes. Serve immediately.

VARIATION: For the vegans, substitute olive oil for the butter. For the carnivores, substitute low-sodium chicken stock for some of the water.

STUFFED SHELLS WITH BUTTERNUT SAUCE

SERVES 4 TO 6   **TIME** 1 HOUR

One 12-oz [340-g] box
jumbo pasta shells

1 tsp olive oil, plus
more for drizzling

4 oz [115 g] ground pork, or
1 cup [100 g] grated zucchini

2 cups [840 g] Cauliflower-
Nut "Ricotta" (page 196)
or low-sodium ricotta

½ cup [15 g] chopped fresh
basil, plus more for garnish

⅛ tsp ground allspice

4 cups [960 ml] Roasted
Pepper and Butternut
Squash Soup (page 243)

Preheat the oven to 375°F [190°C]. Lightly oil a 9-by-12-in [23-by-28-cm] baking dish.

Bring a large pot of water to a boil over high heat and add the pasta shells. Turn the heat to medium-high and cook until al dente, 6 to 8 minutes. Drain the pasta shells in a colander and rinse with cool water.

Meanwhile, add the olive oil to a medium skillet or sauté pan and heat over medium-high heat. When hot, add the ground pork and cook until browned and no longer pink, stirring frequently, 6 to 8 minutes. Drain the fat and set the cooked meat aside in a small bowl.

In a medium bowl, combine the cauliflower "ricotta," basil, cooked pork, and allspice and mix well. Set aside.

Spread 1 cup [240 ml] of the squash soup in the bottom of the prepared baking dish. Fill each pasta shell with the "ricotta" mixture, about 1 Tbsp per shell, and place in the baking dish in a single layer, seam-side up, over the squash soup. Cover the stuffed shells with the remaining 3 cups [720 ml] soup. Drizzle a little olive oil over the top, cover the dish with aluminum foil, and bake until the shells are tender, 15 minutes. Uncover the dish and continue to bake for another 10 minutes. Turn on the broiler for the final 3 minutes to crisp the pasta shells. Garnish with basil, and serve hot.

VARIATION: To cut down on cooking time, mix together 2 cups [480 ml] canned no-salt-added tomato sauce and 2 cups [480 ml] canned no-salt-added butternut squash purée. Stir in some salt-free spices, such as smoked paprika and salt-free garlic powder, and use this mixture in place of the Roasted Red Pepper and Butternut Soup.

COCONUT-CINNAMON ICE CREAM

You can always buy a carton of sodium-free ice cream or sorbet from the store. But like all other low-sodium cooking adventures, making your own tastes a gazillion times better. Plus, it offers you the opportunity to try unique flavors and textures of your choosing, and impress your dinner guests. Other than making the custard, your ice-cream maker and freezer will do the rest of the work for you. So buckle up and give this homemade ice cream a try. You may never buy a carton again.

MAKES ABOUT 5 CUPS [1.2 L]   **TIME** 3 HOURS, 35 MINUTES (MOSTLY INACTIVE TIME)

**3 cups [720 ml] canned
full-fat coconut milk**

2 eggs

¾ cup [150 g] sugar

¼ tsp ground cinnamon

Make an ice bath by filling a large bowl halfway with ice cubes and water. Nestle a medium bowl in the ice bath and put a fine-mesh sieve in the medium bowl.

In a large saucepan, whisk together the coconut milk and eggs. Put the pan over medium-high heat and whisk in the sugar. Use a wooden spoon to stir the mixture until it thickens and registers 175°F [80°C] on a candy thermometer, 6 to 8 minutes. (If you don't have a candy thermometer, check whether the custard is done by dipping a wooden spoon in the custard. While holding the spoon sideways, run your finger along the back of the spoon. If the streak remains without the custard running back into the empty space, it is ready.) Remove the pan from the heat and pour the custard through the fine-mesh sieve to strain out any eggy bits, pushing the custard through with a silicone spatula.

CONTINUED

Add the cinnamon to the custard and whisk until mixed well. Set the custard and ice bath aside to cool for 10 to 15 minutes. Take the custard out of the ice bath, press a piece of plastic wrap directly on the surface of the custard, and refrigerate for 2 hours, or up to overnight.

Using an ice-cream maker, follow the manufacturer's instructions to make the ice cream. Put the finished ice cream in an airtight container and freeze for at least 1 hour before serving.

VARIATION: If you want to add texture, mix 1 cup [100 g] toasted coconut or puffed rice cereal with a little cinnamon, sugar, and a drizzle of agave nectar. Serve sprinkled on top of the ice cream.

PICKLED CHERRIES

For your next happy hour, skip the olives—which can contain around 50 mg of sodium per olive—and make some pickled cherries instead. The combination of tangy balsamic vinegar mixed with the tart fruit makes a great accompaniment to cocktails and pre-dinner cheese platters (for those who can eat cheese). These also make a great edible gift during the holidays. You can leave the stems on for easy snacking or remove the pits from the cherries to make them look more like olives. Eat them on their own, use them in wild rice stuffing, or give them to guests to put in their martinis.

MAKES 2 CUPS [380 G] **TIME** 30 MINUTES (PLUS 48 HOURS FOR PICKLING)

1 orange

½ cup [120 ml] water

½ cup [120 ml] apple cider vinegar

½ cup [120 ml] balsamic vinegar

½ cup [100 g] dark brown sugar

1 tsp peppercorns

½ tsp whole cloves

1 cinnamon stick

2 to 3 cups [280 to 420 g] cherries, stemmed (fresh or frozen unsweetened)

Use a peeler to make ribbons of orange peel. Cut the orange in half and juice the halves into a bowl. Set aside.

In a small saucepan, combine the water, cider vinegar, balsamic vinegar, brown sugar, peppercorns, cloves, cinnamon stick, and ½ cup [60 ml] of the orange juice (discard any extra) and stir to mix well. Bring the pickling liquid to a boil over medium-high heat. Remove the saucepan from the heat and allow the liquid to cool for at least 20 minutes, or longer if you are using plastic containers.

Use a knife to cut a small X in the bottom of the cherries. Stuff the cherries and the orange peel ribbons into a 2-cup [480-ml] heatproof container. Set aside.

When the liquid is lukewarm to the touch, pour it into the container, covering the cherries. (If there is not enough liquid, add a bit more balsamic vinegar.) Put the lid on the container and close tightly. Give the container five or six good shakes to mix up all the pickling juices, and put it in the fridge to cool.

CONTINUED

In 48 hours, the cherries will be ready. Resist the urge to taste before then, because the longer you wait, the more pickled they will be. When they're ready, try to finish them off within 2 weeks, which won't be hard. Serve them in a bowl with toothpicks.

VARIATION: Try other spices next time, like fresh ginger and star anise, to change the flavor and give more pop to these pickles.

NOTE: If you have extra cherries, don't panic. The ones in the container will shrink a little in the warm liquid, so when there's extra space, add the leftover cherries.

THE DINNER PARTY: POLENTA WITH LAMB CHOPS, HARISSA, AND LEMON FENNEL

Polenta makes a perfect starting point for guests with and without dietary restrictions. It takes on a creamy texture even without dairy, and it serves as a rich canvas that complements almost any protein, vegetable, or sauce combination. While I use lamb chops here, if you want less meat, use beans or roasted vegetables instead. Offer Parmesan on the side for guests who like (and can handle) a salty kick. Plate individual portions, present the dish family style, or, for something wild, assemble all of the components on a large, wooden cutting board.

SERVES 4 TO 6   **TIME** 35 MINUTES

LEMON FENNEL

1 bulb fennel

Zest of 1 lemon, plus 2 Tbsp lemon juice

POLENTA

4 cups [960 ml] water

1 cup [140 g] yellow medium-ground cornmeal

½ tsp salt-free garlic powder

Pinch of freshly ground black pepper

Preheat the oven to 400°F [200°C].

To make the Lemon Fennel: Wash the fennel bulb and cut off the knobby bottom. Remove any brown outer layers. Using a mandoline, or really good knife skills, hold the fronds and thinly slice the fennel bulb below the fronds. Put the fennel slices in a medium bowl and add the lemon zest and juice. Put in the refrigerator and let the fennel marinate for 30 minutes.

To make the Polenta: In a large saucepan, bring the water to a boil over medium-high heat. Stirring with a wooden spoon, slowly add the cornmeal to the boiling water. Turn the heat to low and continue stirring until the polenta starts to thicken, about 5 minutes. Add the garlic powder and pepper, and stir again to combine well. Continue to cook the polenta for 20 to 25 minutes, adjusting the heat as needed and stirring every 10 minutes to keep it from sticking or burning on the bottom of the pan. Remove from the heat and keep warm. (Your goal is to have the polenta finished when it's time to eat, since it will get a little gummy if it

LAMB LOIN CHOPS

2 tsp dried dill

2 tsp freshly ground black pepper

8 to 12 small lamb loin chops, each about 1½ in [4 cm] thick

1 Tbsp olive oil or vegetable oil

Fresh herbs: chopped dill, basil, mint, or fennel fronds

Harissa Hot Sauce (page 164) for serving

Grated Parmesan cheese, for non-low-so guests, for serving

sits. But if timing gets off and the polenta gets gummy, just add 1 to 2 Tbsp warm water or a spoonful of the lamb roasting juices to make it creamy again.)

To make the Lamb Loin Chops: In a small mixing bowl, combine the dill and pepper. Pat the lamb chops dry with a paper towel and rub the dill mixture all over each chop. Add the olive oil to a large ovenproof skillet (or two, if needed) and heat over medium-high heat. Add the lamb in a single layer (cook in batches if necessary) and sear until each chop has a golden brown crust, 3 to 4 minutes per side. Use tongs to hold the chops so you can sear the sides of fat, about 1 minute per chop. Lay the chops flat again and put the skillet in the oven to finish cooking, 6 to 8 minutes, depending on the thickness. Remove the skillet from the oven, cover loosely with aluminum foil, and let the lamb rest for 5 minutes.

Spoon the creamy polenta onto four to six plates and lay one or two lamb chops, per person, on top. Spoon some of the rich lamb roasting juices over the lamb and polenta, if desired. Remove the fennel slices from the lemon marinade and place a small handful over the lamb chops. Sprinkle each plate with fresh herbs. Serve with the harissa and Parmesan cheese on the side.

THE CASUAL FIESTA: JERK-ISH FISH TACOS WITH SAUCE, SLAW, AND SALSA

Tacos are my go-to meal for big groups. Almost all of the fixings can be prepared ahead of time and served cold or at room temperature—a big plus for the host or hostess. And they bring a ton of color, texture, and flavor to the table—a big plus for low-so eaters. You can easily adapt these tacos to take advantage of in-season produce or adjust to different dietary needs. And with so many fixing options, guests get to design their own perfect taco. Or two. Or more.

`SERVES` 4 TO 8   `TIME` 1 HOUR, 35 MINUTES

PEACH-JALAPEÑO SAUCE

2 orange bell peppers

1 jalapeño chile

1 cup [170 g] chopped peaches, fresh or thawed frozen

Zest and juice of 1 lime

CARROT-LIME SLAW

2 carrots

1 Tbsp lime zest, plus
1 Tbsp lime juice

CORN-JICAMA SALSA

1 Tbsp coriander seeds

1 tsp vegetable oil

1 Tbsp diced seeded jalapeño chile

1½ cup [210 g] corn kernels, fresh or thawed frozen

To make the Peach-Jalapeño Sauce: Preheat the oven to broil. Line a baking pan with aluminum foil.

Cut the bell peppers and jalapeño in half and remove the stems and seeds. Lay them cut-side down in the prepared baking pan. Broil until charred; remove the jalapeño after 8 to 10 minutes and the bell peppers after 12 to 15 minutes. Put into a medium bowl. Use the foil to cover the bowl and let steam about 15 minutes. After they are cool to the touch, remove and discard the charred skins and roughly chop. Transfer the bell peppers and jalapeño to a blender (or food processor). Add the peaches, lime zest, and lime juice and purée until smooth. Set aside.

To make the Carrot-Lime Slaw: Using a julienne peeler or a regular peeler, cut the carrots into thin ribbons. Put the carrot ribbons in a medium bowl and toss with the lime zest and lime juice. (The slaw can be prepared 1 day ahead for a more intense lime flavor; store in the fridge in an airtight nonreactive container.)

CONTINUED

1 cup [140 g] diced jicama
or cucumber

½ tsp salt-free garlic powder

¼ cup [7 g] finely chopped
fresh cilantro

2 green onions, root ends
trimmed, thinly sliced

1 to 3 corn tortillas per person

JERK-ISH FISH

2 tsp smoked paprika

½ to 1 tsp cayenne pepper
or salt-free chili powder

1 tsp salt-free garlic powder

½ tsp ground cumin

¼ tsp ground cloves

¼ tsp ground cinnamon

¼ tsp freshly ground black pepper

1½ lb [680 g] snapper, cod,
or tilapia fillets

2 tsp vegetable oil

1 peach or mango, cut into
½-in [12-mm] slices

½ cup [35 g] shredded
purple cabbage

½ cup [60 g] diced red onion

Plain Greek yogurt for serving

¼ cup [7 g] chopped
fresh cilantro leaves

2 limes, cut into 4 wedges each

To make the Corn-Jicama Salsa: Heat a large sauté pan or skillet over medium-high heat and toast the coriander seeds until fragrant, about 2 minutes, stirring or shaking the pan frequently. Add the vegetable oil, diced jalapeño, and corn and cook, stirring frequently, for 5 minutes. Transfer the mixture to a medium bowl and let cool for 10 minutes. (If you are using fresh corn kernels, you don't need to heat them first.) Add the jicama, garlic powder, cilantro, and green onions to the bowl. Stir until well combined. Cover tightly and refrigerate until serving, up to 1 day.

Preheat the oven to 350°F [180°C]. Wrap the tortillas tightly in aluminum foil and put in the oven to warm while you make the fish.

To make the Jerk-ish Fish: In a small bowl, mix together the paprika, cayenne, garlic powder, cumin, cloves, cinnamon, and black pepper. Rub this spice mixture all over the fish fillets.

Add the vegetable oil to a large sauté pan or skillet and heat over medium-high heat. Add the fish in batches, cooking until the fillets turn golden in color and flake when pulled with a fork, about 5 minutes per side. Put the cooked fish in a medium serving bowl and cover with foil to keep warm while you cook the rest of the fish. Use a fork to break apart the fillets.

Place the warmed tortillas on a plate, cover them with a kitchen towel to keep them warm, and place on the table. Set out the jalapeño sauce, carrot slaw, corn salsa, fish, and the peach slices, shredded cabbage, diced onion, yogurt, cilantro, and lime wedges. Let your guests build their own tacos.

THE GROUP EFFORT: FLATBREAD WITH FOUR MIX-AND-MATCH SPREADS

Remember: When you personally have a hand in making the meal, the food tastes better. Multiply that by the number of guests at your dinner party and just imagine the kind of flavor boost that results. Not to mention entertainment value. So the next time you invite the gang over, let them roll up their sleeves and get involved with some flatbreads. Prepare the dough and spreads ahead of time—or assign guests spreads to make on their own and bring for sharing—and when it's time, let everyone tie on an apron and get to work on their personal pizzas.

MAKES FOUR 6-BY-10-IN [15-BY-25-CM] CRUSTS   **TIME** 2 TO 3 HOURS (DEPENDING ON THE DOUGH RISING TIME)

½ oz [15 g] active dry yeast

1½ cups [360 ml] warm water

2 Tbsp sugar

2 Tbsp olive oil, plus 1 tsp and more for drizzling

1 tsp salt-free garlic powder

½ tsp freshly ground black pepper

4 cups [480 g] all-purpose flour

Spreads and corresponding toppings (recipes follow)

In large bowl, mix the yeast with the warm water. Let the mixture stand until it bubbles, about 5 minutes. Mix in the sugar, 2 Tbsp olive oil, garlic powder, and pepper. Stir until combined. Add the flour, 1 cup [120 g] at a time, and use your hands to mix the dough until it starts to come together in a ball. (If the dough is too sticky, add a little more flour. If it is too dry, add a little more water.) Put the dough on a lightly floured work surface and knead until it feels smooth and springy, 6 to 8 minutes.

Wipe the large bowl clean and put the dough ball back in it. Pour the 1 tsp olive oil over the top of the dough and use your hands to spread it all over the dough ball. Cover the bowl with plastic wrap or a kitchen towel, and let the dough rise in a warm space until doubled in size, 1 to 2 hours. Cut the dough into four equal parts and shape them into balls. (At this point, you can dust the dough with flour and wrap in wax or parchment paper. Put in a resealable bag and refrigerate for up to 3 days or freeze for up to 3 months. Thaw in the refrigerator and proceed as directed.)

CONTINUED

Preheat the oven to 425°F [220°C]. Line two large cookie sheets with aluminum foil.

Lightly flour the work surface again and use a rolling pin to shape each of the four dough balls into a 6-by-8-in [15-by-20-cm] rectangle about a ¼ in [6 mm] thick. Transfer the dough to the prepared cookie sheets, two per sheet.

Bake the flatbreads until the bottom crust starts to feel firm, 6 to 8 minutes. Take the cookie sheets out of the oven and lower the oven temperature to 375°F [190°C].

Spread one of the spreads onto each flatbread crust, leaving a ¼-in [6-mm] border. Let your guests add additional toppings as desired and finish with a drizzle of olive oil on the top.

Return the flatbreads to the oven to bake until the crust is golden brown and crispy, 12 to 15 minutes. Let cool for 5 minutes. Slice and serve hot.

BROCCOLI AND BASIL SPREAD

MAKES ¾ CUP [165 G]   **TIME** 15 MINUTES

2 cups [180 g] broccoli florets and stems

2 to 3 Tbsp olive oil, plus more for serving

¼ cup [7 g] tightly packed chopped fresh basil leaves

½ tsp salt-free garlic powder

Pinch of freshly ground black pepper

TOPPINGS
CHOPPED FRESH BASIL LEAVES, SALT-FREE PINE NUTS OR SLICED ALMONDS

Fill a medium pot with 2 in [5 cm] water and place a steamer basket in the bottom of the pot above the water. Bring the water to a boil over medium heat. Put the broccoli in the basket, cover, and steam until fork-tender, 6 to 8 minutes. Transfer the broccoli to a blender (or food processor). Add 2 Tbsp of the olive oil, the basil, garlic powder, and pepper. Blend until smooth, scraping down the sides of the bowl with a spatula and adding the remaining 1 Tbsp olive oil if needed.

Store in an airtight container, drizzled with olive oil to prevent browning, in the refrigerator for up to 4 days.

CAULIFLOWER AND MUSHROOM SPREAD

MAKES 1½ CUPS [330 G]   **TIME** 20 MINUTES

2 cups [220 g] cauliflower florets

2 tsp olive oil, plus 2 Tbsp

3 garlic cloves, chopped

1 cup [70 g] sliced stemmed cremini mushrooms

1 Tbsp orange zest, plus 1 Tbsp orange juice

2 to 3 Tbsp fresh parsley leaves

¼ tsp freshly ground black pepper

Pinch of red pepper flakes

TOPPINGS
SLICED SHALLOT, ARUGULA

Fill a medium pot with 2 in [5 cm] water and place a steamer basket in the bottom of the pot above the water. Bring the water to a boil over medium heat. Put the cauliflower in the basket, cover, and steam until fork-tender, 6 to 8 minutes. Transfer the cauliflower to a blender (or food processor).

Meanwhile, heat the 2 tsp olive oil in a medium skillet over medium-high heat. Add the garlic and mushrooms and cook, stirring frequently, until browned, 8 to 10 minutes. Transfer to the blender. Add the 2 Tbsp olive oil, orange zest, orange juice, parsley, black pepper, and red pepper flakes. Blend until smooth, scraping down the sides of the bowl if needed.

Store in an airtight container in the refrigerator for up to 4 days.

BUTTERNUT SQUASH-DUKKA SPICE SPREAD

MAKES 1½ CUPS [330 G]   **TIME** 15 MINUTES

2 cups [280 g] cubed
butternut squash

2 to 3 Tbsp olive oil

2 Tbsp Dukka Spice Mix (page 188)

TOPPINGS
DOLLOPS OF LOW-SODIUM
FARMER'S CHEESE OR RICOTTA,
SLICED TOMATOES

Fill a medium pot with 2 in [5 cm] water and place a steamer basket in the bottom of the pot above the water. Bring the water to a boil over medium heat. Put the squash in the basket, cover, and steam until tender, 10 to 12 minutes. Transfer the squash to a blender (or food processor). Add 2 Tbsp of the olive oil and the dukka. Blend until smooth, scraping down the sides of the bowl and adding the remaining 1 Tbsp olive oil if needed.

Store in an airtight container in the refrigerator for up to 4 days.

CILANTRO-PEA SPREAD

MAKES 1 CUP [220 G]   **TIME** 15 MINUTES

2 cups [280 g] peas, fresh or frozen

¼ cup [7 g] tightly packed
fresh cilantro leaves

½ tsp cumin seeds

¼ tsp salt-free chipotle
chile powder

1 tsp olive oil

Zest and juice of 1 lime

TOPPINGS
JALAPEÑO CHILE SLICES, GRATED
CARROTS, RAW CORN KERNELS

Fill a medium bowl with ice and water and put it in the freezer to chill for 5 minutes to make an ice-water bath.

Meanwhile, bring a medium pot of water to boil over medium-high heat. Add the peas and cook until tender and bright green, 2 to 3 minutes.

Remove the ice-water bath from the freezer and transfer to the counter. Immediately drain the peas and pour them into the ice-water bath. Let cool for 5 to 8 minutes. Drain the peas again and transfer to a blender (or food processor). Add the cilantro, cumin seeds, chile powder, olive oil, lime zest, and 1 tsp of the lime juice. Blend until smooth. Taste and add more lime juice, if needed.

Store in an airtight container in the refrigerator for up to 4 days.

PAVLOVA WHOOPIE PIES WITH MINT WHIPPED CREAM

This dessert is like doing a backflip during the first dance at your wedding (which happened at mine). It's unexpected, it's daring, and it definitely leaves an impression. But don't let the level of difficulty deceive you, because making a pavlova is a lot easier than a backflip. *Pavlova* is just a fancy name for a meringue covered with whipped cream. You can bake the pavlova flat, stack several like a layer cake on a large tray, and serve with forks for your guests, if you like interactive presentations; or even make them into whoopie pies, like I've done here. While this version is spiked with fresh mint whipped cream, a pavlova is a wonderful canvas for trying unusual flavor combinations, sweet or savory. Like peppermint, poppyseed, and even cayenne pepper and chocolate flakes. So stretch, bend those knees, and dive into these pavlova whoopie pies.

MAKES 8 WHOOPIE PIES   **TIME** 2 HOURS

MERINGUES

1 cup [200 g] granulated sugar

½ cup [100 g] packed light brown sugar

1½ Tbsp cornstarch

1½ tsp vanilla extract

2 tsp distilled white vinegar

5 egg whites, at room temperature

MINT WHIPPED CREAM

¼ cup [7 g] lightly packed fresh chopped mint leaves

2 Tbsp granulated sugar

To make the Meringues: Preheat the oven to 275°F [135°C]. Line two large cookie sheets with parchment paper. Using a pencil and the rim of a 2½-in- [6-cm-] diameter drinking glass, trace eight circles on each sheet of parchment (leave plenty of space between each circle), making 16 circles total. Flip the parchment over, so the pencil markings won't get on the meringues.

Whisk the granulated sugar, brown sugar, and cornstarch in a medium bowl until it is lump-free and well combined. (If your brown sugar has hardened, it's best to use a food processor to break up any lumps.) In a small bowl, stir together the vanilla and vinegar. Set aside.

CONTINUED

**2 cups [480 ml] heavy
whipping cream**

¼ cup [20 g] powdered sugar

Using electric beaters and a large mixing bowl or a stand mixer, beat the egg whites on medium speed until they hold soft peaks, 2 to 3 minutes. Increase the speed to medium-high and, while beating the egg whites, add the sugar mixture 1 Tbsp at a time. After all the sugar has been added, beat 1 minute more. Add the vanilla-vinegar mixture and beat at high speed until the batter is glossy and holds stiff peaks, another 3 to 5 minutes.

Use a spatula to spoon ½ to ¾ cup [120 to 180 ml] of meringue, about 2 in [5 cm] high, on each circle on the prepared sheets. Use the spatula to smooth out the meringue circles. Bake for 35 minutes. Turn off the oven, and let the meringues rest in the oven with the door closed for 1 hour. Remove from the oven and let cool.

To make the Mint Whipped Cream: Clean and dry the electric mixer beaters and the mixing bowl. Chill the bowl and beaters in the freezer for 5 minutes.

Meanwhile, combine the mint and granulated sugar in a food processor (or blender). Pulse a few times until you have finely ground mint sugar. Set aside.

Add the whipping cream and powdered sugar to the chilled mixing bowl. Mix on high speed for 2 to 3 minutes, just until the cream gets very thick and holds medium peaks, being careful to not overbeat. (Overmixing heavy whipping cream will cause it to separate. If this happens, don't panic. Fold in a little extra cream and it will come back together.) With a spatula, gently fold in the mint sugar. Refrigerate for up to 1 hour.

Frost one meringue with ¼ cup [60 ml] of the whipped cream. Place another meringue on top, and press gently to form a two-layer whoopie pie. Repeat to assemble eight whoopie pies. Serve immediately.

RECIPES GROUPED BY TYPE

SOUPS

DINNERS

PARTY MEALS

DESSERTS

INDEX